I0670220

Reading the Past
Understanding the Present

Reading the Past
Understanding the Present

EDITED BY

AGNIESZKA ORSZULAK
AGNIESZKA ROMANOWSKA

JAGIELLONIAN UNIVERSITY PRESS

The publication of this volume was financed by the Faculty of Philology of the Jagiellonian University

Reviewer
dr hab. Magdalena Cieślak

Academic supervision
prof. dr hab. Marta Gibińska
dr hab. Agnieszka Romanowska, prof. UJ

Cover design
Małgorzata Flis

ISBN 978-83-233-5001-9
ISBN 978-83-233-7235-6 (e-book)

www.wuj.pl

Jagiellonian University Press
Editorial Offices: Michałowskiego 9/2, 31-126 Kraków
Phone: +48 12 663 23 80, Fax: +48 12 663 23 83
Distribution: Phone: +48 12 631 01 97, Fax: +48 12 631 01 98
Cell Phone: +48 506 006 674, e-mail: sprzedaz@wuj.pl
Bank: PEKAO SA, IBAN PL 80 1240 4722 1111 0000 4856 3325

Table of Contents

PART III
THE THEATRE OF POLITICS

AFTERWORD

Preface

This volume came into being as a result of the NEW FACES project ("Facing Europe in Crisis: Shakespeare's World and Present Challenges"), a three-year-long Erasmus Plus Strategic Partnership of nine European universities, initiated in the academic year 2016/2017. In the seminars and workshops offered during the intensive programme sessions students were encouraged to explore the cultural, political, and economic functions of the early modern theatre, especially the works by William Shakespeare, and its wider historical and literary context. The essays presented in this collection demonstrate how the past and the present, theory and practice, are inherently interwoven and how the understanding of the crises of the past helps to face contemporary local and global contexts. To accentuate the international character of the project and the value of communication among European nations above their differences in order to work through the current problems together, local languages of the partner universities were present, side by side today's *lingua franca*, English, in the form of summaries, abstracts, descriptions of events and in dissemination materials. In this volume this appreciation of unity in diversity is reflected in the abstracts of each text, as they are cited in two languages – English and the native language of the author.

The student essays collected in this book constitute a representative sample of the project's leading topics. Václav Kyllar's paper examines the European migrant crisis, especially the dialogue between the Western society and the immigrants, perceived as the Other. He analyses the problem by referring to Shakespeare's play *The Merchant of Venice*, which showcases the early modern foundations on which Europe stands today. The uneasy relationship between Shylock and the Christians, with its alienation, inequality, and discrimination, mirrors the tensions that can arise from the conflict with a contrasting identity in a heterogeneous society. Jacques Derrida's philosophical work sheds light on encountering the Other and the binary of hospitality and hostility towards them. Kyllar draws an analogy between such a reading of Shylock's situation and the current treatment of immigrants, proposing a re-evaluation of the present-day European politics.

"Shylock, the Undoubtable Other" also focuses on the phenomenon of otherness in Shakespeare's *The Merchant of Venice*. Elahe Mousavian observes that, in the play, this problem is two-sided and although Shylock is portrayed as the main Other, he is not the only one – the Christians also represent the alien side of this relationship. She analyses the language of the play as the point of encounter between the Others and the failure of communication. The concept of hostipitality, proposed by Jacques Derrida, acknowledges the paradox of hospitality and hostility and constitutes the framework for the theoretical debate. Subsequently, the author likens Shylock's experience to the situation of the Afghans in Iran, fleeing from war only to suffer a different form of violence.

Federica Bonora, in her essay "Shakespeare's Art as a Vehicle for Mediation on the Global Refugee Crisis," explores the contemporary refugee crisis and its perception of the Other. She examines the way social theatre connects literary works with the physical world and allows its participants to connect among communities, celebrating diversity and complexity. Shakespeare's plays have proven to be universal and timeless in their portrayal of various social problems, therefore many creators choose them to address present conflicts. Some of the recent adaptations analysed by Bonora employ refugees and immigrants as actors, deriving from their real-life experiences, and providing a deeper understanding of the events happening on stage.

Censorship, Natalya Stocks asserts, has been a prevailing feature of advanced societies and humanity has been subjected to it for centuries. She traces the development of this phenomenon, emphasising its importance in shaping a worldview and defending the established system. Through the analysis of content restriction in Shakespeare's time and the years of the apartheid regime in South Africa, the author demonstrates its cultural, social, and political consequences.

Ana Rita Catalão Guedes focuses in her paper on the conception of death as a cultural phenomenon and the attitudes towards it throughout the centuries. She adopts Philippe Ariès's notion of death as something shameful, unpleasant, and destructive and contrasts it with the vision presented in Shakespeare's *King Lear*. The analysis of the recent BBC Two's adaptation of the play confronts the two approaches and offers a commentary on our modern inability to deal with death.

Tânia Cerqueira comments on the change that has occurred in our perception of death in modern times. This natural part of life, due to its prevalence and universality once calmly accepted as something inevitable, has now become a source of anxiety. In the contemporary Western society, death is a taboo, as stated by Philippe Ariès. Hence, humankind has turned to science and technology in pursuit of immortality, creating different visions of the posthuman. Through the analysis of the film *Warm Bodies* (2013), a retelling of Shakespeare's *Romeo and Juliet*, the author presents the zombie as a violent projection of human emotions regarding natural death and a cautionary tale about the possible outcomes of our search for the eternal life.

Katarzyna Hübner, following René von Schomberg's article "A Vision of Responsible Science" and his concerns about inventions, discusses ethical implications of imitation. She analyses Shakespeare's *The Tempest*, Francis Bacon's *New Atlantis*, and Ridley Scott's *Blade Runner* (1982), focusing on their representation of (ir)resposible science, misuses of imitation, and distribution of knowledge. Through applying the practice of presentism, the author draws an analogy between the events of the past and the current time of Covid-19 pandemic which exposes global alienation and scientific competition. She concludes that responsibility and solidity of ethical standards is fundamental to science nowadays.

Agnieszka Orszulak examines how the understanding of, attitudes towards, and political significance of authority has changed throughout the centuries. Following the classifications of types of authority introduced by Max Weber and Claudia Rapp, she analyses the portrayals of power presented in Shakespeare's history plays – *Richard II*, *Henry IV* part 1 and 2, and *Richard III*, and compares them to the contemporary representatives, the Polish President Andrzej Duda and the American President Donald Trump. This procedure exposes a pattern in the subsequent representations of authority, proving that a satisfying relation between the governing and the governed is yet to be found.

In her paper "Jacek Woszczerowicz's Appropriation of Shakespeare's *Richard III* in Communist Poland," Ewelina Szalecka outlines the turbulent political situation in Poland after the Second World War. She remarks on the significance of the 1947 Shakespeare Festival and its role in representing the Polish culture, as well as expressing the rebellious attitudes in the nation. During the times of political oppression and imposed censorship, many theatre artists used allusions and metaphors to manifest dissatisfaction with the communist leadership. The author analyses one of the most significant theatrical productions of the period, Jacek Woszczerowicz's *Richard III* that redefined the character of Gloucester in modern terms, confirming the historical contemporaneity and universality of this history play.

The volume closes with an extensive description of the project's rationale and objectives and a presentation of some methods and strategies of its realisation. In her text "Strategic Partnership Project as Academic Training Ground" Agnieszka Romanowska argues that the NEW FACES Strategic Partnership proved to be an effective academic training ground that enabled students to develop academic, social, and international competences and skills vital for their involvement in shaping the future of Europe as prospective scholars and as citizens.

The NEW FACES project was an opportunity for students to discover the value of interdisciplinary and international cooperation. They were able to work with a group of European scholars and non-academic institutions in order to gain a better understanding of the contemporary crises and attempt to propose a course of action towards their solution. The selection of seminars and workshops offered each year allowed the participants to develop their intercultural awareness, critical thinking, writing and teamwork skills, as well as to enhance their linguistic competences, crucial for working in the current multilingual environment. The Intensive Programmes resulted in an extensive collection of texts discussing the literary, historical, and political aspects of European crises, some of which are published in this volume.

Agnieszka Orszulak

PART I

Facing the Other
Understanding Ourselves

VÁCLAV KYLLAR

Charles University in Prague

Approaching the Other in Shakespeare's *Merchant of Venice*

Abstract

The purpose of this paper is to analyse William Shakespeare's *Merchant of Venice* and the possible implications it might have for the European migrant crisis and the current state of the European public discourse with regard to our shared identity. The uneasy search for this common European identity and the challenge of the migrant crisis, which shows the strained basis on which any dialogue between Europeans and the Other is built, is related to Shakespeare's play. *Merchant of Venice* has been chosen because it best showcases Shakespeare's attentive description of the early modern European society and the foundations on which Europe stands today with all the inequality and discrimination that was a part of this society.

The main method used for this analysis was close reading of *Merchant of Venice* and of Jacques Derrida's *Of Hospitality* that provides the theoretical framework for this work. Derrida's understanding of the law and hospitality, as well as of the role of the Foreigner guides the inquiry into the uneasy relationship between Shakespeare's Shylock and his Christian counterparts. This relationship is described both in the socio-historical context of early modern Europe, but also in terms of theatrical and dramatic analysis. The conclusion of this inquiry tries to isolate the problem of hospitality and the Other and places it in analogy with the European migrant crisis.

The paper describes the primary dynamic of the Judeo-Christian interaction in Shakespeare's Venice and points to a possible conclusion that can be drawn from the tragic constellation of the broken pact of hospitality that leads to the ambivalent and deeply unnerving ending of the play. The same conclusion can be used as a blueprint for the current social and political situation in Europe. The lack of discussion and mutual deliberation can be seen both in the play and the present Europe and it is possible to search in both for the same causes and possible solutions to this problem.

Keywords: Shakespeare, Derrida, hospitality, Europe, migrant crisis

Souhrn

Účelem tohoto článku je analýza *Kupce benátského* od Williama Shakespeara a možných implikací, které tato hra může mít pro evropskou migrační krizi a současný stav evropského veřejného diskurzu týkajícího se naší sdílené identity. Neklidné hledání této evropské identity a výzva migrační krize, která ukazuje na napjaté základy, na nichž je jakýkoliv dialog mezi Evropany a tím Jiným postaven, je uvedena do souvislosti s Shakespearovou hrou. *Kupec benátský* byl vybrán, protože nejlépe ukazuje Shakespearův pozorný popis společnosti raného novověku a základy, na nichž dnes Evropa stojí, se vší nerovností a diskriminací, která byla součástí této společnosti.

Hlavní metodou využité k této analýze bylo pozorné čtení *Kupce benátského* a *O pohostinnosti* od Jacquesa Derridy, které mé práci poskytne její teoretický rámec. Derridovo chápání zákona a pohostinnosti, stejně jako role Cizince, bude provázet mé šetření neklidného vztahu mezi Shylockem a jeho křesťanskými protějšky. Tento vztah je popsán jak ve společenskohistorickém kontextu raně novověké Evropy, tak skrze divadelní a dramatickou analýzu. V závěru mého šetření se pokusíme izolovat problém pohostinnosti a toho Jiného a postavit jej do analogie s evropskou migrační krizí.

Tento článek popisuje primární dynamiku židovsko-křesťanské interakce v Shakespearových Benátkách a ukazuje na možný závěr, který lze vyvodit z tragické konstelace porušeného paktu pohostinnosti, který vede k ambivalentnímu a hluboce zneklidňujícímu konci hry. Stejný závěr může být použit jako plán pro současnou společenskou a politickou situaci v Evropě. Nedostatek diskuze a vzájemné deliberace spojuje tuto hru a současnou Evropu a v obou případech lze hledat stejné příčiny i možné řešení tohoto problému.

Klíčová slova: Shakespeare, Derrida, pohostinnost, Evropa, migrační krize

Crisis of European Identity?

European Union has faced many challenges since its inception as the European Coal and Steel Community in 1951. The post-war trauma that European societies had to overcome was, for the first time, effectively brought to the communal space. The years following the end of the Second World War saw an increasing move towards democratisation on all levels of the state, which helped to facilitate debate both within individual states and in the European community at large. The ensuing dialogue between many diverse nations and cultures took place to shape a new Europe. The primary challenge of the discussions that surrounded the formation of the European Union was very old and well known to many of its participating nations. However, there was no consensus or ready answer they could share in response to this challenge. It was a question of identity – what unites Europe, what makes us different, where to draw the boundaries between them and us, and what this binary should look like. All of these questions had a long history that went back further to the nineteenth century and each particular nation answered these questions in its unique way. Looking back to the nineteenth century, these answers have played a central role in the politics of the national revolutions, unification movements and wars. The anxiety arising from these questions, or, individually, from the lack of any robust solution available to the inquiring parties, is entangled with the horrors of the Second World War, the Shoah and the ethnic cleansings and expulsions that took place in the aftermath of this conflict.

The project launched at first by ECSC and later by the EU was, among other things, trying to revisit these fundamental questions and provide an answer that would prevent new disasters and hostilities fuelled by nationalistic sentiments from happening. Moreover, although there have been many scholarly inquiries into the precise way in which the EU tried to construct the present European identity (if, indeed, there is any shared identity to talk about), and although the process itself and its basic tenets have been more or less satisfactorily acknowledged by some of these inquiries, this construction is not without serious shortcomings (Colomer 2008, 280-284). The European refugee crisis is, of course, the prime example as to how insufficient even the attempt at building a common European identity has been. However, even though the refugee crisis can be considered at least partly averted by various negotiations which took place during June and July of the year 2018 and earlier, the impact of the migration crisis is still very much alive and present in the everyday lives of many

Europeans, even if only latently. European politics are still divided on the issue of immigration, and many of the current government parties (especially in the member states of the Visegrád Group) maintain their popular support by appealing to the anti-immigration sentiments present in the society. When the crisis started, it revealed the uncomfortable questions that challenged the European identity as constructed (or under construction) in the previous years. All the while the ensuing political turmoil and immediate creation of the "barricade mentality" left little to no space for a consequential re-evaluation and an actual discussion on what this encounter with the Other means to us, as Europeans.

In this essay I shall try to face that problem by referring to two sources – Shakespeare's play *The Merchant of Venice*, and the work and thought of Jacques Derrida, a philosopher who dealt with the question(s) posed by the Other. The goal of the present paper is to approach the difficulties arising from the encounter between the European society that is still forming its identity and the Other (the immigrant) by a juxtaposition with Shakespeare's play, which displays the uneasiness, disturbances and challenges innate to every encounter with the Other. First, I shall analyse selected parts of *The Merchant of Venice* and through a close reading try to identify segments that may throw light on our present predicament in Europe. The play has been chosen for its dramatization of the tensions that can arise from the conflict with the Other in a heterogeneous society, not unlike in present-day Europe. The framework for considering the issue of othering and the problems of accepting or rejecting the Other is a philosophical work that is concerned with the problematic of the meeting with the Other and with the binary of hospitality and hostility towards them. For this purpose, I shall use some of Derrida's philosophical ideas to address the outlined issues.

Shakespeare's time was marked by a series of dramatic changes that swept through English and European societies; the plagues decimated the population, and enclosures forced people into cities; the rise of Reformation divided and interrupted the social and religious fabric of England and Europe, while the nascent capitalism increased the overall social inequality. These events were part of Shakespeare's experience and enhanced the representation of the world in his dramatic works. The effort to make sense of these divisions and changes was one of the reasons why his plays resonated strongly with their contemporary audiences and to a no lesser extent with the generations to come. From the perspective of the twenty-first century, Shakespeare's work affects us with its accurate portrayal of inequality and of the dynamics that drive it. Furthermore, the representation of inequality in Shakespeare's works appears on multiple levels; Shakespeare portrays it both by linguistic means (choices of vocabulary, style and register) as well as through the narratives and identifiable themes. His portrayal of inequality appears to us as both believable and convincing. The ensuing reading of *The Merchant of Venice* should demonstrate what is meant by this particular statement.

The Name of the Other

The Merchant has often been read as a play that shows Shakespeare's sensibility and insight into the complicated relationships with the Other. Shakespeare probably wrote the play between the year 1596 and 1599 as a partial response to a revenge tragedy written by his fellow playwright Christopher Marlowe, called *The Jew of Malta* (Shapiro 1988). The story of *The Merchant* had several sources. Although there were very few (if any) Jews in England in Shakespeare's time, his audiences would have been familiar with many of the stereotypes associated with them (Halio 2008, 3-7). In our times, most of the possible aspects of antisemitism tend to be generally downplayed in favour of the overall emancipatory potential which this play has. This trend of downplaying antisemitism in *The Merchant of Venice* is further reinforced by the astonishing amount of criticism on this topic that has piled up in the last decades (Halio, 9-13). This critical turn is without a doubt a tendency of the late twentieth and twenty-first century and an indirect reaction to the Holocaust, but the potential for the critical power is inherent to the play itself (Halio, 1-3). Throughout the play, one can witness a process of othering both on Shylock's part, but more importantly, on the side of the Christians.

Shylock's public image is moulded by how he is addressed, talked about and imagined as much as in the way he sees himself. The way in which Shylock is presented is worth further examination. When he first enters the stage, he is addressed as Shylock, and Bassanio deals with him as with a merchant, although seemingly of lower status, as one can gather from Bassanio's impatient and sometimes even distrustful questioning (Shakespeare 2008, 1.3.7-8; further references to this work by act, scene, and verse only). Both Jews and usurers had a lower social standing in the medieval society, and so the fact that the Venetians view Shylock as someone of a lesser status is not so surprising; however, antisemitism was not universal and the mores of Shakespeare's times can hardly justify how Shylock is addressed during the rest of this scene (Kaplan 2007, 10-12). Bassanio asks for Shylock's approval "May you stead me? Will you pleasure me? Shall I know your answer?" (1.3.7-8) as he tries to assure Shylock of Antonio's solvency, which is something Shylock questions a moment later (1.3.27). At first, it seems that they engage in a dialogue. However, the conversation quickly develops into a spiteful verbal fight full of contempt that leaves no space for understanding.

Bassanio asks Shylock for money and he knows that Shylock is the only one who can help him in Venice. Even that does not stop him from mocking him (for example by inviting Shylock to dine at a Christian household), questioning his knowledge ("Have you heard any imputation to the contrary?" 1.3.13-14), and viewing him as his inferior – this contempt shows during the penultimate scene at the Venetian court where Bassanio likens Shylock to a devil ("and curb this cruel devil of his will," 4.1.214). At first, Shylock seems to be above these hateful feelings and prejudice and instead acts as a man of his trade, counting and processing the financial risks his loan will carry. Once he moves aside and exposes his thoughts through his soliloquy, one can see that even his mind is caught in a grudge that he holds towards the Christians and Antonio in particular. Shylock's feelings are more lucid and articulated in this regard ("How like a fawning publican he looks. / I hate him because he is a Christian / [...] Cursed be my tribe / if I forgive him," 1.3.38-48). However, that is because he is given the dramatic privilege of his soliloquy, whereas the audience is left to decipher the real extent of Bassanio's and Antonio's dislike of Shylock from their public utterances.

Afterwards, Shylock and Antonio engage in a heated verbal exchange and eventually they cast off their appearances of peaceful citizens and show themselves as hateful enemies. It is important to note that this shift occurs along the lines of a theological debate. First, one can see Shylock recounting the biblical story of Jacob ("When Jacob grazed his uncle Laban's sheep..." 1.3.68) and only when Shylock suggests that his mercantile faculties equal that of Jacob does Antonio retort to linking him to a devil ("the devil can cite Scripture for his purpose / [...] O, what a goodly outside falsehood hath!" 1.3.95-99). The point of friction is the difference in their religions and the fear that one or the other might have a better claim to their shared Scripture. What ensues is, therefore, not a dialogue or a discussion, but an open conflict, as both Shylock and Antonio revive all their old animosities, the power of which surpasses that of their economic motivations and ultimately thwarts even the strictly financial relations between them (best seen in the scene of the trial).

When Antonio approaches Shylock, he uses a variety of names to call him, which demonstrates the way Antonio thinks. He likens him to a devil (1.3.95) or a villain (1.3.97), he addresses him as a dog and a cur (1.3.126), but also as a Hebrew (1.3.175). All the names that Antonio associates with Shylock reflect the unstable and multifaceted position that a Jew had in the medieval and early modern Christian fantasy: a Jew could be something inherently evil or just a lowly servant, but as a "Hebrew" he could just as well be wise and furnished with the qualities of the Prophets from the Old Testament.

Two plausible reasons for the conflict between Antonio and Shylock can be identified – religion and trade techniques – that are accordingly tied to personal and religious ethics and their respective social positions. The first reason for the hatred that Shylock feels towards Antonio (or perhaps Bassanio as the text itself leaves us without any indication) is his Christian faith. Shylock says: "How like a fawning publican he looks. / I hate him for he is a Christian" (1.3.38-39); however, he adds "but more for that in low simplicity, / he lends out money gratis and brings down / the rate of usance here with us in Venice" (1.3.40-42). This remark suggests that his animosity stems partly from a religious difference, but also that the main factor is the difference in approach to trading practices. In the following dialogue, Shylock explains his view on usury to Antonio and justifies himself by his reading of the Scripture. It is important to note that of all the possible things, he chooses to explain his position as a Jew (and therefore a man of the Book) towards usury and thus his trading practices. This is understandable in the discussion of a business proposal (as well as it explains the basic moral and economic background of the practice to the audience). Importantly, Shylock exposes part of his identity as presented to the Other (i.e. Antonio); it consists of both his religion and his profession as a money-lender. Justifying his claim as a usurer by quoting the Bible, he consequently makes the Scripture and the practice of usury inseparable. Antonio replies to this with "This was a venture, sir, that Jacob served for, / A thing not in his power to bring to pass / but swayed and fashioned by the hand of heaven" (1.3.88-90), which in turn shows Antonio's Christian interpretation of the Verse, more akin to the Protestant reading of the Bible.

The competitive, highly structured and fundamentally violent environment of the early modern period or, in other words, of the nascent of capitalism, intertwined with the authorities, practices and world-view inherited from the Middle Ages. On the one hand, an individual was expected to make his wealth with the help of his merits or the fortune of his daring, as the Venetian merchants did whenever they invested in their argosies. However, on the other hand, his position remained deeply rooted in the political and cultural customs of his surroundings and his religion. So if the Jew wanted to venture his capital, the society would not allow it. From this clash of two different world-views sprang the precarious position of many of the early modern Jews. Shylock's role is crucial for the emergence and sustenance of the venture capitalist society that is dependent on his usury precisely because it was otherwise forbidden for all Christians. However, it was indispensable for all venture capitalists. This crux resulted in a vital threat to the Christian dogma that remained in the centre of Western society (Greenblatt 1978, 292-295). Shylock's otherness is, therefore, intrinsically linked both to his religion and to his role in the society. His otherness gives him an almost threatening power, but it excludes him entirely from the Christian community.

Hospitality, Law and Dialogue

To illustrate this deep divide between him and the rest of Venice one might turn to Derrida's essay *Of Hospitality*. There he discusses the status and attributes of a foreigner as he is embodied by Oedipus or Socrates and summarises the predicament of a foreigner like this:

> The Foreigner carries and puts the fearful question, he sees or foresees himself, he knows he is already put into question by the paternal and reasonable authority of the *logos*. The paternal authority of the *logos* gets ready to disarm him, to treat him as mad, and this at the very moment when his question, the question of the Foreigner, only seems to contest in order then to remind people of what ought to be obvious even to the blind! (Derrida 2000, 11)

It would be challenging to see Shylock as an embodiment of the Foreigner that Derrida has in mind. However, this analogy can still help us understand the nature of the relationship between Shylock and the rest of the characters.

When Shylock comes to the court, he brings with him a dagger and a pair of scales – appropriated and perverted attributes of Lady Justice. With them, he also brings his ideals of justice supported by his interpretation of the Scripture and his sense of identity in Venice. This entrance is all the more threatening because the ideals he brings with him draw their authority from the very same Scripture the Christians use. In other words, Shylock "carries and puts the fearful question" by opposing the prevailing sense of justice held by the rest of the court and contrasting it with a different reading that is "his," as it is a constitutive part of his sense of self (his *ipseity*). Shylock believes that he is calling for the universal law when he says "My deeds upon my head! I crave the law, / the penalty and forfeit of my bond" (4.1.203-204), and his stubbornness that is possibly nurtured by his experience of a life of inequality forbids him to listen to any suggestions or pleas of the opposing party.

This understanding of justice is visibly perverted, and the modern audience might find it hard to accept without any further adjustments, to some extent because it represents a very literal interpretation of the law that is usually associated with religious fundamentalism. The Christians try to offer other solutions (such as paying double the amount of the original debt), but seeing that Shylock will not be satisfied by anything else than "the law," Portia decides to use this determination to her advantage. She gives him "the law" that he does not even realise he is demanding, by outwitting him into a full consent without disclosing the full scope of the sentence. One can best see her manoeuvre when she says: "Thyself shall see the act; / for as thou urgest justice, be assured / thou shalt have justice, more than thou desir'st" (4.1.311-313) and later on in the scene "The Jew shall have all justice. Soft! No haste! / He shall have nothing but the penalty!" (4.1.318-319).

When approaching laws from the legalistic point of view that Shylock held unto this point, Portia is undoubtedly right. The moral problems that arise from her involvement are manifold – first of all, her presence is an act of deceit and transgresses the boundaries of law; secondly, she uses the laws of Venice with the knowledge that Shylock is a Jew, and thus not a full citizen, and she does so to sentence him and strip him of his wealth. This predicament leads us to the question that Derrida works with: whether the law is something universal or if there are different sets of laws for every set of people, and, ultimately, if there are two types of law (universal and particular) that is ethically correct when dealing with others. For if there were no special clauses in the Venetian law for "aliens," Shylock would get his rightful bond. When he calls for "the law," he calls for a level and universal treatment before the court of justice, but after he gets disqualified from Portia's understanding of universal law – that of transcending mercy and charity – she, as a representative and mediator for the state of Venice, lets him fall into the clutches of an uneven and, from a modern point of view, an anti-semitic law.

The reaction of the Venetians reveals how Shylock's standing in Venice is perceived and gives us a clue as to what his position in the Venetian society was. By addressing him not as Shylock, but as "the Jew" (4.1.13, 33) and later on as a dog, wolf and so on, he is judged primarily as a Jew and only later as an individual, as Shylock. The primary trait of identification is his Jewishness, that is the most important fact for both Shylock and the Christians. Derrida's understanding of the "contract" between the foreigner and the host shows that it is of a hereditary character and Shylock inherits his position as a guest in the Venetian society (Derrida 2000, 21-22). Although he is an integral part of the early modern capitalist society that has a space for him in both its judicial and ideological apparatus, Venice will never be his home precisely because of these laws that condition his stay. Shylock's questioning of the Venetian law that proves to be a Christian law in more than one sense, with Mercy in its centre, brings him into conflict with his "host" or, in other words, the Christian Venice and leads to the breaking of the pact of hospitality.

This conflict is the point where one comes to the very crux of the problem and where several crucial questions, yet again, arise. Why is Shylock still a guest in a place where, one can assume, he was born and the language of which he can speak just as well as any other Venetian? Do his actions justify different treatment before the court regarding different laws that are intrinsically connected to his status as a guest? And lastly, is the treatment of immigrants in Europe during the recent crisis in any way similar and what could be the implications arising from these points concerning our future in the European community?

An answer to these problematic and entangled questions might be found in Derrida's understanding of law and hospitality. In the latter part of his essay, called "Step of Hospitality / No Hospitality," Derrida introduces the antinomy of hospitality which is a paradox uniting *The* law and the laws. On the one hand, there is the unlimited hospitality that should compel us to offer ourselves to the guest without any rules or conditions, and, on the other hand, there is the hospitality as a pact of the guest and the host. These two concepts stand in opposition and, at the same time, they complement each other as *The* law could not exist without the laws that are articulating it while being guided and inspired themselves (Derrida 2000, 79-81). To welcome someone at home there needs to be a border for the guest to cross and a fundamental binary between the guest and the host, and so there is no dissociation of the two forms of hospitality. The impossibility to resolve this antinomy does not directly equal a failure. The grey area between the particular laws and the complete openness is a place for negotiation between us and the Others, and this can in turn be used as a space where contact and dialogue is possible.

In *The Merchant of Venice*, both Shylock and the Christians fail to find this space where negotiation is possible and where both parties can change to not only coexist but also to live together. I followed some of the scenes where Shylock meets Antonio or the Venetian establishment, and I examined how they approached, addressed and communicated with each other. I also explored the way their communication shaped or reflected upon the Jewish identity of Shylock and, finally, I analysed the Venetian concept of justice and both Shylock's and the Christian discourse regarding the law. Nowhere in the play do the two parties meet: the greatest tragedy of *The Merchant* is the inevitability of the clash between Shylock and the Christians. Shylock is pushed aside by the Christian establishment and none of the characters makes an effort to engage and meet the Other. Derrida's philosophy of hospitality proves useful in theorising and making sense of this situation and points towards a way leading to a possible solution.

The present-day European politics have often made the same mistake as the Christians did in Shakespeare's play and left little to no room for an actual dialogue between them and us and, worse yet, in many cases there has not even been a chance to meet with the Foreigner as several governments took a hard stance against the migration and closed their borders. In order to stop any future disasters or tragedies, such as the ones witnessed in *The Merchant* or during the Second World War, a space where both the hosts and the guests can meet, talk, deliberate and listen to each other has to be found. It is crucial to realise that some ethnic groups and minorities are still practically considered our guests. The dialogue with them should be reinitiated alongside with the work on our shared identity.

One has to open to Others not just because it is right or ethical and because this contact can help both parties, but because only through contact with the Other can we continually find ourselves.

References

Colomer, J.M. 2008. *Comparative European Politics*. New York, NY: Routledge.

Derrida, J. 2000. *Of Hospitality*. Translated by R. Bowlby. Stanford, CA: Stanford University Press.

Greenblatt, S.J. 1978. "Marlowe, Marx, and Anti-Semitism." *Critical Inquiry* 5(2). 291-307.

Halio, J.L. 2008. "Introduction." In: W. Shakespeare, *The Merchant of Venice*. Edited by J.L. Halio. New York, NY: Oxford University Press, 1-83.

Kaplan, M.L. 2007. "Jessica's Mother: Medieval Constructions of Jewish Race and Gender in *The Merchant of Venice*." *Shakespeare Quarterly* 58(1). 1-30.

Shakespeare, W. 2008. *The Merchant of Venice*. Edited by J.L. Halio. New York, NY: Oxford University Press.

Shapiro, J. 1988. "Which is *The Merchant* and which *The Jew*?" *Shakespeare Studies* 20. 269-279.

ELAHE MOUSAVIAN

University of Szeged

Shylock, the Undoubtable Other

Abstract

In Shakespeare's *The Merchant of Venice*, Shylock (the Jew) is the character whose "otherness" is obvious. He is excluded not only by the Christian Venetians, but even by his own daughter. In this study, I would like to focus on Shylock's character as the Other and the way other characters face him. As Martin Buber mentions, dialogue is a good means of understanding the Other. In this play, dialogue is the best structure within which we can explore the way of characters' encounters with Shylock as the Other, as well as Shylock's reactions to other people. It is noteworthy that in the very beginning of the play, facing the Other takes place just because that Other is needed. This may also lead us to think about the concept of "hostipitality" proposed by Derrida. In this case, Shylock is a stranger treated as an enemy rather than a guest. Here, the hostility is two-sided. Both sides (Shylock and the Venetians) keep the distance and approach each other only in case of need. The best scene in which we can observe this paradox of hospitality and hostility is when the Venetians invite Shylock to dinner. Therefore, the way both sides deal with this situation of hostipitality through dialogue as the means of communication must be investigated. On the other hand, examining Shylock's dialogues with himself will offer an insight into the way he defines his own position as the Other. Is he a passive and indifferent Other or a kind of person who wants to do something to change his condition? Finally, the main focus of this study will be the way in which the Other (Shylock) is defined via dialogue and the way hostipitality works in the relation between Shylock and others. I will also discuss the problem of facing the Other in the present context and in a different form to show that people living in the same state, speaking the same language, and having the same religion can also label each other as Others.

Keywords: Other, Shylock, hostipitality

Összefoglaló

Shakespeare *A velencei Kalmár* című művében Shylock (a zsidó) olyan karakter, akinek „Mássága" nyilvánvaló. Nemcsak a velencei keresztények, hanem a saját lánya is kirekeszti. Ebben a tanulmányban Shylock karakterére mint Másikra és a többi szereplő hozzá fűződő viszonyára szeretnék fókuszálni. Ahogy Martin Buber kifejti, a dialógus a Másik megértésének az egyik legjobb módja. Ebben a darabban a dialógus a legjobb struktúra, amelyen keresztül felfedezhetjük, ahogyan a karakterek szembekerülnek Shylockkal mint Másikkal, és hogy Shylock hogyan viszonyul a többiekhez. Érdemes megfigyelni, hogy a mű elején azért néznek szembe a Másikkal, mert szükség van rá. Ez el is vezet a „hosztipitalitás" Derrida által fejtegetett koncepciójához. Ebben az esetben Shylock egy idegen, akit inkább ellenségként, mintsem vendégként kezelnek. Itt az ellenségesség kétoldalú. Mindkét fél (Shylock és a velenceiek) megtartja a távolságot és csak szükség esetén közelítenek egymás felé. A vendéglátás (hoszpitalitás) és ellenségesség (hosztilitás) paradoxonának megfigyelésére a legjobb jelenet az, amikor a velenceiek ebédre invitálják Shylockot. Éppen ezért mindenképp meg kell vizsgálni, hogyan birkózik meg mindkét fél a dialógust mint kommunikációs módot használva a „hosztipitalitás" helyzetével. Másfelől azon dialógusok vizsgálata, amelyeket Shylock hordoz, betekintést engednek abba, hogyan definiálja saját magát a Másikként. Passzív és közömbös Másik-e, vagy egy olyan személy, aki szeretne tenni valamit azért, hogy változzon a szerepe? Végezetül a tanulmány fő fókusza arra fog irányulni, hogyan határozódik meg a Másik (Shylock) a dialóguson keresztül, és hogyan működik a „hosztipitalitás" Shylock és a többiek között. A Másikkal való szembenézés problémájáról napjaink kontextusában, más formában is értekezni fogok, hogy megmutassam, az olyan emberek, akik ugyanabban az államban élnek, ugyanazt a nyelvet beszélik és azonos vallásúak, szintén megbélyegezhetik egymást a Másikként.

Kulcsszavak: Másik, Shylock, hosztipitalitás

Introduction

Otherness, no matter what one would like to think, is never natural. Indeed, most sociological attempts to survey the idea of otherness have tended to schematise it as a part of identity construction. For George Herbert Mead, social identities can be constructed as we interact with other people and then reflect upon those social interactions and exchanges, and different forms of communication between self and other are what create the development of identity and self-image (Mead 1934). From the point of view of Zygmunt Bauman, otherness is more notable for its role in establishing social identities through dichotomies:

> Thus abnormality is the other of the norm, deviation the other of law-abiding, illness the other of health, barbarity the other of civilization, animal the other of the human, woman the other of man, stranger the other of the native, enemy the other of friend, "them" the other of "us," insanity the other of reason, foreigner the other of the state subject, lay public the other of the expert. Both sides depend on each other, but the dependence is not symmetrical. The second side depends on the first for its contrived and enforced isolation. The first depends on the second for its self-assertion. (Bauman 1991, 8)

A good example of the way in which self-identity can be built through the other is Simone de Beauvoir's exploration of otherness: "Otherness is a fundamental category of human thought. Thus it is that no group ever sets itself up as the One without at once setting up the Other over against itself" (de Beauvoir 1956, 16). Indeed, as Andrew Okolier comments, "Social identities are relational; groups typically define themselves in relation to others. This is because identity has little meaning without the 'other.' So, by defining itself a group defines others" (2003, 2).

In Shakespeare's *The Merchant of Venice*, Shylock (the Jew) is the character whose otherness is obvious. He has always been addressed as "Villain Jew" or "Dog Jew" by the Venetians. He is somehow excluded from the society, not only by the Christian Venetians, but even by his own daughter Jessica. Her escape from the father's house could be seen as an escape from a community which is considered to be the Others' community by the dominant Christians, who are in charge and hold power. Therefore, the otherness of Shylock will be even more emphasized when his community loses its members. In Act 3, Scene 1, when Tubal (another Jew) enters, Salarino says: "Here comes another of the tribe: a third cannot be matched, unless the devil himself turn Jew" (Shakespeare 1917, 3.1.77-79; further references to this text are by act, scene, and verse number only). Here we can see how a Venetian describes the Jews both as Others and a minority. This otherness and being in minority is also discernible in the number of Jewish characters and their roles in the whole play. Apart from Shylock, there are two more Jews – Tubal and Jessica. Among them, the latter turns Christian, while Tubal does not play a very important role. Even in the case of Shylock, he is fading out as we approach the end of the play and he disappears completely after his conversion. At the same time there are many Christian characters who have the opportunity to express themselves by the means of dialogue. In this way, we can perceive that the form of the play is in harmony with the content in order to depict the situation of the Others.

It is not simply that Shylock's position as an undoubtable Other should be the only example of otherness in the play. We cannot really decide to ascribe it to Shylock alone, because the Christians are definitely the Others for Shylock. Unlike other forms of otherness, which assume the Other on one side and the non-Others on the other side (and which can therefore acknowledge, but play down, the problem of how the non-Others receive the Other and contrariwise), otherness in this play is a two-sided problem. But, most of all, otherness in this play centres on Shylock: in a sense he is the obvious Other, as he is rejected and excluded both in form and content of the play. It should not be overlooked that one major aspect of his otherness has its roots in his disappearance after the forced conversion. After all, Shylock's withdrawal at the end of the play has really much to do with his otherness, his relegation to the gloomiest fate; it is a fact of exclusion and humiliation, if not of suppression.

The Merchant of Venice and Otherness

In this study, I would like to focus on Shylock's character as the Other and the way the other characters face him. Shylock's attitude towards Christians will also be the matter of attention. While the Venetians refer to Shylock only by negative names such as "dog," "villain" and "devil," for him it is enough to call the Venetians "Christians" to express his attitude. When Antonio asks for a loan and promises to pay back three times more than what he should get, Shylock says: "O father Abram, what these Christians are, / Whose own hard dealings teaches them suspect / The thoughts of others!" (1.3.160-162). Or in the scene at the court, Shylock again hesitates to use Antonio's name: "I take this offer then; pay the bond thrice, / And let the Christian go" (4.1.317-318). But what does it imply? Is being Christian itself enough of an insult or is his enmity towards the Venetians less strong than theirs towards him? Or is it simply a reaction to those who call him Jew all the time?

In this play, dialogue is the best structure within which we can explore the encounter of the Venetians with Shylock as the Other, as well as Shylock's reactions to them as Others. Yet the dialogue does not really function here (for either side) as a means of understanding the Other. For them, the Other has already been defined as a definite enemy with whom no understanding is sought; the dialogue is only a way of confronting, abusing and deceiving. It is noteworthy to see that at the very beginning of the play, the dialogue with the Other takes place only because that Other is needed. Interestingly, this is the only moment when Venetians treat the Other with some respect in order to get what they want:

> Bass. Ay, sir, for three months.
> Shy. For three months; well?
> Bass. For the which, as I told you, Antonio shall be bound.
> Shy. Antonio shall become bound; well?
> Bass. May you stead me? will you pleasure me? Shall I know your answer? (1.3.2-8)

This is a crucial moment of the play in the sense that it is the only moment in which Shylock is treated with respect, being addressed as "sir." Nevertheless, Bassanio seems to be anxious and impatient while wearing the mask of respect towards the Jew. Even Shylock himself is aware of his position as the Other who is needed when he says to Antonio:

> Signior Antonio, many a time and oft
> In the Rialto you have rated me
> About my moneys and my usances:
> Still have I borne it with a patient shrug,
> For sufferance is the badge of all our tribe.
> You call me misbeliever, cut-throat dog,
> And spet upon my Jewish gaberdine,
> And all for use of that which is mine own.
> Well then, it now appears you need my help. (1.3.106-114)

The concept of hostipitality proposed by Derrida may serve as a useful key to a different interpretation, however. Hospitality, according to Derrida, is a word which carries its own contradiction. It means that the guest is a welcomed stranger treated as a friend or ally, but the guest may also be a stranger treated as an enemy. Thus the terms hospitality/hostility and friend/enemy seem to merge into each other. In other words, it is the right of a stranger not to be treated with hostility when he arrives on someone else's territory, but at the same time the host maintains his or her authority. It means that it is the host who defines the conditions and laws of hospitality, therefore, there will not be any unconditional welcome. In this way, there are limitations upon the situation of hospitality and it depends on the person's reactions to the rules of the host that identifies him as an enemy or as a friend (Derrida 2010, 3-4). On such reading, Shylock is a stranger treated as an enemy rather than a guest. As someone who has been accused of usury, he admits he is not positioned as a friend, and he is the Venetians' particular enemy. Indeed, who Shylock is to the Venetians is inextricably blended with how he will engage in the host's environment, and it will affect their talk and their encounter. Yet, the hostility is on both sides because Shylock and the Venetians keep the distance and approach each other only in case of need.

The best scene in which we can observe this paradox of hospitality and hostility is when the Venetians invite Shylock to dinner. The way both sides deal with this situation of hostipitality in the dialogue as the means of communication must be investigated. Since hostility here is mutual, communication becomes questionable. Shylock's response to the invitation demonstrates his attitude clearly:

> Yes, to smell pork; to eat of the habitation which your prophet the Nazarite conjured the devil into. I will buy with you, sell with you, talk with you, walk with you, and so following; but I will not eat with you, drink with you, nor pray with you. (1.3.34-38)

This passage defines Shylock's limitations in his relation with the Venetians. An important point to mention here is that religion itself can be a suitable ground to differentiate people. The followers of different religions usually regard one another as Others. This may lead them to call the other side "devil" since they believe themselves to be on the side of God. There are many instances in the play where the Venetians indicate the otherness of Shylock by associating him with devil or seeing in him the devil himself. For example,

Salanio says when he sees Shylock: “Let me say ‘amen’ betimes, lest the devil cross my prayer, for here he comes in the likeness of a Jew” (3.1.20-22). Is there any similarity between the devil and the Other? Devil is the Other himself since he was rejected by God and the community of angels and in most religions he is known as the fallen angel. Therefore, devil is the representation of the extreme Other with whom all Others are associated.

Looking at things from a different perspective, the examination of Shylock’s monologue offers an insight into the way he himself defines his position as the Other. Is he a passive and indifferent Other or a kind of person who wants to do something to change his position? As we mentioned before, for Shylock calling the Venetians “Christians” is sufficient to show contempt and hatred towards them. In one of his monologues, he says:

> These be the Christian husbands! I have a daughter;
> Would any of the stock of Barrabas
> Had been her husband rather than a Christian! (4.1.293-296)

And elsewhere when meeting Antonio, he says to himself:

> How like a fawning publican he looks!
> I hate him for he is a Christian,
> But more for that in low simplicity
> He lends out money gratis and brings down
> The rate of usance here with us in Venice.
> If I can catch him once upon the hip,
> I will feed fat the ancient grudge I bear him.
> He hates our sacred nation, and he rails.
> Even there where merchants most do congregate.
> On me, my bargains and my well-won thrift,
> which he calls interest. Cursed be my tribe,
> If I forgive him! (1.3.41-52)

Although he considers himself superior to Christians, he has to deal with them in a different way, because they are the ones in power. In one of his arguments with them he tries to prove that Jews, like Christians, are human beings:

> Hath not a Jew eyes? hath not a Jew hands, organs, dimensions, senses, affections, passions? Fed with the same food, hurt with the same weapons, subject to

> the same diseases, healed by the same means, warmed and cooled by the same winter and summer, as a Christian is? If you prick us, do we not bleed? If you tickle us, do we not laugh? If you poison us, do we not die? And if you wrong us, shall we not revenge? If we are like you in the rest, we will resemble you in that. (3.1.57-67)

Regardless of the speaker (Shylock), this speech could be a manifest of equality. It eloquently explains the very obvious but forgotten similarities of all human beings. These essential similarities are usually forgotten when people decide to define Others as different and therefore worse.

We may ask if Shylock as the Other has any voice in this text? Is he passive or active regarding his situation as the Other? There is not one definite answer to this question since his position changes during the play. At the beginning, he has an active role with many dialogues and monologues to express himself and his enmity towards Christians. But as we get closer to the end of the play, he speaks less and gradually disappears from the scene. This asymmetry of his role in the play says a lot about the way he faces his otherness. The very argumentative character of Shylock turns to a passive one. The turning point of this change takes place in the court. When he realizes that the doctor is not as objective as he thought, he is ready to accept everything without any argument. The critical situation of needing the Other also plays an important role in this change. The Venetians gave the voice to Shylock till he was needed. Antonio in the court says:

> For the commodity that strangers have
> With us in Venice, if it be denied,
> Will much impeach the justice of the state;
> Since that the trade and profit of the city
> Consisteth of all nations. (3.3.27-31)

His concern is all about profit and the Other is important here, because he is needed. Shylock becomes passive when he is sentenced and forced to be converted. His disappearance after the conversion may be interpreted as the absorption of a minority by the majority. He is not even an Other anymore. He is now absorbed by the Christian society and he does not have a voice as he is no longer needed. Or even worse, he becomes nobody.

It is interesting to take a critical look at the actions of the Venetians. They seem to act against their own religion. They keep talking about mercy but when it comes to face the Other, fraud is accepted. They seem to want to change Shylock to be one of them from the very beginning. Antonio says: "This Hebrew will turn Christian: he grows kind" (1.3.178). The Venetians in a way push the Jew to redefine his stance as the Other. At the same time they will consistently treat him as the hated Other. Again, Shylock is aware of their ways and he keeps his own otherness carefully. He says to his daughter before leaving for dinner with the Venetians:

> I am bid forth to supper, Jessica:
> There are my keys. But wherefore should I go?
> I am not bid for love; they flatter me:
> But yet I'll go in hate, to feed upon
> The prodigal Christian. (2.5.11-15)

When given opportunities to talk about his otherness in critical ways, Shylock not only shows an understanding of his situation as the Other, but he also depicts the Venetians' weaknesses. Yet, verbal expression is only one of many languages of the play. Shakespeare used the end of the play – that is, "Shylock's disappearance after his conversion" – to demonstrate that the Venetians keep regarding Shylock as the undoubtable Other even after his forced conversion.

Facing the Other: From Shakespeare's Play to the Present-day Crises

In Levinas's eyes, the Other is the one who is essentially different and foreign to us. He also sees the Other as an ethical teacher in the sense that we can learn from and about the Other (Levinas 1969, 51). But defining and facing the Other is not always as easy as this. It means that the Other is not necessarily defined by his or her obvious differences. Rather than simply differentiating and stigmatizing the Other, we actively construct the meaning of the term. What I think we should keep in mind is that Others might not be necessarily different from us and still be considered as Others, because we define them as such.

On the other hand, seeing the Other as an ethical teacher is a very idealistic proposition; I doubt that it may happen often, perhaps in some individual relations. In the social context, the Other is mostly a learner rather than a teacher. The Others are supposed to learn to behave as the majority if they want to survive in that society. In this sense, stigmatizing people as Others means that they lack something, that they are not very welcome by the majority, or at least treated with suspicion. Even if they change themselves to be adapted to the rest of the society, they are not totally accepted. As mentioned before, Otherness does not always mean being totally different. The encounter with the Other does happen even when that Other shares the same language, culture and religion with the majority. Considering the social and historical context of the Jews and the Venetians, we should realize that they were not very different in the sense that they lived together in the same state for a long time, they spoke the same language (Shylock can easily communicate with the members of the Christian society) and they even had the same religious roots, as Christianity grew out of the Judaic tradition and so its adherents pray to the same God.

The meeting with the Other in our world is not only about differences. It is true that when we talk about the crisis of facing the Other in Europe, this Other is the one coming from a non-European society with a different language, culture and most often with a different religion. But it is not always like this everywhere else in the world. To demonstrate the complexity of the concept of Other, I would like to mention the case of otherness of the Afghans in Iran. The Afghans and the Persians share the same language and religion. Yet, the Afghans in Iran are refugees or immigrants who have fled from the war. Their population in Iran is more than two million. They are usually employed in a limited number of dangerous and poorly paid manual labour jobs, regardless of their education and skills. Often, they suffer various forms of violence in their everyday life in Iran exactly because they are considered the Others. In her report on Afghan refugees in Iran, Janne Bjerre Christensen writes:

> Although the negative experiences of being Afghan in Iran depend on the geopolitical games, and the fluctuating and unpredictable policies of the Iranian state, it is of course tightly connected to the denigrating attitudes and outright racism, which they meet in the Iranian population – heavily influenced by populist policies and financial crises. The Afghans, I have interviewed in Denmark, speak of widespread discrimination, humiliations, physical attacks and racism (nejâdparasti). They emphasise the lack of dignity and of being constantly considered less worthy than the Iranians. "It's a kind of shame to say, 'I'm Afghan,'" A said. S emphasised: "Being an Afghan is like being a criminal." "They called us afghâni kasif, 'dirty Afghan,' and afghâni ashghâl, 'Afghan trash.' We feel really

> humiliated. They don't think we're human at all. Animals in Iran are treated better than we are," R told me. (Bjerre Christensen 2016, 33)

If all those people, the Afghans and the Persians, share the same background, why should they feel to be so very different? There must be reasons and motives other than just obvious differences responsible for the division into us and others. One should consider power relations and economic problems. The analysed play can shed some light on this issue – Shylock is not hated only because he is a Jew but also because he is a usurer and he makes money. Economically, he is a serious rival for Christians. The Afghans are not hated just because they are foreigners and strangers. They are Others because they are regarded as inferior to the Iranians culturally. They are simply Others because they have no power and no money. The crisis can also be related to the issue of self-identification, which was discussed in the beginning of this essay. As self is defined in relation to the Other and as these two are usually seen as opposites, degrading the other may be a way of self-aggrandizement. Therefore, both Christians in the play and contemporary Iranians identify themselves as superior by using their social power to degrade the Other even though they share similar backgrounds with those considered as Others.

Finally, there is a real danger that the crisis of otherness will grow as technology, science, and society develop. We may face new forms of otherness while we are trying to find solutions to the current ones. An additional complication is the development of science, which raises yet another problem of Otherness. The development of zoology highlighted the difference between the human and the animal. The development of biology emphasizes the difference between men and women. The development of psychology shows us the differences between the child and the adult and between all human beings. With the development of societies and cultures and lifestyles we shall be subjected to more and different kinds of otherness. Knowing the differences in itself is beneficial in a sense that it teaches us how to behave and how to learn from each different person or community. But we should always be aware of the role of power in defining the Other. Maybe otherness will not be a crisis anymore only in the case of abolishing the power hierarchy, which allows some people to think that their differences are privileges and Others' differences are weaknesses.

References

Bauman, Z. 1991. *Modernity and Ambivalence.* Ithaca, NY: Cornell University Press.

Bjerre Christensen, J. 2016. *Guests or Trash: Iran's Precarious Policies Towards the Afghan Refugees in the Wake of Sanctions and Regional Wars.* Copenhagen: Danish Institute for International Studies.

de Beauvoir, S. 1956. *The Second Sex.* Translated and edited by H.M. Parshley. London: Jonathan Cape.

Derrida, J. 2010. "Hostipitality." *Angelaki: Journal of the Theoretical Humanities* 5(3). 3-18.

Levinas, E. 1969. *Totality and Infinity: An Essay on Exteriority.* Translated by A. Lingis. Pittsburgh: Duquesne University Press.

Mead, G.H. 1934. *Mind, Self, and Society.* Edited by Charles W. Morris. Chicago: University of Chicago Press.

Okolier, A.C. (ed.). 2003. *Identity and Power in Africa and the Caribbean.* N.p.: Psychology Press.

Shakespeare, W. 1917. *The Merchant of Venice.* Edited by Ch. Knox Pooler. London: Methuen.

FEDERICA BONORA

University of Ferrara

Shakespeare's Art as a Vehicle for Mediation on the Global Refugee Crisis

Abstract

This article explores the contemporary refugee crisis, the theme of the encounter with the Other and the theatre as an experiential approach that can educate people to understanding, acceptance and empathy. In this work William Shakespeare serves as a foil for a discussion of past and present forms of life, fiction and narrative that accompany the escape routes of refugees seeking refuge and relief. The article opens with general observations on the refugee crisis in Europe and its depiction of the Other. Further, it considers the social theatre as a special place that can lead to a community relationship with a plurality of identities, which are strengthened by the encounter between diversity and complexity. William Shakespeare's works make viewers aware of the complexity of some social problems that still exist today. Some of his plays are still linked to social, political, and economic issues of our time, such as otherness, racism, migration, the refugees. What makes Shakespeare so special is that the playwright does not deliberately provide concrete solutions to these problems, but in fact offers various perspectives and many possibilities for reflection. It is the task of the reader/spectator to find a possible solution to these issues. For example, the play *The Book of Sir Thomas More* can be read as a type of narrative that, using empathy and the refugee's image, can be used by schools, theatre workshops, and associations with a pro-refugee and intercultural purpose. The theatre is a space of total freedom and a place where one can be welcomed, recognised, accepted for the identity that represents us. Social theatre promotes the defence of human dignity and it is a source of real integration and understanding. This type of theatre also looks for the psychophysical well-being of the members of the communities through the identification of communicative, expressive and relational practices, which are capable of mitigating the individual stress, fears and malaise. This article aims to demonstrate that the recent adaptations of Shakespeare's works are able to promote a true encounter between cultures as well as the psychological well-being and empowerment of its participants. Some examples of Shakespearean re-imaginations with refugee actors and immigrant communities are, for example, Nawar Bulbul's *King Lear*, Bulbul's *Romeo and Juliet* (via Skype), and Jessica Bauman's *As You Like It*.

Keywords: refugees, theatre, William Shakespeare, crisis, otherness

Sommario

Questo elaborato esplora la crisi contemporanea dei rifugiati, il tema dell'incontro con l'Altro e il teatro come un approccio esperienziale che può educare le persone alla comprensione, all'accettazione e all'empatia. In questo lavoro William Shakespeare funge da complemento per la discussione sulle forme di narrazioni di vita e di fantasia, passate e presenti, che accompagnano le vie di fuga dei rifugiati in cerca di rifugio e di soccorso. Questo articolo si è aperto con un'osservazione generale della crisi dei rifugiati in Europa e della sua percezione e presentazione dell'Altro. In questo lavoro si osserva in particolare modo il teatro sociale inteso come luogo speciale che può condurre ad una relazione comunitaria di pluralità identitarie, che risultano rafforzate grazie all'incontro tra diversità e complessità. Le opere teatrali di William Shakespeare rendono gli spettatori consapevoli della complessità di alcuni problemi sociali che esistono ancora oggi. Alcune delle sue opere teatrali sono ancora legate a questioni sociali, politiche, economiche del nostro tempo, come l'alterità, il razzismo, l'esodo, i rifugiati. Ciò che rende Shakespeare così speciale è che il drammaturgo inglese non fornisce di proposito soluzioni concrete a questi problemi, ma di fatto offre varie prospettive e molte possibilità di riflessione. Spetta al lettore/spettatore il compito di ricercare tali soluzioni. Ad esempio, l'opera teatrale *The Book of Sir Thomas More* può essere letta come un tipo di narrazione che, utilizzando l'empatia e l'immagine del rifugiato, può essere utilizzata da scuole, laboratori teatrali e associazioni con un fine pro-rifugiati e interculturale. La festa del teatro è uno spazio di totale libertà e un luogo dove si può essere accolti, riconosciuti, accettati per l'identità che ci rappresenta. Il teatro sociale favorisce la difesa della dignità umana ed è fonte di reale integrazione e comprensione. Questo tipo di teatro ricerca inoltre il benessere psicofisico dei membri delle comunità mediante l'individuazione di pratiche comunicative, espressive e relazionali, capaci di calmierare lo stress individuale, paure e malesseri. Questo articolo intende dimostrare che i recenti adattamenti delle opere del Bardo siano in grado di promuovere un vero incontro tra le culture nonché il benessere psicologico e l'empowerment dei suoi partecipanti. Alcuni esempi di adattamenti shakesperiani con profughi-attori e comunità di immigrati sono, ad esempio, il *King Lear* e il *Romeo and Juliet* (via Skype) di Nawar Bulbul, *As You Like It* di Jessica Bauman.

Parole chiave: rifugiati, teatro, William Shakespeare, crisi, alterità

Introduction

In this paper, I am going to analyse some processes leading to the eradication of prejudice, hostility, and rejection in our contemporary society. I believe people need to be more concerned about migration issues and therefore this essay will propose a discussion of the incessant crisis of encountering the Other, which raises from racial differences and the plight of human beings situated on the periphery of social exclusion. The article draws mainly on William Shakespeare, whose plays make people aware of the complexity of some problems which exist today. Several of his works are directly related to social and political issues of our times, such as otherness, racism, refugeedom, and migration. Theatre could encourage a real meeting among cultures, a better understanding of the current problems the European Union is facing, of social development through migration, of the issue of human dignity and well-being of migrants. As one cannot live without eating, so one cannot have a reasonable quality of life without the mechanisms of representation, and theatre is a place that provides this kind of nourishment. It is the place where people rediscover the self, one's own history, one's own dimension of subject, and the role people play in the community to which they belong. In this paper, I am going to argue that Shakespeare's art plays an important role: it represents the crises of our time; in some plays we can hear refugees' voices, which can educate people and become testimony to experimenting with new Shakespearean adaptations. Through narration in the theatre, people can be made aware of the problems of our time.

Recently, some of the most famous works of Shakespeare – *As You Like It*, *Hamlet*, *King Lear*, *The Tempest*, *Romeo and Juliet*, to name a few – have been produced in various theatres or refugee camps around the world. At this point, it is crucial to make an appropriate division of the adaptations of Shakespeare's plays that will be analysed here: 1) adaptations with actor-refugees; 2) plays adapted with a pro-refugee purpose; 3) plays which are shown to an audience composed of people in marginal spaces such as refugee camps; 4) social theatre workshops that use the works of Shakespeare to let the young participants find their own voice. Shakespeare's art has also been used in a didactic and experiential approach which can educate new generations of students in understanding, acceptance and empathy towards others.

Crises

Europe is coping with the situation of refugees displaced from their home, on their way to Europe. Fleeing from poverty, war, terrorism, climate change in Africa, Middle East and Asia, they look for shelter on the grounds of humanitarian ideals. The current situation is unprecedented in history: a wave of desperate, expropriated people, made up of men, women, children and infants, who cross the Mediterranean by precarious means of transport, only to arrive to Europe at the geographically and economically weakest points (the coasts of Greece, Italy and Spain). Most of these refugees wish to reach Northern Europe, which is currently the strongest geographical and economic area on the European continent. The European heads of state and politicians, such as Viktor Orbán and Matteo Salvini, protest against the European Union's migration policy: the Hungarian Prime Minister has erected the border barrier between Hungary and Serbia, while the former Italian Interior Minister closed the ports during his term in office. In the disorderly camp of Horgos, the transition zone on the border between Serbia and Hungary, refugees are waiting to learn their fate. The migration crisis was exacerbated again with the Turkish invasion of north-eastern Syria in October 2019. Turkish President Recep Tayyip Erdoğan responded with harsh words to the statement of condemnation issued by EU Foreign Minister Federica Mogherini. Erdoğan angrily threatened to send 3.6 million refugees to Europe, if the EU tried to present Turkey's operation as an invasion (Giorgio 2019). Turkey offers hospitality to about half of the 5.6 million Syrian refugees. In March 2020, about 35,000 migrants have gathered at Turkey's borders with the

EU since the Turkish president broke the 2016 pact under which Brussels promised to pay six billion euros in return for hosting (or retaining) refugees fleeing Syria (Boffey 2020). Erdoğan has also accused the European Union in recent months of lack of solidarity with his military operations in Syria and asserted that Turkey would have already spent about forty billion euros in housing refugees in his country (Boffey 2020).

For Alfred Hornung, asylum or bread-and-water seekers, exiles, stateless refugees are thus reduced to a subhuman status, "haunted by the problem of identity" (Hornung 2017, 617). Hornung argues that these vulnerable people share the status of outcasts and outlaws, trying to find salvation in the form of transactional and transcultural belonging. The status of refugees can be linked to the "liquid life" category of the sociologist Zygmunt Bauman, which is linked to the quick patterns of consumption of a liquid modern society. Following Bauman's reasoning, the refugees live in a sort of "liquid life," based on "a precarious life, lived under conditions of constant uncertainty" (Bauman 2005, 2). The philosopher Judith Butler claimed in *Frames of War* that the term "precarious" is "operative in imprisonment and torture, but also in the politics of immigration, according to which certain lives are perceived as lives while others, though apparently living, fail to assume perceptual form as such" (Butler 2004, 24).

We must ask ourselves what is the meaning of the word "crisis" – a fundamental term for the discussion of this paper. A definition of "crisis" in the English language is provided by the Oxford Dictionary: "a time of great danger, difficulty or uncertainty when problems must be solved or important decisions must be made" (Hornby 2000, 298). The crisis is the point at which we recognize that things must change, circulate, evolve: it is a time when we discuss and try to find solutions to the problem, taking concrete decisions and opening up new perspectives. According to Marta Gibińska, the crisis leads to the possible development of a state of instability or danger, dealing with social, economic, political or international issues, which usually lead to a radical change (Gibińska 2018, 1). Moreover, the crisis can cause an emotional or circumstantial upheaval in a person's life; in this dramatic and significant moment the involved people must make a difficult and/or important decision. Countless crises have always characterized the European cultures. It is worth remembering some crucial crises and consequent migrations that accompanied our European history: the Edict of Expulsion of the Jews from the Kingdom of England (1290); the Alhambra Decree (1492), which expelled the Jews from Spain; the exodus of the Huguenots from France after the Edict of Fontainebleau (1685); the immigration to the United States of European emigrants in colonial times; the Great Depression (1873-1895); the 1929 Crisis; mass evacuations, forced displacement, expulsions and deportations during the Second World War; the Holocaust; the Financial Crisis in Europe linked to the Great Recession between 2006 and 2013; the so-called "brain drain" in different periods; and, finally, the European Migrants' Crisis from 2013 to the present.

German journalist Ralph Bollmann (2015) recently compared the historic migration of 1500 years ago with the current situation in Europe. In his comparison, Bollman refers to the status of the Roman Empire in the fourth century as a prosperous and open society characterized by migration flows. The Romans did not want to face up to their migration crisis and did not give hospitality to the migrants, despite the fact that the Roman Empire had been a cosmopolitan power. Consequently, the Romans panicked and rejected the refugees for good. Although they were protected by natural walls, such as the Limes and the South Sea – the so-called "Mare Nostrum" – the Visigoths eventually invaded the Roman Empire and took Rome. In agreement with other historians, Bollman links the decline of the Roman Empire to its inability to integrate with the "barbarians." The classical version of this theory of decay comes from the Roman author Publius Cornelius Tacitus. In his work *La Germania – De origine et situ Germanorum*, the Roman historian described the inhabitants of the North as savages: the Germans drink too much, they argue too often, they have no civilization, they seek only the Romans' money. The *Frankfurter Allgemeine Zeitung* journalist believes that Tacitus was very much concerned about a possible arrival of the Germans (Bollmann 2015). On the other hand, Tacitus also expressed admiration for their uncorrupted nature and their courage in battle, praised the strict monogamy of the Germans, the simplicity of their costumes, and the high value of their hospitality, which intensely contrasted with the rampant immorality and decadence of Roman customs. *La Germania* shows both moral and political traits of the German folks, and it is likely to highlight the danger to Rome posed by the people bordering the Empire. It is also interesting to note that the term used by German scholars to describe what was once known as the "barbarian invasions" is "*Völkerwanderung*," which literally means "wandering of peoples." Nowadays, authors prefer to use the term "migratory period."

At these critical times, various European countries are forced to face crises, threats, as well as constant change and reorientation, and they must react in solidarity in order to find new resolutions. For Gibińska, the European political, social and economic environment today appears to be a highly unreliable one, characterized by an unstable structure within it. European societies must deal with both positive and negative values, which leads to doubts, feelings of disharmony and, in the worst cases, direct dislike or hostility (Gibińska 2018, 1). For Richard Chapman (2018, 3), the "crisis" of European refugees owes its particular intensity to a variety of factors, not least to the presence of economic problems that are difficult to resolve and most likely exacerbated by austerity policies that hit mostly the lower classes of European society. As a result, society is experiencing a state of insecurity and anxiety, especially the working class, which is afraid of losing jobs and it has little confidence in public political institutions and trade unions. It is, therefore, a difficult context, which gives fertile ground for various political propagandas, fake news and hate speech. Miguel Ramalhete Gomes (2018, 3) even speaks of a new contemporary fascism fomented by crises such as globalization, the destruction of industry, the establishment of a regulated market in neoliberal Western economies, mass unemployment and the desperation of the working classes. For Chapman (2018, 3), the specificities of the refugee crises should make people reflect on the concept of "other" and the different levels of otherness perceived by host communities. He goes on to say that a bipolar "us and them" reading of the migratory event in Europe moves far away from the truth, not only for moral considerations, but simply because "us and them" is a naive dichotomy, which denies or hides the complexities and nuances of otherness in any migratory experience (Chapman 2018, 3). Gibińska (2018, 1) believes that, in the face of such a crisis, some people can react by developing adaptive capacities that can lead to passive attitudes of abandonment, or even indifference and exclusion. For Gibińska, this position is very dangerous because indifference and passivity never help to resolve critical situations in the crisis. In this regard, she adds: "It is important to realize that crisis forces us to review the accepted values and ingrained habits, making us aware of their adequacy or inadequacy and pushing us to (re)define our moral stance. Passivity is no solution. We have to act" (Gibińska 2018, 2). According to Gibińska (2018, 1), the phenomenon of the crisis is unavoidable, it is a normal state of life in society, and we must learn to live with it, deal with it, and to be able to use it to our own advantage. Therefore, at these difficult times for the European Union, from both economic, political and social points of view, we must take particular responsibility for making the correct decisions. Giandonato Caggiano (2019) maintains that in the growing humanitarian crisis the most serious violations of human rights are taking place, while the adequate international legal instruments are lacking. He claims that states are developing alternative measures to compensate for the difficulties of offering asylum on a large scale, such as offering temporary protection rather than full refugee status, establishing safe havens, border assistance and deploying peacekeeping and humanitarian assistance management troops (Caggiano 2019). One example might clarify this concept. Following Zsolt Tóth, it is important to emphasize Orbán's position on refugees:

> According to Orbán, the difference is simply that while migrants do not have the slightest respect for Hungary's borders and violently threaten the Hungarian nation with their invasion, refugees respectfully stop at the country's entrance and politely request a refugee status. Ironically, having a refugee status equates to being locked up in the transit zone, which resembles a prison fabricated from containers. [...] In addition, new legislation came into effect in the beginning of July 2018, according to which refugee status in Hungary is denied to those who have already entered another safe transit country. This affected two refugee families in August, who were not granted refugee status but were handed over to the Aliens Policy Authority within the transit zone. The difference in status meant that only the children and the breast-feeding women received food. Not even the leader of the Hungarian Evangelical Fellowship, Gábor Iványi, was allowed to give food to these families. (Tóth 2019, 7-8)

In contrast to Orbán, the Swedish Prime Minister Stefan Löfven showed a different position on the migration crisis. Löfven declared to a crowd in Stockholm on 6 September 2015, "My Europe takes in people fleeing from war, my Europe does not build walls" (qtd. in Crouch 2016). Sweden has always welcomed refugees and in 2015 had accepted more refugees per capita than any other country: almost 163,000 people, mainly from Syria, Afghanistan and Iraq, asked for asylum in Sweden that year. But three months and nearly 80,000 asylum seekers later, Stockholm decided to slash the flow to about 1,000 refugees a week since the Swedish system could not cope (Crouch 2016). According to Caggiano (2019), in order to face the current refugee crisis, it is necessary for the European Union to contribute and stimulate dialogue on the adoption of the new forms of international protection and the attribution of new powers to international bodies.

A very important crisis that is faced every day by all European citizens is the crisis of encountering the Other, that is the confrontation with a human being whose physical appearance, mental and cultural structure, language and behaviour put us in a defensive position, because we recognize the Other as "not I/not we." For those who take a defensive attitude, these new refugees would carry the so-called "otherness," that is a potential threat to the religious and ethical assumptions of the Christian tradition and the European people's values. In the last decade the anti-Semitic sentiment has also grown in Europe, with the following tragic events: the anti-Semitic attacks on a synagogue on 9 October 2019 in Halle, Germany; the terrorist attack on the Hypercacher in Paris, shortly after the attack on *Charlie Hebdo*'s headquarters in 2015; the attack on the Jewish school in Toulouse in 2012; and demonstrations by extreme right-wing parties in front of the Auschwitz concentration camp in 2019. During the commemorations in Auschwitz for the International Day of Remembrance on 27 January 2019, a group of militants of the Polish extreme right-wing nationalist group gathered outside the former Nazi extermination camp to protest against the Polish government, accusing it of remembering only the Jews and not the Polish victims (Del Re 2019). The group of Polish nationalists, led by Piotr Rybak, also tried to enter the former Nazi concentration camp shouting "Poland for Poles" ("Auschwitz" 2019).[1] The group of extreme right-wing protesters was promptly prevented from entering the museum by the police, separating it also from the counter-protesters who came with the banner "Stop Fascism" ("Auschwitz" 2019). Other extreme right-wing demonstrations have taken place in the European Union in recent years: in Dresden in 2017, in Chemnitz in August 2018. The demonstrations in Chemnitz are linked to the killing of Daniel H., a resident of Chemnitz, who died after being stabbed by two men, one of Syrian nationality and the other of Iraqi nationality. In the demonstrations in Chemnitz, people perceived as foreigners were chased through the streets and greeted with the Nazi salute, which is illegal in Germany. Konstantin von Notz of the Bündnis 90/Die Grünen Party (Alliance 90/The Greens) judged the Interior Minister Horst Seehofer's silence as "scandalous." Von Notz accused Seehofer of contributing to the xenophobic mood with his anti-migrant stance (Connolly 2018). This situation would be related to Angela Merkel's open doors policy towards refugees undertaken in the summer of 2015. Chancellor Merkel has become a figure of hatred for the extreme right parties; she condemned the insurgents, telling the reporters:

1 All translations from Italian are provided by the author.

"What we have seen is something which has no place in a constitutional democracy. [...] We have video recordings of [people] hunting down others, of unruly assemblies, and hate in the streets, and that has nothing to do with our constitutional state" (Connolly 2018).

There are numerous reasons to believe that in Italy racism is a current phenomenon. The Senator of the political party Lega (Northern League) – Tony Iwobi, has been offended on Facebook by racist and derisory insults. Iwobi has been described as the "Django black," "backyard nigger," "enslaved nigger," "mannequin," "Uncle Tom" (Mirakyan 2019). On the other hand, former Senate vice-president Roberto Calderoli had offended Cécile Kyenge, the former Minister of Integration, saying in July 2013 at the Northern League party in Treviglio: "When I think of Kyenge I think of an orangutan" (Rame 2019). Given the controversy, Calderoli tried to defend himself by stating that this was only "a funny joke" (Manfré 2013). As a result, he was sentenced in the first instance to one year and six months in prison and the judges acknowledged the aggravating racial circumstances (Rame 2019). However, Kyenge decided not to become a civil party and therefore no compensation of an economic nature was provided. Consequently, the sentence has been suspended and there will be no mention in the criminal record of the Northern League Senator Calderoli (Rame 2019). Kyenge commented that it was an encouraging sentence for all those who fight against racism (Rame 2019). The former Minister of Integration also added that racism could and had to be fought by legal as well as civil, civic and political means (Rame 2019). "Racism," the Italian politician concluded, "must be condemned wherever it shows itself" (Monari 2020). Moreover, after the threats on the Internet and the exposition of the banner of the Italian extreme-right party *Forza nuova* in front of the Milan City Hall in November 2019, the prefect Renato Saccone decided to assign security protection to the senator of Jewish origin, Liliana Segre, the Holocaust survivor of the Auschwitz concentration camp. On 30 October 2019, Liliana Segre put a motion for the establishment of an extraordinary Commission for the fight against intolerance, racism, anti-Semitism and incitement to hatred and violence ("Istituzione Commissione" 2019). Eurispes Italy 2020 Report shows that 16.1% of Italians minimize the importance of the Shoah, while 15.6% deny it ("Eurispes" 2020). According to this report, between 2004 and 2020 there is an increase in those who believe that the Holocaust never happened (from 2.7% to 15.6%).

Shakespearean Adaptations *With* and *For* Refugees

Many plays and drama projects suggest that William Shakespeare's plays, especially tragedies and comedies, can be represented as adaptations that include contemporary issues. According to Harold Bloom, Shakespeare is a unique playwright, because of his discovery of man through the exercise of language and thought: "He wrote the best poetry and the best prose in English, or perhaps in any Western language. That is inseparable from his cognitive strength; he thought more comprehensively and originally than any other writer" (Bloom 1998, xviii). The dramatist's genius was able to create completely different, but self-consistent voices for his more than one hundred major characters and many hundreds of utterly distinctive minor personages (Bloom 1998, xviii). This part of my essay explores the following issues: 1) some significant Shakespearian adaptations with actor-refugees; 2) Shakespearian works adapted with a pro-refugee purpose; 3) Shakespearian plays which are shown to an audience made up of people on the fringes of society; 4) social theatre workshops that also use the works of Shakespeare to help refugees and give fresh voice to young participants rendered mute by the horrors of war.

Shakespearian adaptations with actor-refugees

Shakespearian adaptations with actor-refugees are the result of various experiments whose aims are to increase their audience's empathic skills and put viewers in the victims' shoes. Jessica Bauman, theatre director of the New Feet Productions, produced a new interesting re-imagination of William Shakespeare's *As You Like It* named *Arden/Everywhere* (Bauman 2017b). It was hosted by Baruch Performing Arts Center in New York in the fall of 2017, which led her to work with refugees and immigrant communities from all over the world – sixteen actors from nine different countries. *Arden/Everywhere* is a story about refugees, which Bauman spent more than three years working on. The theatre director investigated the text of Shakespeare's play through a series of workshops, holding her ideas up to the close scrutiny of a table work (New Feet Productions staged reading, 2015; Drama League Rough Draft residency, 2016); she also explored how a movement vocabulary rooted in soccer informs the storytelling (Holes in the Wall retreat, 2017). She taught refugees, asylum seekers and immigrants in New York City (International Center, FEGS, Refugee Youth Summer Academy, Arab-American Association, Baruch Performing Arts Center) and ran a theatre workshop at Kakuma Refugee Camp in Kenya with Film Aid International. *Arden/Everywhere* offers a unique experience that links all too often neglected stories of refugees and immigrants with Shakespeare's classics. To work on the show gave refugees and immigrants, which were eager to perform, the opportunity to express themselves, whatever their previous experiences might have been. *Arden/Everywhere* allowed Bauman to work directly on the experiences of refugees through special techniques, such as play and storytelling, to stimulate the imagination and the narrative of their traumatic experience. The aim of this cooperation was to connect her audience with the painful world of dislocation and to discover simple truths of human life such as resilience, reconciliation and love. Bauman discovered a new way to explore stories, overcoming the classical approach of telling difficult tales that could be found in the media. She asserted that every stage of the process had revealed something crucial to her about the story she needed to tell. Working with ESL students and resettled refugees taught her the importance of hearing stories from the people who have actually lived them. For this reason, she declared,

> From the young people I taught at RYSA, I discovered the importance of soccer. The Drama League residency allowed me to deeply investigate Audrey and Phebe; in our production, they were not simply the butt of the jokes (stupid and slutty, or arrogant and ugly), but characters with agency and complexity. A devised piece created in a workshop for immigrant actors at Baruch PAC led to the stories of cast members being included in the final production. (Bauman 2017a)

The experience with the refugees in Kakuma showed her that in all human beings, hardship and joy live together in intimate proximity. Bauman realized that her job was to tell this story and she declared "that every human experience we all lay claim to is also happening for refugees" (Bauman 2017a). For Bauman, the full array of experience offered by Shakespeare in *As You Like It* belonged both to a refugee camp and the vision of Arden. This adaptation was able to create a community of spectators from different experiences and contexts. Apart from the show, it provided a starting point for a series of experiences involving communities: theatrical workshops, post-show talk-back, assistance and political commitment on refugee issues, theatrical aperitifs, potlucks and shared meals, convivial moments.

Can Shakespeare heal the wounds of war? Can the words of the great poet really ease the sorrows of young Syrians who fled the war? This is what Nawar Bulbul, the famous Syrian actor and director, ponders and hopes.

Bulbul is the theatre expert who directed one hundred Syrian children in his Arabic-language adaptation of *King Lear* on 27 March 2014 (Dickson 2015). This *King Lear* was performed in Zaatari, Jordan, near the Syrian border, the same UNHCR camp where Bulbul himself was a refugee. The adaptation, translated into literary Arabic, was an attempt to help counteract the effects of war, which caused young Syrians to lose vital years of education. Bulbul's goal was to save Zaatari's children from boredom and mental laziness. According to the UN data, more than half of the 587,000 refugees registered in Jordan were under the age of eighteen: about 60,000 of those young people lived in Zaatari camp, where only one in four children regularly sat at a school desk (Hubbard 2014). Children who did not attend school expanded the ranks of that "lost generation" which risks remaining, in part, illiterate. "There are particles of good in even the worst things. It's up to men to know how to extract it carefully," declared the Syrian actor, paraphrasing a verse from *Henry V* (Meringolo 2014). It was this conviction that drove the director to put aside anger and apathy to create a better world. The Syrian actor decided to roll up his sleeves and build a Shakespeare's tent – a special place to welcome refugee children who were keen on becoming actors. In this exceptional spot Bulbul introduced the hundred children of Zaatari to the Bard's works, especially to *King Lear*. Like *Hamlet*, *King Lear* is a tragedy that deals with the themes of madness, torn families, loss of land – themes and issues that characterize the experiences of many refugees (Dickson 2015).

Another performance with refugees directed by Bulbul is the re-imagination of *Romeo and Juliet* played by two young Syrians, who were divided by war and reunited in real time via Skype during the time of acting. The attic of the hospice had been transformed into Verona. A wounded young boy (Romeo), a patient of a hospice for Syrian refugees in Amman, Jordan, performed with the image of a girl (Juliet) on a screen (Taneja 2015). She lived in the besieged city of Homs, Syria. On the screen her head with the veil was masked to protect her identity from the regime of Bashar al-Assad. The audience of this peculiar *Romeo and Juliet* was made up of young people who had been seriously injured. Some of them had lost their limbs in the bombed-out Homs and were carried up by their caretakers to see the performance. During the play, there were interruptions, but then the connection would return. Some passages have been specially inserted into the text to meet the challenge posed by the spatial fragmentation and geographical location. It is also important to emphasize how Taneja described Roxanne, a girl playing Juliet's companion, who, at the sight of the corpses of the two lovers killed by poison, cried: "Enough killing! Enough blood! Why are you killing us? We want to live like the rest of the world!" and many of the audience started to cry (Taneja 2015). There was also an interesting connection between Friar Lawrence and Father Frans van der Lugt. The latter was the Jesuit priest killed by the Assad regime in 2014.

Shakespearian works reimagined with a pro-refugee purpose

As regards Shakespearian works re-adapted with a pro-refugee aim, I would like to begin with *As You Like It* commissioned by Leister's Curve Theatre and performed by Dash Art Company in 2009, which offered a journey into a very different England. The production was about contrasting aspects of immigration, the hard realities of lives in which migrants are subjected to a tyrannical environment, and the hopes they continue to have. According to Peter Kirwan (2009, 86-87), Dash Art Company used the text to stress the cultural diversity of contemporary England rather than its rural past. This play is also very interesting for its idea of "Eutopia." First of all, it explores what it means to be a European citizen today. Then, it celebrates change and diversity in Europe. Dash Art Company's re-imagination also encourages a new understanding of *As You Like It* and the opportunity to find new voices which could reach a wider range of communities. For Janice Valls-Russell (2019, 18-19), Dash Art Company reflects how different traditions and cultures can cooperate together, integrating a feeling of closeness. The comedy shows undoubtedly Shakespeare's familiarity with migration and the presence of refugees in England and in Europe. Mercedes Sapuppo (2019) finds in this play some clear examples of the migrant's plight. For instance, Duke Senior, who is exiled from his dukedom and lives surrounded by his company in a forest, gives a speech to "his co-mates and brothers in exile" (Shakespeare 2006, 2.1.1; further references to Shakespeare's works will be by title and corresponding act, scene, and verse number). In addition, Adam symbolizes the plight of the banished people: he exemplifies the refugee's difficult journey and the problems of finding nourishment when he exclaims "I can go no further. O, I die for food. / Here I lie down and measure out my grave" (*As You Like It* 2.6.2-3). In the play Adam's story is told, whereas the refugees' stories tend to go untold, as many of them perish in the middle of the Mediterranean Sea. Like Duke Senior and his party, in Calais, France, refugees gathered in improvised camps around the port (about 1,500 refugees in December 2018), attempting to cross the Channel by boat (Townsend 2018).

Some people have come to the shores of England in boats from northern France, with traffickers charging each of them up to 6,000 pounds a trip. With the intensification of controls along the English Channel, the journeys of hope often take alternative routes. In recent years some migrants have been trying to reach Britain crammed into the containers on ships or the rears of trucks.

Another re-adapted Shakespearean play with a pro-refugee objective is Sea-change Theatre's *The Tempest*, which represents the migrants who arrive to Europe as stranded characters. According to the official website of Sea-change Theatre, they define themselves as "an all-female company who create bold new work through reimagined classical texts" ("The Tempest" 2016). This company aims to celebrate diversity and challenge hetero-norms and gender roles. Sea-change Theatre's first production was an adaptation of Shakespeare's *The Tempest*, which was performed at Skala Eressos Women's Festival in September 2016 in Lesbos, Greece. For that performance the company brought together a professional team of theatre-makers and local people to celebrate both Shakespearean and Greek culture on the 400th anniversary of Shakespeare's death. The company used the shipwreck to develop a story of refugees. Sue Frumin, who adapted the play, decided to accentuate Sycorax's status as an immigrant – a "foul witch" and "blue-eyed hag" from Algiers (*The Tempest* 1.2.304-317) – and Miranda's status as an exiled refugee. Frumin's decision to emphasize the character of Sycorax allowed for an exploration of the current discordant attitudes to freedom of movement. The central story of Sycorax, a woman exiled from her own country, referred specifically to the plight of many refugees, who are held in camps on the Greek islands, having washed up on the Greek shores, for instance on Lesbos, since 2013.

Shakespearian plays shown to refugee audiences in marginal spaces

By examining Shakespearian works which are shown to an audience made up of refugees in conflict zones, it is worth noting interesting versions of *Hamlet* performed in Jordan and *King Lear* played in the West Bank (Dickson 2015). *Hamlet*, starring actors from London's Globe Theatre, was staged in a UNHCR refugee camp in Zaatari, Jordan, created specifically to house nearly 120,000 displaced Syrians. The Globe Theatre's *Hamlet* was performed in 197 countries, to more than 255,000 people and travelled over 180,000 miles (Dromgoole 2014). The tour was sponsored by

UNESCO for its commitment to local communities and its promotion of cultural education. *Hamlet* performed by The Globe was shown in Northern Europe, South America, Africa, Australasia, the Pacific and Asia. The show was offered free of charge to local audiences wherever possible. It should be emphasized that this work was staged for many people considered exiled and marginalized. In this section The Globe's performance in Zaatari is discussed. The photographer Sarah Lee worked on site and her pictures, which had great resonance in England, show the performance of the actors playing Hamlet and the faces of the spectators in the refugee camp (Lee and Fidler 2015). Lee's particularly striking photograph shows the intensity of the actress who impersonates Ophelia sinking into madness, and at the same time it captures the wonder and amazement in the attentive looks of the refugees: women, children, teenagers, elderly, and men; a young Syrian manages to capture Ophelia's madness on his smartphone.

Dominic Dromgoole, the former artistic director of Shakespeare's Globe Theatre in London (2005-2016), recounts vividly how the refugee camp was hit by a sandstorm and the show had to be interrupted, so that families could reunite with their relatives and check with the camp workers the tents' security status (Dickson 2015). Lee made a complete report of the theatrical experience in Zaatari and her images taken in the sandstorm are worthy of admiration (Lee and Fidler 2015, fig. 2 and 3). Dromgoole reminisces in his book *Hamlet Globe to Globe*: "As Hamlet died, at that exact moment, another noise softly filled the room, a gentle and percussive thap-thappity-thap on the roof. As Hamlet died, the rains came." (2017, 334). He also states that in 1608 *Hamlet* was staged on a boat – the *Red Dragon* – off the coast of Yemen, proving that the spirit of itinerant theatre has always been a part of William Shakespeare's theatrical art (Dromgoole 2014).

In September 2012, the German director Thomas Ostermeier staged his *Hamlet* in Camp Jenin in Ramallah, West Bank. His company performed the show and stayed for a few days to hold a workshop with young Palestinian actors on the relationship between Hamlet and Ophelia. During these two events at Janin camp, Ostermeier created a documentary *Hamlet in Palestine* (2017) with the collaboration of Nicolas Klotz. The documentary explores Ostermeier's visit to a Palestinian prison and his journey to Tel Aviv to try to understand what happened to his friend Julio Mer-Khamis, the director of the Freedom Theatre killed in April 2012 in Janin camp. The murder took place in front of Mer-Khamis's daughter and her nanny. The Freedom Theatre was an association which taught theatrical arts to Palestinian children and adolescents. The German director claims to have met many trapped and angry young people in Ramallah, who looked like Prince Hamlet. Without any freedom of movement, these young men were regarded by the Israeli government as dangerous suspects, while in their homes and in the mosques they were solicited by father figures, who urged them to act in the name of revenge (Dickson 2015). According to some interviewees, the people of Freedom Theatre could understand the real problems of Palestine (Carrasco 2017). During the interviews, we learn that the Freedom Theatre was threatened by both the Israeli and Palestinian governments. The fate of Julio Mer-Khamis reinforces the parallel between Shakespeare's work and the Israeli-Palestinian conflict: if you cannot trust your relatives, friends, your mother, you cannot trust anyone; consequently, you risk going mad (Carrasco 2017). Hamlet uses the theatre as a form of provocation, to get his uncle Claudius to confess to his father's murder. Carrasco believes that the Freedom Theatre tried to do the same with the Israeli and Palestinian governments and analogous expedient is used by Ostermeier and Klotz in their documentary film.

Social theatre workshops using Shakespearean plays to give fresh voice to young refugees rendered mute by war

As for social theatre workshops that employ Shakespeare's plays to make the participants find their own voice, the work of Capuchin Social Theatre – Caring For Life through Arts by Brother Stefano Luca and his CapST Methodology must be mentioned here. Helping young Syrians in Beirut, Brother Stefano works on the concept of hospitality through social theatre. Social theatre is today a form of contemporary theatre and is considered by scholars as "necessary." Claudio Bernardi states:

> Social theatre is concerned with the expression, training and interaction of people, groups and communities, through performance activities that include different genres of theatre, play, party, ritual, sport, dance, cultural events and manifestations [...]. Social theatre is part of the current anthropological commitment whose strong points are the social construction of the person; the dynamics of interpersonal relationships and intersubjective understanding; the structure of communities and small-scale social forms; it is therefore proposed as an action or liturgy of communities, threatened with extinction by the homogenization and personalization of culture by the media society, and

> as a search for the psychophysical well-being of the members of any community through the identification of communicative, expressive and relational practices, able to mitigate the malaise and individual stress typical of Western society. (Bernardi 1998, 157)

Brother Stefano Luca is also the director of the documentary project *Undhur ilay / see me / guardami*, work carried out at the JRS FVDL Center in Beirut in 2018, in collaboration with Jesuit Refugee Service and sponsored by the Capuchin Friars Minor. This documentary talks about the social theatre workshop conducted by Brother Stefano with fifteen young Syrian refugees. In the film *Undhur ilay / see me / guardami* the director of CapST gives testimony to how war imprisons young people in a limbo of loneliness.[2] During the seminar *La società a teatro* on 20 December 2019 at the Teatro Comunale in Ferrara, Italy, Brother Stefano showed to an audience the key elements of his work in conflict zones, which has been analysed through the CapST methodology.[3] The workshop in Lebanon lasted ten weeks and involved a total of fifteen young people and an operator. The theatrical action took place at the FVDL centre (a Jesuit school), located in Sinn al-Fin, near Bourj Hammoud, a village and municipality in Lebanon located in the al-Matn district, largely inhabited by Syrian migrants and refugees since the 1950s. Historically, the Syrians had slaughtered many Lebanese in older conflicts. Following the Syrian civil war, which began on 15 March 2011, Lebanon made a strong humane gesture by hosting Syrian refugees. The Syrian refugees living in Lebanon have a dual nature: some of them try to return to Syria; others, however, do not wish to return to their country of origin, as they hope to emigrate to the Western countries. The Lebanon's Jesuits immediately realized that a school in Sinn-al-Fin was missing; therefore, they took steps to open a school as soon as possible. In Lebanon, Brother Stefano had the opportunity to experience social theatre, which aimed at taking care of people and communities. In the workshop implemented in Lebanon, the theatre expert

2 "Productions." *Capuchin Social Theatre*. http://www.capsocialtheatre.org/productions.html. Accessed 23 October 2020.

3 The film "Undhur ilay / see me / guardami" presented during the seminar *La società a teatro* on 20 December 2019 in *Teatro Comunale di Ferrara*, http://www.teatrocomunaleferrara.it/events/event/undhur-ilay-see-me-guardami/, accessed 13 August 2020. The video (unpublished) was shown during the following seminar: http://www.teatrocomunaleferrara.it/events/event/undhur-ilay-see-me-guardami/, accessed 13 August 2020. The trailer is available on youtube: https://www.youtube.com/watch?v=L6d3rPOxjf4. Details about the CapST methodology presented below come from the seminar's content (unpublished).

had the objective of letting the Syrian refugees find their own voice and hope, since war had the strength to disintegrate speech, and the possibility to express themselves. War, imprisonment and violence have always reduced freedom and eliminated communication. Hoping to achieve recognition of the Other and relations built on communication and physical dialogue, Brother Stefano worked on the theatrical word through specific interventions aimed at involving the whole community. During the 2019 seminar in Ferrara (*La società a teatro* 2019), Brother Stefano listed the following points, fundamental for the realization of his workshop with the CapST methodology:

1) Constitution of a group (the union of two distinct groups of adolescents);
2) Building up life skills;
3) Focusing on aggressiveness, discrimination, hope, self-esteem, trust and suspension of judgment;
4) Re-writing the text (in this case, William Shakespeare, *The Merchant of Venice*, 3.1.48-61).

The young participants introduced such changes to the famous speech as "mocked by my accent," "turned my friends into my enemies... because I am Syrian," "they defrauded me of my respect, that I owed to myself, trust." In the seminar of 20 December 2019, coordinated by *La società a teatro*, Brother Stefano pointed out that Shylock's monologue was also read and rewritten in another social theatre workshop with "Child Soldiers" in Rwanda, 2016. The most interesting contributions of Child Soldiers in relation to this monologue are as follows: "Do we not love our village?" "Do our families not work?" "We are human beings, we are children, not soldiers." It is important to highlight how these young people felt when judged and exposed because of the condition they were living in; they suffered from very low self-esteem.

The process elaborated by the CapST methodology created a strong psychological presence of the team, which activated some specific interventions focused on caring. From the workshop's beginning, the adolescents' families had been helpful and cooperative, and they gave Brother Stefano full trust, signing the privacy documents for the filming purposes. The community event took place in the neighbourhood inside a small square and was video recorded, basically for two reasons: 1) to get a video track; 2) to generate confidence in those who did not want to be filmed face-to-face.

Some girls and boys participated in the reading of their reimagined Shylock's monologue; others participated in it without showing their faces to the camera, and some adolescents decided not to participate in the video recording at all. At the end of the work, some girls regretted not participating actively in the recording.

It is important to emphasize the feedback activity which concerned the social theatre workshop. During the seminar Brother Stefano asked himself some important questions regarding the choice of Shakespeare's Shylock monologue for this work, like: How did the adolescents accept the text? Did they identify themselves? Did the text have a strong effect on the children? On the whole, Brother Stefano was satisfied with the choices he had made. The young participants had certainly benefited from that significant experience. The question "How did the children accept the text?" was answered, "Without much effort."

In conclusion, in the Syrian refugees' words vibrated the echoes of the contemporary migrant's fate: unrecognized, mocked, desperate, despised, but also unwanted, not unlike the sentiments expressed by the original Shylock. According to Riccardo Calimani (2016, 11), Shylock, an imaginary, but plausible character, made of flesh and blood, hatred and revenge, is extraordinarily modern, as he demands equality in diversity, highlighting his identity, first and foremost, as a human being. This example suggests that traumatized refugees can be supported through Shakespearean theatre. Peter Brook (2019) has left some impressive lines: "Shakespeare doesn't belong to the past. If his material is valid, it is valid now. It is like coal [...] but the meaningfulness of a piece of coal to us starts and finishes with its combustion, giving us the light and the heat that we want. And that to me is Shakespeare" (82).

Social Theatre with Refugees in the UK

Theatre is an excellent tool to give voice to marginalized people, who want to share their real experience with one or more specific communities and/or groups of people. In 2017, in the city of London, Ella Smith and Emma West organized "Shakespeare Shorts," a theatre event in which they paired scenes from Shakespearean plays together with modern-day refugee stories – read by a one-night-only, never-to-be-repeated company of actors – in order to raise money for the UN Refugee Agency. The show incorporated live theatre, video stories, and projections. Smith and West, both actors and producers, wanted to harness the power of storytelling to bring tangible help to refugees. As they declare at the official site of "Shakespeare Shorts," their mission is the following:

> Storytelling remains one of mankind's most powerful tools & Shakespeare is the playwright of compassion. He is a friend to the dispossessed and a scourge to those who inflict cruelty. Most importantly, he highlights our shared humanity. With the refugee crisis growing around the world, it is time to act. (Smith and West 2019)

The evidence suggests that Shakespearean plays are quite adaptable to the contemporary crisis issues and they help create a platform for refugees to express their own realities.

Some experts argue that these narrations must come from the refugees themselves. Lois Keidan (2008) believes that these "socially engaged practices are a way of empowering the disempowered and including the excluded, and [they] can achieve radical and remarkable transformation." These blended practices are useful, but they take time to be implemented. Besides, they do not provide long-term solutions, especially when cooperating with young and emotionally vulnerable people. For that reason, it is advisable that directors, staff, and actors cooperate with social assistants, educators and volunteers, who are significant figures for refugees and asylum seekers. Working with associations, NGOs, and communities, theatre companies become "facilitators" and tend to avoid paternalistic attitudes, which end up prolonging situations of social exclusion and a sense of inferiority (Henriques Coutinho and Pompeo Nogueira 2013, 175). The theatre staff must be trained with training days, weekly debriefing sessions, evaluation meetings. The staff evaluates the work according to the established ethical framework, skills and planning strategies. People with less experience benefit from those with more experience through cooperative learning.

Unlike art-based therapies which involve specialized therapists and specific patients as trauma victims, participatory and community theatre activities are art projects and they do not propose therapeutic and health-related goals. Participatory theatre presents itself, in the wide and diversified panorama of Performing Arts, as a practice capable of redefining the role of the spectators, overcoming the distinction between those who act and those who attend the performance. Those who take part in a participatory theatre performance take part as spectators, that is, they are to all intents and purposes both a protagonist and a co-author of the scene's dynamics (Henriques Coutinho and Pompeo Nogueira 2013, 175). Participatory theatre, therefore, gathers all those artistic expressions in which the theatrical fact moves around a fundamental principle: to involve the spectator and make him or her aware of his or her role. Some of the most extreme experiences of participatory theatre are characterized by a marked passage of artistic responsibility to the audience: the spectator joins the actors or, in the most radical cases, can even replace professional performers (Pocosgnich 2018). The experiential factor is fundamental in this type of theatre, which differs from other types of theatre thanks to an amplification of the active experience, that is, the very possibility of making the success of the artistic event change through the audience's action (Pocosgnich 2018). Participatory theatre is a useful tool to unite communities of spectators and to make them aware of one or more social themes to be shared. When the community factor takes on a proper importance, participatory theatre is naturally linked to other forms of social theatre (Pocosgnich 2018). Taking inspiration from some practises developed by Dorothy Heathcote, participatory theatre involves the setting of specific boundaries between the fiction of the stage and the space occupied by the audience in their real life, for example the emotional security of the participants, their confidence during the performance, the empowerment of the participants, the centrality of open and genuine reflection, a pedagogy based on Questioning (Rifkin 2010, 30-31). Questioning is a technique that is at the heart of teaching and learning; it is a key tool in creating a dialogue with patients and students. Questions are asked to find out what people know and to guide their thinking carefully. Through this Questioning process the participants are helped to bring out their memories, thoughts and energies which they intend to release. With this technique, experts stimulate learning and self-knowledge. A theatrical conductor can decide to submit their actors to specific questions to improve their performance. However, theatre specialists must be careful not to let participants relive situations of discomfort or traumatic events.

The experience of Stella Barnes, former director of the Oval House Theatre, is fundamental to the present paper. The philosophy and methodology used by Barnes is based on role-play, person-in-role, forum theatre, storytelling and physical theatre techniques in order to involve young people in a physical, emotional and intellectual way. In her essay "Drawing a Line.

A Discussion of Ethics in Participatory Arts with Young Refugees" Barnes criticizes the way some of her colleagues' dramatization of true refugee stories have been directed (2009, 34). As an example, she reports a dramatization of two African women in London, both victims of persecution and genocide. In the show one of the women began to tell her story and describe her life, her family, her friends, and all the terrible things those people have suffered. Exploiting the space of the stage and through gestures, both women re-lived their own suffering: soldiers chasing women, dead bodies, fear. At a certain point, the monologue of one of the women was interrupted: the woman's voice trembled, she found it difficult to speak, she sought contact with the director. A heavy silence fell on the audience. The woman breathed and struggled, tried to recite the next lines, her voice broke again and she started to cry. Then, she stopped and looked at the director again and said she could not carry on. The director spurred her on and said, "Yes, you can. You've done it before" (Barnes 2009, 34). The show resumed and was completed, but Barnes and her colleagues were united in their disapproval and shocked by what they witnessed. Barnes believes that the two women did not play a role or a character, but they played themselves. What the theatre expert witnessed was not fiction, but a life re-enacted for an audience. The emotion, the fear, the trauma: they were all real. The former director of the Oval Theatre wonders what the theatre company was trying to achieve and what were the ethical choices of the theatrical work. Indeed, many theatre projects for young refugee artists require participants to use their own life stories as resources for the project. Many young refugees involved in theatre are asked to (re)play their real life in drama. These projects are usually called: your story, your journey, memory box (Barnes 2009, 35). The message that is conveyed to the participants of some theatre workshops is as follows: "I want to know your story; I want to know something you remember from the past; I want to know what home means to you; I want to know what happened to you; I want to know your journey; I want to know your trauma" (35). Some artists therefore define themselves as recipients of stories, and others define themselves as "story listener" (35). For Barnes most people who have the privilege of living in a safe area also have the curiosity to learn about the dramatic and intimate stories of those who have suffered: "We have a desire to know what happened to them [refugees] and we feel privileged if someone chooses to disclose their story to us" (35). However, Barnes carefully avoids the hidden stories of refugees becoming the focus of her participatory theatre projects. She believes refugee stories can provide a powerful material for theatre and exciting art, but those who decide to do this kind of collaboration must learn to hold back and not to cross an important limit: in the theatre workshop all participants are to be considered equal and no one must exploit refugee stories for artistic purposes (35). Therefore, theatre experts should not focus on the traumatic experience itself to assure emotional and psychological safety of asylum seekers.

Barnes's method deals with not asking the young participants to use their past experiences directly; thus, she prefers working on the aspects of present and future life. If the show is linked to real issues, the theatre expert encourages the use of metaphors, symbolism, folk tales as an approach to preserve refugees' health and prevent unnecessary suffering (Barnes 2009, 35) We must, therefore, distinguish between fiction and reality, between the literal and the symbolic or metaphorical, between the specific and the universal. It is, then, advisable to work with fiction, since it has certain characteristics, such as that of removing negative thoughts and protecting against pain. Telling a fictional story in an adaptation of a play can be an empowering and deeply creative process (40). Nevertheless, some artists have criticized Barnes's position, stating that her work tends to be too cautious and that she actively limits the participants' creativity through her concern to make the work safe. Following a fruitful discussion between Barnes and various specialists in the field, it emerged that in some cases young refugees can take risks in art projects. The theatre expert points out that individuals or groups are not required to take personal risks; however, they can choose to do so if they wish. It is also important to highlight that the workshops' themes in the Oval Theatre are decided in agreement with the participants, since the theatre project is based on the relationship with the group rather than for the group (35).

Finally, it is clear that the theatrical conductors must pay attention to their audience's feelings, which could face an uncomfortable situation during the theatrical performance. Theatre directors must think carefully about the narrative choices to be put on stage. As Gillian Whitlock (2015b) suggests, in many places the refugees' out-of-life narratives, cause anxiety and politics of the Other's fear because they disturb "our comfort zones" (173). The refugees' out-of-life narratives could therefore irritate the "comfort zones" of the people attending the stage event. The narrations that should be avoided are those that could be offensive, shocking, gruesome and/or visceral to the audience.

The Concept of Hospitality in *The Book of Sir Thomas More*

The Book of Sir Thomas More is a little-known manuscript attributed to the Bard, which was never staged or produced. According to Stephen Greenblatt (2017), the play was probably banned from performance by the censor. The work was rediscovered in the spring of 2016, when the British Library digitized and uploaded online *The Book of Sir Thomas More*, along with 299 other handwritten documents. The manuscript of *Sir Thomas More* was shown to the public in 2016 at an exhibition at the British Library dedicated to Shakespeare, as part of the commemoration of the 400th anniversary of Shakespeare's death. Later, Ian McKellen recorded a video released by BBC Two's "Shakespeare Live!" program on 23 April 2016. This was acclaimed by the media as "Shakespeare's handwritten 'plea for humanity'"; *The Book* reappeared in the media on 20 June 2018, on the occasion of the World Refugee Day, in a short film created by the International Rescue Committee and Shakespeare's Globe ("What is The Strangers' Case?" 2018). The video shows famous actors and refugees from Syria, Sierra Leone and South Sudan playing some lines of *The Book of Sir Thomas More*. The verses are clearly dedicated to migrants or, more precisely, they deal with the experience of refugees in England in the sixteenth century. Lord Chancellor Thomas More addresses an angry mob of Londoners, who struggle to stop the immigration of "strangers." The Lord Chancellor tries to reason with the mob, calling for empathy and greater understanding in two expressive speeches:

> You'll put down strangers,
> Kill them, cut their throats, possess their houses,
> And lead the majesty of law in lyam
> To slip him like a hound. Alas, alas! Say now the King
> As he is clement if th'offender mourn,
> Should so much come too short of your great trespass
> As but to banish you: whither would you go?
> What country, by the nature of your error,
> Should give you harbour? Go you to France or Flanders,
> To any German province, Spain or Portugal,
> Nay, anywhere that not adheres to England:
> Why, you must needs be strangers. Would you be pleased
> To find a nation of such barbarous temper,
> That, breaking out in hideous violence,

Would not afford you an abode on earth,
Whet their detested knives against your throats,
Spurn you like dogs, and like as if that God
Owed not nor made not you, nor that the claimants
Were not all appropriate to your comforts,
But chartered unto them, what would you think
To be thus used? This is the strangers' case;
And this your mountanish inhumanity. (2.4.134-155)

Grant them removed, and grant that this your noise
Hath chid down all the majesty of England;
Imagine that you see the wretched strangers,
Their babies at their backs and their poor luggage,
Plodding tooth ports and costs for transportation,
And that you sit as kings in your desires,
Authority quite silent by your brawl,
And you in ruff of your opinions clothed;
What had you got? I'll tell you. You had taught
How insolence and strong hand should prevail,
How order should be quelled; and by this pattern
Not one of you should live an aged man,
For other ruffians, as their fancies wrought,
With self same hand, self reasons, and self right,
Would shark on you, and men like ravenous fishes
Would feed on one another. (2.6.84-97)

This scene had a direct reference to current manifestations of people demanding expulsion of migrants from the country in the town of Goro, Ferrara, Italy in 2016, when a group of people manifested against parish hospitality and created some barricades to block the arrival of the refugees' bus, which included some pregnant women and children (Francalacci 2016). Unlike in *The Book*, no one intervened on behalf of the refugees. Gillian Whitlock evoked Jacques Derrida's awareness of the contradictory nature of the exercise of hospitality, which concerned the responses to the immigration wave from Africa into France and the French demonstrations in 1996 (Whitlock 2015a, 247-248). For Derrida, the global politics of forced migration initiate possibilities of not only sociality and reciprocity, but also of violence and control; new spaces of hospitality are mingled with militant enforcement of border controls (Whitlock 2015a, 247-248).

In Shakespeare's time, many refugees escaped the European religious wars finding their way to England, while black men and women moved to England in sufficient numbers to be defined as a public nuisance at the time. The Bard lived and worked with people of different background. *The Book of Sir Thomas More* bears witness that Shakespeare as a playwright reflected on life and migration. Furthermore, Shakespeare must have known More's theories of a utopian thinker, his viewpoint of an experienced politician, and his beliefs of a religious person. Paola Spinozzi notes:

> More defends Christianity and believes that the expression of religious spirituality is the foundation of civil society, yet his preference is for freedom of belief, as practiced by the Utopians, who ignore the Revelation. The Lord High Chancellor who died after choosing not to relinquish his Catholic faith portrays a utopian society in which all religious cults can be professed. (Spinozzi 2016, 596)

It is quite possible that *The Book of Sir Thomas More* has a pro-refugee purpose. History repeats itself: migrations have always existed, causing the same feelings in every historical era. Greenblatt (2017, n.p.) emphasizes the following verses, "Imagine that you see the wretched strangers, / Their babies at their backs and their poor luggage, / Plodding to the ports and coasts for transportation," seeing in them the collapse of distance between the natives and the foreigners;[4] walls falter and fall; a ghetto is razed to the ground. Yet, this migration phenomenon led to the emergence of anti-immigrant protests in the city of London. Reading Shakespeare's words today, we can clearly see a connection to the situation of the refugees from Syria, Africa and Asia who risked their lives during the sea crossing to Europe. More's words strive to create empathy between his audience and the migrants, asking the citizens of London to imagine themselves in the same situation as the refugees. The lines of More's speech, written four hundred years ago, are topical, and confirm the immortality of the great English poet, who speaks of universal feelings, in which readers and spectators can recognize each other centuries later: love, hatred, revenge, jealousy, pity. Greenblatt (2017) argues that such language is obviously no substitute for a coherent, safe and humane international refugee policy, which is run by constitutional lawyers, experienced diplomats and wise and dignified leaders. Nevertheless, the universal feelings evoked by Shakespeare connect with Edward Said's childhood dream, as expressed

4 French protestants and foreigners seeking political asylum in England during the Elizabethan era.

in *Out of Place*, "I wish we could have been all-Arab, or all-European and American, or all-Orthodox Christian, or all-Muslim, or all-Egyptian, and so on" (Said 2000, 5).

Conclusion

Shakespeare's plays demonstrate that immigrants have always been important to European society and so they can help people challenge the hatred and the fear of the Other in Europe. A play such as *The Book of Sir Thomas More* shows that Shakespeare was familiar with the phenomenon of migration in the sixteenth-century England. All people should be encouraged by the great playwright's words. What makes Shakespeare so special, however, is that the dramatic genius does not provide solutions to issues, but he offers several perspectives and possibilities. The evidence suggests it is people's responsibility to find answers to problems such as extremisms, xenophobic rhetoric, mental and physical boundaries as fences and walls. Young generations must be able to picture alternatives: dialogue and "educating own's judgement" are essential. Examining Shakespeare's verses and themes in schools, universities and theatre workshops is, in my humble opinion, necessary. In times of crisis schools and theatres have the moral duty to fight racism and discrimination and promote a culture of inclusiveness, cooperative learning, metacognitive evaluation and reflection. Social and participatory theatre relies on new ideas, records of life, emotions, and represents a new kind of hospitality. In some new adaptations of Shakespeare's plays we can distinguish theatrical experiments with refugees. In this regard, it is worth mentioning Nawar Bulbul's *King Lear*, who, through the Bard's verses, fights school drop-out, illiteracy and gives voice to those who do not have it, and Jessica Bauman's adaptation of *As You Like It*, namely *Arden/Everywhere*, where she tried to connect her audience with the simple truths of human life: resilience, reconciliation and love. Another interesting Shakespearean re-imagination is Bulbul's *Romeo and Juliet*, a tragedy played via Skype by two young Syrians with a spatial and geographical fragmentation. In addition, Brother Stefano Luca with his CapST Methodology has given hope back to some Syrian adolescents, giving them a new fresh voice through theatre strategies, psychological skills and verses of *The Merchant of Venice*. Crucial to this research is also the position of Stella Barnes, the former director of the Oval Theatre in London, who works with refugees. When young people feel safe, they can take creative and sometimes personal risks; they can take unexplored paths to make sense of their theatrical experience and help them with their own life. If the play has links to real themes, Barnes suggests the use of metaphors, symbolism, folk tales, as an approach to preserve the refugees' mental health and avoid further suffering. Telling a fictional story in a theatrical adaptation can be a deeply empowering and creative process. It is pivotal to analyse the processes that lead to the eradication of prejudice, hostility and rejection in our contemporary society: we must identify the values of the other and expect our values to be equally recognized. Understanding the mechanisms behind the refugee crisis is an increasingly important task, because even though the number of refugees arriving now is at a minimum compared to previous years, the crisis is far from over. Climate change, wars, epidemics and socio-economic crises contribute to the influx of refugees to Europe, even though the European Union is not yet able to reach a unanimous consensus on how to deal with this crisis. In conclusion, this article ends with Pope Francis's statement after his visit to Lesbos in April 2016: "We must never forget, however, that migrants, rather than simply being a statistic, are first of all persons who have faces, names and individual stories" ("Francis" 2016).

References

"Auschwitz, corteo di nazionalisti polacchi al campo di sterminio nazista. Schermaglie con antifascisti." 2019. *Il Fatto Quotidiano*. https://www.ilfattoquotidiano.it/2019/01/27/auschwitz-corteo-di-nazionalisti-polacchi-al-campo-di-sterminio-nazista-schermaglie-con-antifascisti/4927910/. Accessed 23 October 2020.

Barnes, S. 2009. "Drawing a Line: Discussion of Ethics in Participatory Arts." In: S. Barnes, *Participatory Arts with Young Refugees*. London: Arts in Education, 34-40.

Bauman, J. 2017a. "*Arden/Everywhere* by William Shakespeare." http://jessicabauman.net/theater/as-you-like-it/. Accessed 28 July 2019.

——. 2017b. "The 'As You Like It' Project." http://ardeneverywhere.com/. Accessed 28 July 2019.

Bauman, Z. 2005. *Liquid Life*. Cambridge: Polity Press.

Bernardi, C. 1998. "Il teatro sociale." In: C. Bernardi and B. Cuminetti (eds.), *L'ora di teatro. Orientamenti europei ed esperienze italiane nelle istituzioni educative*. Milano: Euresis, 157-171.

Bloom, H. 1998. *Shakespeare: The Invention of the Human*. New York: Riverhead Books.

Boffey, D. 2020. "EU and Turkey Hold 'Frank' Talks Over Border Opening for Refugees." https://www.theguardian.com/world/2020/mar/09/turkey-erdogan-holds-talks-with-eu-leaders-over-border-opening. Accessed 12 March 2020.

Bollmann, R. 2015. “Die Völkerwanderung.” https://www.faz.net/aktuell/wirtschaft/wirtschaftspolitik/die-voelkerwanderung-ein-begriff-macht-karriere-13874687.html. Accessed 22 September 2019.

Brook, P. 2019. *The Shifting Point. Forty Years of Theatrical Exploration, 1946–87.* London: Bloomsbury.

Butler, J. 2004. *Frames of War: When is Life Grievable?* London: Verso.

Caggiano, G. 2019. “Migrazioni e diritto internazionale.” www.cestim.it. Accessed 28 October 2019.

Calimani, R. 2016. *Storia del ghetto di Venezia.* Segrate: Mondadori.

Carrasco, N. 2017. “Cinéma du Réel 2017: *Hamlet in Palestine* by Nicolas Klotz and Thomas Ostermeier.” https://desistfilm.com/hamlet-in-palestine-by-nicolas-klotz-and-thomas-ostermeier/. Accessed 29 July 2019.

Chapman, R. 2018. “Crisis and Otherness: The Role of Language.” halshs-02145009. https://halshs.archives-ouvertes.fr/halshs-02145009/document. Accessed 14 July 2019.

Connolly, K. 2018. “German Police Criticised as Country Reels from Far-Right Violence.” https://www.theguardian.com/world/2018/aug/28/german-police-criticised-as-country-reels-from-far-right-violence. Accessed 28 October 2019.

Crouch, D. 2016. “Sweden and Denmark Crack Down on Refugees at Borders.” https://www.theguardian.com/world/2016/jan/03/sweden-to-impose-id-checks-on-travellers-from-denmark. Accessed 4 August 2020.

Del Re, P. 2019. “Polonia, corteo dell’ultradestra tenta di entrare a Auschwitz.” https://www.repubblica.it/esteri/2019/01/27/news/polonia_corteo_dell_ultra-destra_tenta_di_entrare_a_auschwitz-217613024/. Accessed 28 October 2019.

Dickson, A. 2015. “War, Migration and Revenge.” https://www.theguardian.com/commentisfree/2015/oct/30/war-migration-revenge-shakespeare-world-syrian-refugee-camps. Accessed 29 July 2019.

Dromgoole, D. 2014. “*Hamlet* by William Shakespeare, About the Project.” http://globetoglobe.shakespearesglobe.com/hamlet/about-the-project. Accessed 28 July 2019.

——. 2017. “Performing *Hamlet* in a Sandstorm at a Syrian Refugee Camp.” https://lithub.com/performing-hamlet-in-a-sandstorm-at-a-syrian-refugee-camp/. Accessed 29 July 2019.

“Eurispes: risultati del Rapporto Italia 2020.” 2020. Eurispes. https://eurispes.eu/news/eurispes-risultati-del-rapporto-italia-2020/. Accessed 4 July 2020.

Francalacci, N. 2016. “Il no ai migranti di Goro e Gorino.” https://www.panorama.it/news/cronaca/ferrara-si-ribella-ai-migranti-barricate/. Accessed 29 July 2019.

“Francis Greets the Population of Lesbos: Immigrants Are Not Numbers, but People, Faces, Names and Stories.” 2016. Holy See Press Office. https://press.vatican.va/content/salastampa/en/bollettino/pubblico/2016/04/16/160416c.html. Accessed 13 February 2020.

Gibińska, M. 2018. "Crisis: Meeting the Other and the Philosophy of Dialogue." halshs-02145012f. Accessed 17 June 2019.

Giorgio, M. 2019. "Ve la do io l'invasione, Erdogan spara sui civili e minaccia l'Europa." https://ilmanifesto.it/erdogan-agli-europei-zitti-o-vi-mandiamo-36-milioni-di-migranti/. Accessed 28 October 2019.

Greenblatt, S. 2017. "Shakespeare's Cure for Xenophobia." https://www.newyorker.com/magazine/2017/07/10/shakespeares-cure-for-xenophobia. Accessed 4 January 2020.

Henriques Coutinho, M., and M. Pompeo Nogueira. 2013. "The Use of Dialogical Approaches for Community Theatre by the Group Nós de Morro, in the Vidigal Favela of Rio de Janeiro." In: T. Prentki and S. Preston (eds.), *The Applied Theatre Reader*. London: Routledge, 171-177.

Hornby, A.S. 2000. *Oxford Advanced Learner's Dictionary of Current English*. Oxford: Oxford University Press.

Hornung, A. 2017. "Out of Life: Routes, Refugees, Rescue." *a/b: Auto/Biography Studies* 32(3). 603-623.

Hubbard, B. 2014. "Behind Barbed Wire, Shakespeare Inspires a Cast of Young Syrians." https://www.nytimes.com/2014/04/01/world/middleeast/behind-barbed-wire-shakespeare-inspires-a-cast-of-young-syrians.html. Accessed 29 July 2019.

"Istituzione Commissione straordinaria contrasto fenomeni intolleranza: approvata mozione Segre in Aula." 2019. Senato della Repubblica. http://www.senato.it/notizia?comunicato=64001. Accessed 28 October 2019.

Keidan, L. 2008. "The Ethics of Socially Engaged Art." https://www.theguardian.com/stage/theatreblog/2008/may/08/theethicsofsociallyengaged. Accessed 16 October 2019.

Kirwan, P. 2009. "Review of *As You Like It*." *Cahiers Élisabéthains* 75(1). 86-87.

La società a teatro. 2019. Seminar at the Teatro Comunale in Ferrara. 20 December 2019. www.teatrocomunaleferrara.it/events/event/undhur-ilay-see-me-guardami. Accessed 13 August 2020.

Lee, S., and M. Fidler. 2015. "All the World's a Stage: The Globe's *Hamlet* Plays in a Jordanian Refugee Camp." https://www.theguardian.com/artanddesign/ng-interactive/2015/oct/29/undiscovered-country-the-globe-travelling-hamlet-jordan-refugee-camp. Accessed 28 July 2019.

Manfré, E. 2013. "Calderoli: 'Kyenge orango? Una battuta simpatica.'" https://video.repubblica.it/politica/calderoli-kyenge-orango-una-battuta-simpatica/134863/133403. Accessed 20 September 2020.

Meringolo, A. 2014. "Shakespeare a Zaatari." https://www.reset.it/reset-doc/shakespeare-a-zaatari-campo-profughi-giordania-nawar-bulbul. Accessed 13 February 2020.

Mirakyan, N. 2019. "Senatore Iwobi della Lega risponde agli insulti razzisti tramite Sputnik." https://it.sputniknews.com/intervista/201911138292935-senatore-iwobi-della-lega-risponde-agli-insulti-razzisti-tramite-sputnik/. Accessed 15 May 2020.

Monari, F. 2020. "Insulti razzisti a Kyenge, Calderoli condannato in primo grado." https://www.modenaindiretta.it/insulti-razzisti-kyenge-calderoli-condannato-primo-grado-video/. Accessed 20 September 2020.

Pocosgnich, A. 2018. "Non sparate sullo spettatore. Esempi di Teatro partecipativo a Pergine." https://www.teatroecritica.net/2018/07/non-sparate-sullo-spettatore-esempi-di-teatro-partecipativo-a-pergine/. Accessed 13 February 2020.

Ramalhete Gomes, M. 2018. "Learned Goths and Roman Exports: *Titus Andronicus* and Presentism in the 2010s." halshs-02145023. https://halshs.archives-ouvertes.fr/halshs-02145023/document. Accessed 13 February 2020.

Rame, S. 2019. "Diede dell'"orango' alla Kyenge: Calderoli condannato a 18 mesi." https://www.ilgiornale.it/news/politica/diede-dellorango-kyenge-calderoli-condannato-18-mesi-1628756.html. Accessed 20 September 2020.

Rifkin, F. 2010. *The Ethics of Participatory Theatre in Higher Education: A Framework for Learning and Teaching.* London: The Higher Education Academy.

Said, E. 2000. *Out of Place: A Memoir.* New York: Vintage.

Sapuppo, M. 2019. "How Shakespeare Helps Us Challenge the Far-Right in Europe." http://www.publicseminar.org/2019/06/how-shakespeare-helps-us-challenge-the-far-right-in-europe/. Accessed 29 July 2019.

Shakespeare, W. 2006. *As You Like It.* Edited by J. Dusinberre. London: Bloomsbury.

——. 2010. *The Merchant of Venice.* Edited by J. Drakakis. London–New York: Bloomsbury.

——. 1623. *The Tempest.* http://inamidst.com/shaks/tempest/folio. Accessed 20 September 2020.

Smith, E., and E. West. *Shakespeare Shorts.* https://www.shakespeareforrefugees.com. Accessed 13 July 2019.

Spinozzi, P. 2016. "'Acerba illa vita velut carcere atque aculeo.' Health or Death in More's *Libellus vere aureus*: Early Modern Thought and Contemporary Debate." *Utopian Studies* 27(3). 586-600.

Taneja, P. 2015. "Sweet Sorrow as Star-crossed Lovers in Syria and Jordan Connect via Skype." https://www.theguardian.com/stage/theatreblog/2015/apr/14/romeo-and-juliet-staged-in-amman-and-homs. Accessed 29 July 2019.

"The Tempest." 2016. Sea-change Theatre. https://www.sea-changetheatre.com/the-tempest. Accessed 27 July 2019.

Tóth, Z. 2019. "Identities Under Siege: A Comment on the Hungarian Attitude Towards Refugees Informed by Shakespeare's *Othello.*" halshs-02148417. Accessed 28 October 2019.

Townsend, M. 2018. "Police with Batons and Teargas Force Migrants to Flee Calais Camp." https://www.theguardian.com/world/2018/dec/01/french-police-step-up-calais-refugee-evictions. Accessed 29 July 2019.

"Undhur ilay / see me / guardami." 2019. *Teatro Comunale di Ferrara.* http://www.teatrocomunaleferrara.it/events/event/undhur-ilay-see-me-guardami/. Accessed 13 August 2020.

Valls-Russell, J. 2019. "Working with Shakespeare: The Ethics of Community Engagement and Participatory Theatre." halshs-02148427. Accessed 19 July 2019.

"What Is The Strangers' Case?" 2018. International Rescue Committee. https://www.rescue-uk.org/article/what-strangers-case. Accessed 2 November 2019.

Whitlock, G. 2015a. *Postcolonial Life Narratives.* Oxford: Oxford University Press.

——. 2015b. *The Hospitality of Cyberspace: Mobilizing Asylum Seekers Testimony Online.* Oxford: Oxford University Press.

NATALYA STOCKS

Jagiellonian University

Shakespeare, Censorship and South Africa

Abstract

People have been subjected to content restriction for centuries. This paper attempts to introduce the development of this phenomenon and the way it functioned during Shakespeare's lifetime and in the years of the apartheid regime in South Africa. Regardless of the place and time, censorship operates in a similar manner and constitutes an important tool for shaping a society and defending an oppressive system. The paper focuses on the censorship of plays. It discusses the influence of the causal nexus of theatre's censorship on the society and the impact of Shakespeare's plays on shaping the first leader of the post-apartheid South Africa. Research on censorship and its influence on various societies in different historical periods is necessary to better understand this phenomenon and to use the knowledge about the past to avoid censorship dominating freedom of speech in the present-day world.

Keywords: Shakespeare, RSA, censorship, apartheid, theatre

Streszczenie

Ludzkość przez wieki była ofiarą ograniczeń związanych z cenzurą. Artykuł ma na celu przybliżenie rozwoju cenzury, a także jej sposobu funkcjonowania w czasach Szekspira oraz w epoce reżimu apartheidu w RPA. Cenzura działa w podobny sposób niezależnie od miejsca i czasu jej stosowania i stanowi ważne narzędzie w kształtowaniu społeczeństwa oraz ochronie opresyjnego ustroju. Tekst skupia się na cenzurze sztuk teatralnych, badając wpływ, jaki na społeczeństwo mają efekty cenzury stosowanej w środowisku teatralnym. Mówi także o roli twórczości Szekspira w życiu pierwszego lidera Republiki Południowej Afryki po upadku apartheidu. Badania na temat cenzury oraz jej wpływu na różnorodne społeczeństwa w odmiennych czasach pozwalają lepiej zrozumieć to zjawisko, aby móc skuteczniej ograniczać wpływ cenzury na wolność słowa w obecnych czasach.

Słowa kluczowe: Szekspir, RPA, cenzura, apartheid, teatr

Introduction

In my article, I will discuss and compare theatre censorship; the main focus will be placed on the plays by William Shakespeare and their performances in Elizabethan and Jacobean England and in South Africa during the apartheid era. Also, I will try to demonstrate how Shakespeare's creativity is still up to date when addressing modern problems by explaining the influence of his plays on shaping the worldview of the South African freedom fighters. Issues concerning the execution of censorship in Shakespeare's times and the apartheid era will be addressed, such as the reasons for censoring plays, who was most censored and why, what was the most controversial play in South Africa during the apartheid era, as well as the reason why a set of complete works by William Shakespeare was once called the "Robben Island Bible."

A Definition of Censorship

Censorship is nothing new as writers have been subjected to content restriction for many centuries. Nowadays, not much has changed and governments still practise limiting various means of expression. In the present day this procedure differs slightly in methodology and execution in comparison to the times of Shakespeare or the apartheid era in South Africa that will be analysed in this paper, yet, the essence of it remains the same – censorship has been and still is used as a tool to limit various spheres of freedom. As much as censorship is undesirable from the perspective of the society, more often than not it is deemed to be necessary in order to help preserve the prevailing political system or beliefs that make it possible to run an orderly state in a desired way. To censor means to suppress in order to impose one's ideas on others without opposition, as the following definition explains more extensively:

> Censorship is the changing or the suppression or prohibition of speech or writing that is deemed subversive of the common good. It occurs in all manifestations of authority to some degree, but in modern times it has been of special importance in its relation to government and the rule of law. (Anastaplo n.d.)

While censorship has evolved throughout the ages, the general idea of its aim and execution has not changed at all. The perfect evidence of this fact is that it is still possible to find common elements between censorship in the present day, censorship in the Shakespearean era or even in ancient times and that the topics censorship has always been particularly sensitive about – such as, religion, politics and morality – have not changed much. Socrates was one of the earliest recorded victims of censorship, supposedly preaching controversial, even atheist content, which made him infamous among the Athenian society. Back then, censorship was considered an honourable act, which helped shape the society in a way that ensured the accentuation of the right virtues. Socrates was not afraid to speak his mind and continued to do so, while he was aware he was entering shallow waters: "While I breathe and I am able to, I certainly will not stop philosophising" (Plato 2007, 161).

He bestowed too much faith on the open-mindedness of his folk, and soon he was sentenced to death by drinking poison for the supposed demoralization of the Athenian youth who came to listen to his teachings. Throughout the years, other civilizations have learned and repeated the pattern and started to expand the scope of censorship into various areas of society, exploring the promising possibilities of control and authority that came with it.

Censorship in the Times of Shakespeare

The period between the sixteenth and the seventeenth centuries, the times of Shakespeare, was characterised by widespread censorship of plays – as they were the easiest to understand for the often illiterate recipients and had the biggest outreach to the masses. The rulers knew that feeding thought-provoking or even rebellious content to the clearly underprivileged society and making them aware of that fact was a recipe for social unrest and possibly riotous mayhem. Therefore, the censorship office held an essential role in the process of maintaining a relatively peaceful reign in the Elizabethan and Jacobean era. The heavy burden of responsibility placed upon it encouraged the office to be strict in the execution of its duties, which was possible by dividing the main censorship office into numerous sub-groups, as suggested by Michelle O'Callaghan (2000), "Censorship itself was multiform in the sense that there was not one censorship that served the whole state but rather multiple censorships that operated in the service of a range of interest groups" (83). The official seat of the decision-maker and main executor of censorship, until the early seventeenth century, was held by the Master of the Revels and there was no appeal against his decision – at the stage of pre-production censorship and many plays have failed to meet the prevailing standards without the censor's intrusion. Playwrights would encounter the ruthless scythe of the blacking-out office that would slice out whole excerpts, forcing corrections or paraphrases of undesirable fragments or even whole pages of the plays' contents.

During Shakespeare's lifetime, the seat of the Master of the Revels was held by Sir Edmund Tilney. He was trusted by Queen Elizabeth and, being part of her inner circle, made sure to be scrupulous when performing his duties of preventing riotous moods by ensuring safe contents of the plays. During the reign of Queen Elizabeth, new regulations were introduced, mainly extending the authority of the Master of the Revels, but which also rendered plays to be examined in search of undesirable content mainly in the form of "either matters of religion or of the governance of the estate of the common weal" (Best n.d.), what is more, it was necessary to obtain a licence to perform a play. Shakespeare's texts are believed to have been tampered with by the censors, especially when taking into consideration the context of his two plays – *Richard II* and both parts of *Henry IV*. Supposedly, the scene in Shakespeare's *Richard II* in which Richard is deposed was the one that Queen Elizabeth desired to be hushed, as it thematically connected to the Earl of Sussex's failed revolt against the Queen in 1601, as mentioned by Jean-Christophe Mayer (2004) in his article on the "Parliament Scaene": "None of the editions printed during the reign of Elizabeth I (1558-1603) contained the scene at the heart of Act 4, scene 1 (lines 155-318) in which King Richard is deposed by his own Parliament" (28). The play was staged incomplete and the full version of it was allowed only after Elizabeth's death. *Henry IV* was yet another case of such censorship, because of the discontent caused by the choice of names for the characters in the play, namely: Oldcastle, Harvey and Russell, who were real historical figures and whose descendants objected against the unfavourable representation of their ancestors. As a result, Shakespeare decided to change the characters' names to Falstaff, Bardolph and Peto.

Censors had a whole set of rules and regulations at their disposal. The play had to undergo a close examination before being accepted with the official blessing of the censorship office. The attention of the censors was especially fixed on elements critical of the monarchy and legitimacy, on blasphemy, aspects that could provoke uprisings, and any references to living (especially influential) people. At first glance it would seem to be a simple, yet well-organised system, but that was not quite the case. Even though the authority of the censor was significant, it was not regulated clearly enough to be able to prevent any eventuality of undesirable content leaking out. Also, there were other parties with just as much power at play, who also had their part in the decision-making process. The power to censor was not in the hands of just one person, as the Church, monarchs, publishers and, obviously, the Revel's Office could prevent the play from being staged as well. As mentioned by O'Callaghan (2000), censorship in the Elizabethan and Jacobean era was a "crazy quilt of proclamations, patents, trade regulations, judicial decrees, and Privy Council and parliamentary actions patched together by sometimes common and sometimes competing threads of religious, economic, political and private interests" (91). Yet, paradoxically, the owner of the theatre who was willing to produce a play that was controversial in the production phase could simply decide to stage it without seeking the approval of any other authority. In some cases plays were published outside of England only to circumvent the pre-production stage of censorship and go straight to production, which was subject to lesser number of restrictions (O'Callaghan 2000, 92). It was a risky move though, as it could result in banning of the play, penalties for authors and actors or, in extreme cases, even a shutdown of the facility.

In Shakespeare's time, no official set of rules or determinants existed for evaluating the text in an objective and equal way for each of the plays and the approach towards the piece very much depended on the background of the potentially offended person who played the role of the censor. For example, a church official was more likely to ban an excerpt that had a blasphemous touch to it than a monarch who would be mostly concerned about the critique of his or hers legitimacy. Being friendly with a particular censor also helped when pushing the play through the suppressive procedures, as censorship at the time was far from objective and regulated, often dependant on a whim of certain personages. Knowing how to work the ties and acquaintances was a skill that every self-respecting playwright had to learn, in order to gain an official staging licence and release their works in the original shape, with having as little taken or added as possible. Shakespeare was considered to be one of the trusted playwrights and he participated in revising some of the plays at the time. His name is, for example, on the list of agents examining the content of *The Booke of Sir Thomas More*, the history play whose first version was written by Anthony Munday.

He added some significant excerpts to the play initially withdrawn by Sir Edmund Tilney, yet even after the joint efforts of Shakespeare and other editors, there is no proof that the play was ever staged. A new episode for censorship began some hundred years after Shakespeare's death, with Lord Chamberlain assuming the duties and replacing the Master of the Revels. His position remained intact until the late twentieth century and casual banning of stage performances began a new, challenging era for performative arts and play censorship in England.

Censorship in Apartheid South Africa

The genius of Shakespeare is unquestionable. The way his works spread across the globe and influenced millions of people is extraordinary. Even in places most distant from Shakespeare's homeland, such as South Africa, he is placed among the most influential literary classics. Shakespeare wandered all the way to the south of the African continent together with the colonisation of South Africa by the British settlers which started in the late eighteenth century. Apart from introducing the British currency and language to its inhabitants, it also brought a new culture and a rich literary supply as a bonus. Yet, a time was about to come when Shakespeare's plays would yet again fall into the snares of censorship, hundreds of years after their first release, all due to the happenings taking place in twentieth-century South Africa. In the years 1948-1994, South Africa found itself under the rule of the apartheid regime. The following definition accurately portrays the character of apartheid as a:

> policy that governed relations between South Africa's white minority and non-white majority and sanctioned racial segregation and political and economic

> discrimination against nonwhites. The implementation of apartheid, often called "separate development" since the 1960s, was made possible through the Population Registration Act of 1950, which classified all South Africans as either Bantu (all Black Africans), Coloured (those of mixed race), or white. A fourth category – Asian (Indian and Pakistani) – was later added. ("Apartheid," *Encyclopædia Britannica*)

During this period, censorship was at its highest and it was neatly executed on all kinds of artistic works. An official bureau for censorship in South Africa was established in 1963, some years after the nationalistic government has taken over with full legitimacy. The censorship office, under the name of the Republic of Letters, was set with a task of protecting the apartheid image from all "seditious, obscene, and blasphemous representations" (Lenta 2010), which could harm its reputation.

Content restriction in South Africa in terms of its functioning has been compared to the Soviet institution of Glavlit, which aimed at exercising complete control over all the published media. Censorship in South Africa did not go so far, but it succeeded in hindering the creative outlet of artists, when censorship, together with oppression, reached its peak in the 1980s, limiting to the extreme freedom of speech and veracity of information. During this period everything was heavily censored or even banned; books, press, digital media, particular journalists and writers, no matter the race and political standing, all in response to the growing social unrest in South Africa, caused by years of social inequality and isolation of the black and coloured population by the apartheid regime. When it comes to the system administering the doings of the censorship office, like in Shakespearean times, there was no strict set of regulations that would apply to all the works, and censors were granted a lot of freedom as to what and how to censor. Often a decision to treat a work in a particular manner was strictly subjective and was determined by the censor's personal attraction or animosity towards an author, and in the majority of cases no explanation was provided for the censor's decision to ban a work. However, there were certain aspects that censors were especially sensitive to when, being faithful to the phrase "better safe than sorry," they would ban or heavily censor a piece of writing if they as little as suspected that there could be a hidden revolutionary meaning to it, or if a sentence emitted a hint of criticism of the system, especially if the text was written by a native author. These are some general markers introduced in The Publications Act of 1978 that were meant to make it easier for the censors, publishing houses and the general public to recognise an undesirable publication:

> (a) it is "indecent or obscene or offensive or harmful to public morals";
> (b) it is "blasphemous or offensive to the religious convictions or feelings" of a "section";
> (c) it "brings any section [...] into ridicule or contempt";
> (d) it is harmful to inter-section relations;
> (e) it prejudices security, welfare, peace and good order;
> (f) it discloses part of a judicial proceeding in which offensive material is quoted. (Coetzee 1990, 2)

Feedback provided by art was meant to serve a purpose and echo support for the regime in order to preserve a positive image of the system governing the country. Just like in the Elizabethan times, riots and social unrest were to be avoided at all cost, and the censorship apparatus was burdened with the task of preventing such events.

> Conversely the censorship system has caused many writers to flee South Africa. Such exiles can no longer draw on their experiences or the language and thought of South Africa. The continued control of those who stay has had the effect of driving Black writers underground and reinforcing that wall built between Black experience and grievance and those Whites who wish to know about them. The banning, for example, of *Confused Mhlaba* by Khayalethu Mqayisa, on the grounds that the play harmed race relations and compromised the safety of the State, showed, according to the defence, that real events were being withheld from White South Africans and that the banning itself hurt race relations as it reduced the potential for mutual understanding. Not only is all South Africa denied access to thinking of radical Black Africa and formative political and social thinking in the Free World, but Whites are to remain ignorant of the feelings of fellow citizens. Literature written by Blacks, dealing in depth with the Black condition, is immediately a target for suppression. (Merrett 1982, 4)

All the aspects mentioned above affected also theatre and staging plays. Just like representatives of other branches of arts, playwrights and actors were oppressed and prosecuted by the government and the supporters of the system. Some faced heavy fines and others were imprisoned, many were banned from work or fled the country in the heat of events with a ban placed upon them preventing their return and curbing any influence they and their art had on the South African societies ("South African theatre"

2007). The realities of the creative struggle in South Africa were harsh and because of the restrictions placed upon them, as mentioned by Jack Klaff (2014), many prominent artists were forcefully excluded from fighting the system from within, and writers such as Lewis Nkosi, Nat Nakasa and Bloke Modisane were among the talents lost for theatre. Literature in South Africa was in a way divided, there were black and white liberation writers who concentrated on depicting the injustices of apartheid, however, as it was in the case of black and white authors – representatives of each group undertook a different approach to the matter. White authors focused on the need for change and the visions of the future if the rules governing the country remain unchanged, whilst native African literature contained more encouragement for action and hope for a better future. Theatre, especially in the 1970s, was important and dangerous because it was a place where two, instituted as separate, societies met together, and the message of the plays, and the way they were delivered, was the same for all, having a universal and not necessarily directly anti-apartheid meaning, which initially spared it from the claws of the law ("Theatre and Apartheid" 2019). However, such theatres and their audience were strongly discouraged to spread riotous content, as it was common for actors and viewers alike to be arrested after the performance for participating in activities opposing the system; police patrols were placed in front of theatre buildings, which discouraged the audience to enter as they knew that there was a possibility of them being arrested for non-specified period of time upon leaving.

Although plays that condemned the system were produced, the problem was the place of their staging. Consequently, not many of the actual victims of apartheid reached the audience, for black districts, such as Soweto, had hardly any infrastructure to host more demanding productions. Another problem was the intense police activity in the native districts, which made it very difficult to organise performances ("South African theatre" 2007). An element of paradox was also present behind the curtains, because even though the plays touched upon apartheid problems, some theatres did not allow African actors or creative stage workers to work on the performances. One of many examples would be the National Theatre, which, starting in 1947, was one of the biggest institutions prohibiting black participation. The constant handicap of black South African artists in getting a say in the white-dominated areas caused a new phenomenon to emerge, the rise of black township theatre movement starting in the 1950s. As long as until the fall of apartheid, many African and non-African small-scale plays were staged, often moving from one venue to another in short spans of time. Popular venues were church halls, since often they could host a large audience and were inconspicuous. The themes of the plays were predominantly about contemporary injustices of apartheid, such as in *Sizwe Banzi Is Dead* and *The Island*, which won international critical acclaim. There were also stage performances regarding various other themes, such as alcoholism, love and crime, such as *Woza Albert!*, which won the attention of the public thanks to its unique plot telling the story of Jesus' second coming, this time to the apartheid South Africa. The performances mentioned above were the most successful, as they managed to get staged internationally, but not many other plays had the same luck, for theatre groups were harassed on regular basis and suffered shortages of staff, whose members were systematically imprisoned. Also, plays were banned or allowed to be performed to very small audiences, which prevented the spread of inflammatory moods of defiance ("South African theatre" 2007). In the 1970s, The Market Theatre and The Space were pioneers in establishing an artistic non-racial venue in the otherwise racially separated country. While The Space's existence was short-lived due to financial problems, the impact those two theatres had on raising awareness among the society was enormous. In the words of Janice Honeyman, one of the ex-members of The Space Theatre:

> Some plays almost became political rallies. The responses to them were so immediate and visceral, and sometimes affected their outlook to South African life considerably. And so, I do think theatre has played a huge part in changing attitudes in South Africa, and eventually, along with The Struggle, in changing the government. (Honeyman qtd. in "Theatre and Apartheid" 2019)

Theatre in South Africa constituted one of the most powerful anti-apartheid tools for voicing problems of the oppressed, and, just like all other forms of public discourse, it suffered oppression and struggled to reach its audience until the fall of apartheid in 1994. Arthur Miller once said that the "mission of the theatre, after all, is to change, to raise the consciousness of people to their human possibilities" (qtd. in Isherwood and McKinley 2005). From a historical perspective, it can be stated that the South African scene survived and succeeded in fulfilling this task and that, as it will be demonstrated in the following section, Shakespeare's plays also had its share in this.

Shakespeare in South Africa

The second half of the 1980s was characterised by the most intensive internal problems in South Africa. The separatist government was waging a regular war with the media and townships, which ever since the massacre in Soweto were an arena of protests and uprisings. Peaceful resistance proved to be futile, the African National Congress went underground and initiated guerrilla actions, sabotaging various organs of social control and committing terrorist attacks, which resulted in the spread of violence. The governmental control and censorship were never as omnipresent and heavily executed as in this period before the transition. These moods and the sensation of an upcoming change were among the reasons why the Market Theatre decided to make a perilous move, with William Shakespeare as one of the main conspirators. In 1987 the Johannesburg Market Theatre decided to stage *Othello*, a drama about racial prejudice. This ground-breaking production was directed by Janet Suzman and became one of the precursors of the upcoming era of racial equality. The production attracted crowds of all ethnic backgrounds, excited and amazed with the release of such a performance, in which a thing unseen before would happen before their eyes – the dark-skinned Moor, played by a black actor (John Kani) gets involved with a Venetian (white) woman. The scene with Kani and his Desdemona, Joanna Weinberg, united in a passionate kiss was heavily controversial to the audience. This act of public physical exchange of emotions in a performance was shocking to many, as it had only been in 1985 that the South African government under Pieter Willem Botha repealed the ban on interracial marriages, at the same time upholding strict racial segregation and colour-determined urban districts. The play provoked strong and varied feelings for the five weeks during which it was running. Some people would leave the building in rage, bombarding the theatre's mailbox with hatred-filled letters, while others saluted the performance with surges of praise. Even though the controversial production turned out to be a tremendous success that was acclaimed by the audience worldwide, the pre-production human factor should be taken into consideration to add a larger perspective to the performance and production of the play.

Initially, John Kani was hesitant to take on the role of Othello and, when asked by Suzman, responded: "I carry 11 stab wounds on my body, have survived assassination, been detained and have to be careful even walking the street because everybody wants me dead. So thank you, but I am not going to do this play" ("Theatre and Apartheid" 2019). In the past he was ambushed by the apartheid police after performing in his co-authored production of the famous *Sizwe Banzi Is Dead*, and also attacked on other occasions for his defiance initiatives. Kani was perfectly aware of the danger which participating in one of the most controversial productions that this country had ever known might score him. However, there was also another side to him, which called for action: "When I am offered work, I am very selective. I want my work to contribute toward creating a better society, toward bringing people together. That is always the first consideration, not the money" (qtd. in Battersby 1987). Kani knew that *Othello* might have been just what the South African society needed at this point of history and, in the end, decided to accept the part in the play. "I took a deep breath and agreed," Mr. Kani said. "Then my heart started thumping and I immediately knew how much trouble I was in for. [...] But I looked on the light side and said, 'There goes the native causing more trouble, and this time he has Shakespeare to do it for him'" (qtd. in Battersby 1987). In these days it was dangerous to be on the wrong side of the wall, it was dangerous to be a black South African, and it was definitely dangerous to be a black South African who had something to say, especially if it involved the criticism of the system. Therefore, preparing the play was a strong experience for both Suzman and Kani. This shared act of defiance required a lot of trust on both sides, for, in those days, they were representatives of two different societies, and though both sides had much to lose, one of them could lose it all if things went wrong.

There is no better play by Shakespeare to tell the tragedy and experience of suffering and isolation of a foreigner in a faraway land than *Othello.* In this case, what makes the situation so much worse is the fact that the protagonist may identify with the stranger, although he is in his own country: "Like Othello in Venice, Kani said, he feels himself to be an outsider in his own land. He said he was immediately able to identify with Othello through his experience as a black South African: 'They make us feel aliens in our own land of birth by taking away our citizenship'" (Battersby 1987). This was the message that shook the audience to the core and this was the forbidden truth that everyone in South Africa knew, but was not ready to talk about. *Othello*, as directed by Janet Suzman, at the time of its release stirred the society with the realisation of the inevitably upcoming change. South Africa's graduate shift towards democracy in the 1990s met with violent turmoil after which the society began the process of building the future of a "Rainbow Nation," in which all members of the society would enjoy equal rights and must learn to co-exist together on new terms, after years of isolation and violence. The artistic community's apartheid struggle was a long road to freedom that resulted in freedom of speech and expression for the generations to come.

The "Robben Island Bible"

The most recognisable African National Congress activist and definitely one of the most prominent South African citizens was also influenced by Shakespeare, and this experience had an impact on the whole South African society of the time. This person is, of course, Nelson Mandela, the first South African President chosen in the free for all races elections in 1994. Before becoming a head of state, Mandela had faced imprisonment for 27 years, having been found guilty of treason and anti-apartheid revolutionary action during the Rivonia Trial in 1964. He narrowly evaded the death sentence and was instead faced with a life sentence, which was later shortened thanks to the proclamation of amnesia in the twilight of apartheid. During his stay on Robben Island, on which he was imprisoned for the majority of his sentence, Mandela had access to the so-called "Robben Island Bible," which was basically a collection of works by William Shakespeare. In his article, Ashwin Desai (2019) explains how it ended up in the hands of the future leader of South Africa. The name given to this particular set of Shakespeare's works is not accidental. The system that governed distribution of books to prisoners in Mandela's prison was what could easily be called post-publishing censorship. Literature was generally banned on Robben Island, although there was one exception – religious texts. Apart from Nelson Mandela, there is another protagonist in this story, namely, Sonny Venktrathnam, who once asked his wife to send him the complete works of Shakespeare, although he knew that the chances of the collection ending up in his hands were slim. Upon confiscation, Venktrathnam managed to persuade the prison guard that the book was "the Bible by William Shakespeare" and succeeded in getting it back. He then covered the book with images of Hindu gods, to advance the disguise. This decision made by the guard provided Mandela and his fellow inmates with entertainment and ample material for debate and political inspiration in the upcoming years. Each of the prisoners would choose an excerpt from a play which would constitute their "motto," and the plays were interpreted in a way so that they would correspond to the actual situation in South Africa. Shakespeare's universality created a perfect ground for analysis and criticism of the system governing the country (Desai 2019).

After having been released from prison, the ex-political convicts would quote Shakespeare in their speeches condemning apartheid. The passage that Nelson Mandela highlighted in the "Bible," which had a special meaning to him, came from *Julius Caesar*:

> Cowards die many times before their deaths;
> The valiant never taste of death but once.
> Of all the wonders that I yet have heard
> It seems to me most strange that men should fear;
> Seeing that death, a necessary end,
> Will come when it will come. (2.2.32-37)

But it definitely was not the only one that he remembered and related to, as even before his imprisonment on Robben Island, in the infamous Rivonia Trial, he quoted from *Measure for Measure*: "Be absolute for death; either death or life / Shall thereby be the sweeter" (3.1.5-6), and on another occasion, during business negotiations, from *The Merchant of Venice*: "Hath not a Jew eyes?" (3.1.57). A book that by chance found its way to the future leader of South African freedom movement had a definite impact on the fate of his oppressed country. How could it be otherwise, since it was the only text that he and his fellow prisoners had access to for so many years?

Conclusion

In my article, I have tried to build a bridge between censorship during Shakespeare's times and in South Africa in the period of apartheid. This subject is close to the heart of many South-African citizens who have been victims to the system's propaganda and also to me, personally, as my family roots originate from this country. It should be stated that the purposeful omission, manipulation and censorship of information has led to an erroneous understanding of the past political and social situation in South Africa for its citizens of both races and caused it to deepen the misunderstanding and isolation of the two societies. This resulted in growing anger, unrest and finally bloodshed in the struggle to be heard. The issue of censorship is very topical in the present world and continues to be a challenging problem in the modern era of supposed democracy and freedom, therefore all nations around the world must enforce the fight against it with one simple tool – education, and hope that history will not have the chance to repeat itself. One of the most famous quotes by Nelson Mandela is: “Education is the most powerful weapon which you can use to change the world” (1990, Madison Park Speech). While looking at this quote in the context of apartheid, one can say he is most definitely right, but it has to be said that only non-biased education can undertake this role. Settling for anything less, as it was in the case of the Bantu education, will mean an ultimate defeat of freedom of speech, truthfulness of information and hope for a democratic future for the upcoming generations.

References

Anastaplo, G. n.d. “Censorship.” *Encyclopædia Britannica*. https://www.britannica.com/topic/censorship. Accessed 20 July 2020.

“Apartheid.” n.d. *Encyclopædia Britannica*. https://www.britannica.com/topic/apartheid. Accessed 20 July 2020.

Battersby, J.D. 1987. “The Drama of Staging ‘Othello’ in Johannesburg.” https://www.nytimes.com/1987/10/26/theater/the-drama-of-staging-othello-in-johannesburg.html. Accessed 20 June 2020.

Best, M. n.d. “Censorship.” https://internetshakespeare.uvic.ca/Library/SLT/literature/publishing/censorship.html. Accessed 2 August 2020.

Coetzee, J.M. 1990. “Censorship in South Africa.” *English in Africa* 17(1). 1-20.

Desai, A. 2019. “Sonny Venkatrathnam, Anti-Apartheid Crusader With a Shakespearian ‘Gita.’” thewire.in/world/sonny-venkatrathnam-anti-apartheid-crusader-with-a-shakespearian-gita. Accessed 18 August 2020.

Isherwood, Ch., and J. McKinley. 2005. “Arthur Miller, Legendary American Playwright, Is Dead at 89.” https://www.nytimes.com/2005/02/11/theater/arthur-miller-legendary-american-playwright-is-dead-at-89.html. Accessed 23 June 2020.

Klaff, J. 2014. “Acting against Apartheid: The Enduring Power of South African Protest Theatre.” www.theguardian.com/stage/2014/jun/20/acting-against-apartheid-south-african-protest-theatre. Accessed 20 July 2020.

Lenta, P. 2010. “Introduction: Law and South African Literature.” https://www.thefreelibrary.com/Introduction%3A+law+and+South+African+literature.-a0244951478. Accessed 20 July 2020.

Mandela, N. 1990, June 23. “Education Is the Most Powerful Weapon which You Can Use to Change the World.” Speech, Madison Park High School, Boston.

Mayer, J.-Ch. 2004. “The ‘Parliament Sceane’ in Shakespeare’s *King Richard II*.” *XVII-XVIII. Revue de la Société d’études anglo-américaines des XVIIe et XVIIIe siècles* 59(1). 27-42. https://www.persee.fr/doc/xvii_0291-3798_2004_num_59_1_1993. Accessed 20 June 2020.

Merrett, C.E. 1982. "Political Censorship in South Africa: Aims and Consequences." http://www.sahistory.org.za/sites/default/files/DC/remar82.3/remar82.3.pdf. Accessed 20 July 2020.

O'Callaghan, M. 2000. "Publication: Print and Manuscript." In: M. Hattaway (ed.), *A Companion to Renaissance Literature and Culture.* Oxford: Blackwell, 81-94.

Plato. 2007. "Apology." In: *Euthyphro, Apology, Crito, Phaedo, Phaedrus.* Translated by H.N. Fowler. Cambridge, MA: Harvard University Press.

Shakespeare, W. 2005. *Julius Caesar.* Edited by N. Sanders. London: Penguin.

——. 2005. *Measure for Measure.* Edited by J.M. Nosworthy. London: Penguin.

——. 2005. *Othello.* Edited by K. Muir. London: Penguin.

——. 2005. *The Merchant of Venice.* Edited by W. Moelwyn Merchant. London: Penguin.

"South African theatre." 2007. Brand South Africa. www.brandsouthafrica.com/people-culture/culture/theatre. Accessed 20 July 2020.

"Theatre and Apartheid." 2019. Royal Shakespeare Company. www.rsc.org.uk/news/archive/theatre-and-apartheid. Accessed 30 June 2020.

PART II

Life and Death Between Human and Posthuman

ANA RITA CATALÃO GUEDES
University of Porto

"He but usurped his life": The Shameful Death in BBC Two's *King Lear*

Abstract

The aim of this paper is to analyse the 2018 BBC Two's *King Lear* as a commentary on our modern inability to deal with death. Although the Covid-19 pandemic has forced us to confront death on a scale unprecedented in our lifetime, our conception of death as a cultural phenomenon still differs radically from that of our predecessors. Contemporary society tends to perceive it as a private and invisible affair rather than as a visible and ubiquitous occurrence, as it was in the early modern period. In *The Hour of Our Death* (1981), Philippe Ariès defined modern Western attitudes towards death as being characterized by a deep sense of shame. People cannot reconcile the inevitability of death with progress, and so they have learned to hide it and to see it as something inherently negative, unsanitary and shameful. This conception of death is at the very core of the BBC Two's *King Lear* (2018), which sets William Shakespeare's play in a modern setting. In *King Lear* (2018), the protagonist's madness is almost explicitly coded as some form of dementia. Lear spouts abuse at his daughters, plants inappropriate kisses on others, and his inability to recognize Kent is framed as a symptom of some sort of degenerative disorder.

In this paper, I will contrast Lear's original status as the outdated patriarch, who must contend with the passive role assigned to the old, with the modern Lear's obvious echoes of the Western society's inability to deal with those who are old and dying. As Kellehear argues in *A Social History of Dying* (2007), reaching very old age was always associated with a specific set of problems, but the increasing number of old people in modern Western societies has shaped the responses to the issue. Many now end up institutionalized, isolated and stripped from the opportunity to have a "good death." This, too, has added to the idea of death as something shameful. In light of this, I argue that *King Lear* (2018) contains echoes of the way Western society deals with its dying elderly population, and highlights a distinctively twenty-first-century crisis.

Keywords: *King Lear*, Shakespeare, Shakespeare on film, dementia, death and culture, old age

Resumo

O objetivo deste artigo é discutir a adaptação da BBC Two de *King Lear* (2018) enquanto comentário à incapacidade moderna de lidar com a morte. Embora a pandemia de 2019/2020 nos tenha forçado a confrontar o fenómeno morte numa escala sem precedentes, a conceção atual da morte enquanto fenómeno cultural continua a diferir radicalmente da dos nossos antepassados. Em vez de ser visível e omnipresente, como era no período inicial da idade moderna europeia, temos hoje tendência a pensar nela como um fenómeno privado e invisível. Em *The Hour of Our Death* (1981), Philippe Ariès definiu as atitudes contemporâneas da sociedade ocidental em relação à morte como sendo pautadas por um imenso sentimento de vergonha. Não se consegue reconciliar a inevitabilidade da morte com o progresso, por isso ela é escondida e vista como algo inerentemente negativo, sujo e vergonhoso. Esta visão da morte está no âmago de *King Lear* (2018) da BBC Two, que traz a peça de Shakespeare ao século XXI. Em *King Lear* (2018), a loucura do protagonista é retratada de forma quase explícita como uma forma de demência. Lear é abusivo com as filhas, dá beijos inapropriados aos outros, e a sua incapacidade de reconhecer Kent aparenta ser um sintoma de uma qualquer doença degenerativa.

Neste artigo, compara-se o estatuto original de Lear enquanto patriarca obsoleto que deve resignar-se à passividade e irrelevância com a forma como o Lear moderno reflete a incapacidade da sociedade ocidental de lidar com os velhos e moribundos. Tal como Kellehear argumenta em *A Social History of Dying* (2007), chegar a uma idade avançada sempre trouxe problemas, mas o número cada vez maior de pessoas idosas nas sociedades ocidentais tem mudado as respostas a estas dificuldades. Muitos terminam agora as suas vidas institucionalizados, isolados e privados da oportunidade de ter uma "boa morte". Também isto tem contribuído para a ideia da morte enquanto algo vergonhoso. Assim, pode argumentar-se que *King Lear* (2018), reflete a forma como a sociedade ocidental lida com a sua população idosa moribunda, destacando uma crise singular do século XXI.

Palavras-chave: *Rei Lear*, Shakespeare, Shakespeare no cinema, demência, morte e cultura, envelhecimento

Introduction

The story of Lear did not start with William Shakespeare. The trials of Leir, a pre-Roman Briton king, are already told in *Historia Regum Brittaniae*, around 1135. The play *The moste famous Chronicle hystorye of Leire kinge of England and His Three Daughters* (Halio 1992, 1), written and first performed in the 1590s, also returns to the story of the king who divides his kingdom between his daughters and is betrayed by them.

Shakespeare's *King Lear*, likely written around 1605, changes the story substantially. In addition to including the Gloucester/Edmund/Edgar subplot, the playwright changes the happy ending and strips away "every possible consolation from the action to present it with the starkest reality" (Halio 1992, 3). For all its older sources, it is easy to see the relevance that the tale of a decrepit, tyrannical father might have already held for Shakespeare's contemporaries. As Jay L. Halio (1992) states further: "*King Lear* is not only about a monarch and his divided realm but also about a father, his property and his three daughters" (4). It is possible to read it as a family drama, but there was definitely a timely quality to it. Halio adds that there were contemporary analogues: disputes over wills, attempts of daughters to pronounce their fathers mad. Getting to an advanced age might not have been awfully common in Shakespeare's time, but in a mercantile, ever-changing London, whose pace and conventions could already elude the old, the mental and physical tolls of age were bound to be topical themes. The long reign of Elizabeth I gave old age further "publicity" as a theme (Martin 2012, 177). And yet, with the dramatic increase of life expectancy, *King Lear*'s picture of an old, mad patriarch has never been as vivid as it is today. Modern adaptions inevitably allude to the echoes of clinical dementia in its protagonist's behaviour, as well as to our modern struggles in dealing with the decline of old age and death. Such is the case of Richard Eyre's 2018 screen adaptation of the play.

Before proceeding to an inquiry on what a twenty-first-century Lear reveals about the modern conceptions of death and old age, one must discuss the character in the light of the early modern ideas on those same themes.

Even the chronological definition of "old age," determined by cultural and material conditions, has shifted. Yet, while old age certainly had an earlier threshold in the late medieval/early modern period, the generally held idea of a "thirty-five-year lifespan" is highly misleading. Life expectancy was significantly cut by the staggering rates of infant mortality, but those who survived infancy had a decent chance of reaching what one now regards as middle age. Moreover, though in drastically smaller numbers, some did survive into what one now considers "old" age (Martin 2012, 5). Indeed, though some schemes defined people as old after the age of forty, medieval legislative texts define the onset of old age as between the ages of sixty and seventy (Shahar 1998, 43). Being "old" granted one the exemption from military service and various administrative duties, as well as from payment of several taxes. This is not particularly different from the World Health Organization's indication of sixty-five as the chronological age after which one is considered elderly in most developed countries ("Proposed Working Definition" 2012). Now, like before, this number is linked to legal definitions. The biological age after which one is considered "old" coincides with the one after which people are eligible for retirement and benefits.

Though not necessarily reliable, it is Lear himself who claims to be around eighty years old: "fourscore and upward, not an hour more nor less" (Shakespeare 1992, 4.6.58; subsequent references by act, scene, and verse number only are to this edition). He is, by both the early modern and the twenty-first-century standards, old. And while the increasing number of elderly people has created particular stigmas, aging past a certain point never came without them. In her contribution to the book *Old Age from Antiquity to Post-Modernity*, Shulamith Shahar (1998) argues that the notion of a "golden age for the elderly in the past" is a myth (59). There was, in Shakespeare's time, the general idea that the old were to step aside and abandon earthly matters. In religious and didactic texts, the physical decline that came with age was seen both as a punishment caused by man's original sin and an opportunity for its expiation. The deterioration of senses such as sight, hearing or taste made temptation difficult. For the old, self-mutilation and flagellation are no longer needed to castigate the flesh and extinguish the passions. Decrepitude achieves this by itself. As Shahar states further, the expectations for an old person in this context are,

> that he accept his ageing and the plights it entails without complaint, free himself of worldly ambitions, not to behave like the young and especially avoid the sin of the flesh, achieve a sense of resignation, repent and concentrate on his approaching death and the salvation of his soul. There was, however, one more expectation that had a clearer social significance. The old person was expected to withdraw to the margins and make way for the younger ones. (Shahar 1998, 52)

Old age made one redundant. In this context, Christopher Martin offers an unconventional interpretation according to which Lear is not doomed by dementia or decline in themselves, but by his struggle against this very narrative. According to Martin, it is Lear's inability to fully step aside and conform to the role of the redundant, decrepit patriarch that leads to his troubles. Lear struggles because he refuses to withdraw to the margins after splitting the kingdom between his daughters, because he clings to his soldiers and his dignity instead of accepting the passive role his age assigns him. Regan and Goneril retaliate by projecting their gerontophobic ideas onto him nonetheless, characterizing him as a foolish, senile old man. They "script a narrative that best suits their youthful convenience and act together to make it official, for all practical purposes" (Martin 2012, 157). Because he refuses to retire quietly, Lear is forced to suffer and struggle, to play out the sad spectacle of senescence in public. Martin summarizes it by claiming that:

> As embodiments of old age, [the old] must contend with the literal obscenity of their "unsightly" statures before a society that nonetheless fears the inevitable reality they represent and wishes to consolidate its power (while shoring up its self-image) by preserving them as controlled spectacles. The title character's struggle to marshal his own formidable constitution against the public and private roles that the ascending generation would constitute for him in particular emerges as one of the tragedy's most potent dramatic achievements. (Martin 2012, 140)

This is not, as will be discussed later, quite the interpretation that the 2018 film chooses to follow. Hopkins' Lear is, indeed, decaying, going mad from the very start. But it is nonetheless interesting to consider the parallels between the gerontophobic ideas of the past and those of the twenty-first century. Martin (2012) puts it best when he states that "secularisation and the 'ageing of the population' notwithstanding, the images, the attitudes and expectations of old people have changed less than the social realities underlying them" (59). Then, just as now, the old were to be kept as far from sight as possible.

Lear as a "Geriatric Lunatic"

While *King Lear* is already a strong contender for the title of Shakespeare's bleakest play, the BBC Two's 2018 adaptation by Richard Eyre capitalizes on its darkness. Although the movie condenses the original text of the Folio version, which it mainly draws from, in order to run just short of two hours, it does not downplay the disconcerting aura that has always defined the play.

The setting is modern England, but one under a military dictatorship, a world of uniformed men and urban squalor. These are not quite the fascist aesthetics of the 1995 *Richard III*, but a different variation, somewhat reminiscent of the dystopias that have served as a background for many blockbusters in the past decade. There is, however, nothing particularly futuristic about the way this world is presented. Lear is a dictator, war medals shinning in his initially pristine uniform. Gloucester becomes a scheming minister and Albany and Cornwall generals, while Edmund starts out as a rank and file soldier trying to climb the ladder to power. Images of smoking buildings and war-torn cities pass through the screen when Cordelia and France's invasion eventually comes. They do not strike us as particularly distant, but as eerily reminiscent of the war footage broadcast by the mass media. Lear becomes an old man pushing a shopping cart in a derelict area. Edgar ends up sleeping in a tent, in a setting that evokes both a refugee camp and the living arrangements of many rough sleepers. The settings and costumes are nearly colourless, punctuated by shades of red and emerald only in the earlier scenes that depict the luxury in which Goneril and Regan live. The cinematography, too, becomes all the bleaker and more saturated as the plot progresses, leaving only a white light in the very last scene.

Eyre's *King Lear* is a competent film, though perhaps not much more. While starring renowned actors, such as Anthony Hopkins in the titular role, as well as Emily Watson and Emma Thompson as the two sisters, the adaptation was met with moderate critical response. The modernized aesthetics is apparently not enough to make the text resonate with some viewers (Cumming 2018). But the main feature of the critical focus was always bound to be the central performance. If Hamlet is the Shakespearean part to which every young actor aspires, then Lear is the crowning glory at the end of a long career, an intense role that takes up a massive amount of the original text. *The Art Desk*'s reviewer praises Hopkins' Lear as a character that is "irascible, irrational, pugnacious, and not used to having his slightest whim contradicted" (Sweeting 2018). He highlights this combustible portrayal as the adaptation's greatest merit, and points out that it follows the form of portraying Lear's "morbid decline as a progression through the clinical stages of dementia."[1] In *The Guardian*, one of the most enthusiastic reviewers openly acknowledges the implication of dementia present in the adaptation, adding that it is a feature not only of Hopkins' "clinically precise" portrayal, but of most modern depictions of Lear (Lawson 2018). The term "dementia" describes a variety of brain disorders which progressively lead to brain damage and to a gradual deterioration of the individual's functional capacity ("Health at a Glance" 2016). It is the malady with which "we now diagnose the king," the reviewer claims (Lawson 2018).

In 1986, Jonathan Miller had already given an actor intent on playing Lear directions that drew upon his knowledge of "geriatric lunatics" (Hess 1987, 215). This interpretation now seems more common than ever. In fact, before playing Lear at the National Theatre in 2014, the actor Simon Russell Beale underwent a fair amount of research about the topic (Furness 2014). It was not only dementia which helped inform his portrayal of the character, but a specific type of it: Dementia with Lewy Bodies (DLB). According to the Alzheimer's Association, DLB accounts for 10 to 25 percent of the cases of dementia ("Dementia with Lewy Bodies" n.d.). It shares symptoms of both Parkinson's and Alzheimer's, and entails some unique ones. Patients with DLB may exhibit physical symptoms similar to Parkinson's patients, such as a hunched posture, rigid muscles and balance problems. Although memory loss may be less significant than in Alzheimer's, there will be changes in thinking and reasoning, as well as quick variations between alertness and confusion. Hallucinations, both visual and

1 A portrayal that radically differs from Martin's (2012) interpretation of the original text, which argues that Lear is dangerous exactly because he refuses to decline.

auditory, also come with the condition. Patients will experience delusions. They may violently act out dreams.

Hopkins' portrayal may not have been informed by this specific condition, but it is reminiscent of it nonetheless. His Lear exhibits irrational rages and delusions. Already in the "love contest" scene he is brutish and delusional, quick to fly into a rage when Cordelia refuses to flatter him. Hopkins highlights the unstable nature of Lear's emotions by alternating angry, passionate readings of his lines with colder, more mocking ones. His Lear has a malevolent glint in his eye. He exhibits the paranoia that many DLB patients do, turning on his favoured child upon the first contradiction. Yet, his decline only advances from there. While in this first scene he is still a powerful figure, donning a military uniform, Hopkins' Lear is seen next at his eldest daughter's castle, sunk deeply into an oversized coat. It's an image which already suggests his loss of relevance and authority. Furthermore, it signals his loss of identity. Lear is no longer a king, he is no longer a military man, he has lost parts of himself, mirroring the way one does in all sorts of dementia. However, the biggest signs of this loss of his sense of self and propriety come in his confrontation with Goneril. Upon being reprimanded for bringing his noisy, riotous soldiers into her home, Lear is loud, disdainful and rude, even belching to indicate his contempt for her. Yet, it is when uttering the celebrated lines that execrate the fruits of his daughter's womb that Hopkins' Lear becomes physically aggressive, actually grabbing her from behind to touch the cursed spot in her belly. After his confrontation with Goneril, Lear is exhausted, utterly confused. At first, he listens almost silently to the Fool's ramblings, only muttering that he "did her wrong" in an apparent reference to his daughter Cordelia, who is long since gone. "Oh, let me not be mad," he then begs, "sweet heavens, keep me in temper" (*King Lear* 2018, 00:31:36-00:32:45).[2] The heinous scene repeats itself later on, when with "the torrent of vile abuse he heaps on Regan when she's none too enthusiastic about inviting him and his entourage to crash at her place" (Sweeting 2018).

Yet, the truly convincing evidence of Lear's condition comes when Goneril arrives to join forces with her sister. Lear plants a full-mouthed kiss on his horrified daughter's lips in the middle of an argument. A shot shows

2 It is worth mentioning that one could not, in good faith, ignore the signals that attribute part of Lear's behaviour to a dependence on alcohol. Many scenes, such as the one where he first appears in Regan's palace, show Hopkins' Lear taking a sip from a flask.

even Kent and the Fool looking tense and unsure, silent as so many are in the presence of the more humiliating and inappropriate symptoms of dementia. Other features of the text are also read differently in the light of these actions. His failure to recognize Kent as Caius, somewhat mystifying unless one assumes that there is some sort of cognitive decline involved, is portrayed as a symptom. Finally, in his reunion with Cordelia, the line "He wakes" (4.6.39) takes on a non-literal meaning. Lear is not asleep, but rather sitting in a chair with his eyes half open. Awaking in the film is not awaking from a sleep, but rather a momentary bout of clarity and alertness in an otherwise cognitively impaired person. Furthermore, the Lear of this particular scene dons a white hospital robe. Shakespeare's tragic hero is at last a frail, demented, institutionalized old man.

The Fear of Death

In his canonical work on the nature of the cultural conceptions of death in the Western world throughout the last millennium, Philippe Ariès (1981, 718) defines the late twentieth-century approach to death as being one of avoidance and shame. Death, he suggests, has become a modern taboo in the same manner that sex had been one for the Victorians. It is relegated to hospitals, rendered distasteful, stripped of mourning rituals and looked upon with feigned indifference. It is invisible. Indeed, part of this revulsion can be tied to the idea stressed throughout Ariès's book - that it is the most rational of times which seems the most afraid of death. Towards the twentieth century, the author claims, people "began to believe that there was no limit to the power of technology, either in man or in nature" (Ariès 1981, 760). Technology, he argues, erodes the domain of death and creates the illusion that it has been abolished. Alas, it has not, and its reality clashes with the prevalent belief in the power of technology and its capacity to change man and nature.

The late twentieth and the early twenty-first century have seen remarkable technological, scientific and even medical progress. People have witnessed the near eradication of highly infectious diseases, such as polio and measles, in the so-called developed world. In 1980, as Ariès wrote in his book, testing positive for HIV would have amounted to a death sentence. Today, a person with HIV can manage their condition through medication, as if it were a chronic illness, and a few patients across the world have even been cured, in the sense of having tested negative for the virus after having lived with it for a long period of time (Madavilli 2020). Cancer survival rates have also been steadily growing ("Cancer Survival Rates" 2014). And yet, despite all this progress, one is still only delaying the inevitable. Humanity remains unable to tame nature. No one can fully escape from the ravages of death and disease, and the ultimate knowledge that the progress society prides itself on cannot transcend this final obstacle has turned the cultural attitude towards death into one of shame. Death is a harsh truth one is unable to face. It is something to be hidden behind the sanitized walls of the hospital and under false indifference. It is ugly.

In the BBC Two film version, Lear's physical and cognitive decay is a harbinger of death and, therefore, something to contain and conceal. One could evoke Regan's lines: "O sir, you are old / Nature in you stands on the very verge / Of his confine / You should be ruled and led / By some discretion that discerns your state / Better than you yourself" (2.4.139-144). Indeed, Emily Watson's Regan utters these words in such a condescending and saccharine manner that one cannot help being reminded of the barrage of nurses, caretakers and social workers that often surround the elderly in their last days in the twenty-first century.

Unlike in the nineteenth century, in which the Romantic idea of the beautiful death had softened the focus on the ravages of age and disease, there is nowadays a recovery of the horror of physical decay. As Ariès (1981) claims, this actually contains parallels with Shakespeare's times, as "fifteenth and sixteenth centuries had felt a sense of repulsion in the face of the decrepitude of old age, the ravages of disease, the devastating effects of insomnia, decaying teeth, and bad breath" (728). There was also a moral and religious aspect to this fear, as "according to Christian doctrine man forfeited immortality and was condemned to the subsequent process of ageing because of Original Sin" (Martin 2012, 44). But Ariès argues that there was a fundamental difference. He claims that the people of those times were actually more horrified by the cadaver's decomposition and the horror of the newly discovered interior of man. Our current fear is different. The "decomposition after death is transferred to the period before death, the agony" (Ariès 1981, 729).

Although Ariès himself does not follow this line of thought, one might draw connections between this modern disgust of physical decay with what Mike Featherstone (1982) calls consumer society's obsession with "body maintenance" (19). If the body is proclaimed plastic, something to be improved or maintained and displayed, then even "natural" signs of aging such as wrinkled and sagging flesh become something of a sign of moral laxitude, something to be combated. One can draw a comparison here. If in the late medieval and early modern period aging was both a punishment from God after Man had committed the original sin and a sign of the judgment to come, it is now proof that one has "let themselves go," that they have not invested sufficient effort into preserving their body. Either way, senescence is implicitly associated with immorality. But not even the wealthiest and most dedicated can completely stave off the ravages of age. Indeed, in this context, "it is hardly surprising that ageing and death are viewed so negatively – they are unwelcome reminders of the inevitable decay and defeat that are in store, even for the most vigilant of Individuals" (Featherstone 1982, 20). Thus, the 2018 film emphasizes every year of Hopkins' age, sinking him into the aforementioned oversized coats and often focusing on his wrinkled face. His eldest daughters, however, are impeccably well-groomed women, no longer young, but still clear practitioners of body maintenance. The sight of the decrepit, diminished Lear clearly fills them with contempt.

If people live longer than ever, why does showing signs of it horrify them so much? There are, of course, many complex reasons, but one can easily point out that the great increase of life expectancy in the developed world, brought on by technological and medical advancement, has also brought its own problems. Oftentimes, the people who do manage to grow very old are severely limited in both mind and body. As Allan Kellehear (2007, 204) states, dying in old age has always been accompanied by a specific set of difficulties for those who have been able to achieve that longevity, but the additional issue here is that there is a huge and increasing number of people in this situation. While he acknowledges that well-managed deaths for old people continue to exist in hospitals, homes and hospices around the world, what Allan Kellehear (2007) calls "long dying" from old age with an assortment of diseases and general physical and mental decay, often produces "journeys of dying that are extremely difficult, testing and stigmatizing" (207). As the author explains:

> Deaths in nursing homes or living and dying with dementia, whatever its ultimate causes, are not styles of dying that are readily made "good" by a dying person who is confused or has a seriously imperfect memory. Nor is such dying amenable to being well managed by carers who either burn out at home with depression and stress (Black and Almeida 2004) or who simply institutionalize

their elderly, leave them unattended or provide them with minimal care. (Kellehear 2007, 204)

Dementia is, as one can readily tell, an inescapable part of the problem. In Europe alone, there were an estimated 9.6 million people living with dementia in 2015 ("Health at a Glance" 2016) and its prevalence is bound to increase in the countries in which life expectancy is rising the highest. The condition is now a part of our modern conception of a dirty and shameful death. For these people, who have lived too long or survived imperfectly according to the criteria of others, dying becomes a "terrifying this-world journey" (Kellehear 2007, 212). This is, one would argue, the very journey that Lear goes through in the 2018 film.

Regan and Goneril: The Burden of the Father

It has been previously established in this article that dementia and, with it, the modern problems of prolonged dying are already alluded to in the 2018 film adaptation of *King Lear*. But one might also draw a connection between Regan and Goneril's inability to handle their father and the modern society's inability to handle what it sees as a dirty, shameful death and, consequently, those who are suffering through it.

In order to make this point, one has to establish that Regan and Goneril are portrayed far more sympathetically in the movie than they are in most adaptions. In fact, *The Independent*'s reviewer emphasizes that what is "most fresh but coherent is Eyre's interpretation of the three sisters as women absolutely at the end of their tether. Regan and Goneril are not mere evil harpies, nor is Cordelia a sweet saint" (Williams 2018). Indeed, the "love contest" of the first scene (1.1.29-276) is marked by rolling eyes and conspiring glances between the characters behind Lear's back. Cordelia herself seems quite done with the entire affair. Her refusal to abide by her father's demand of a declaration of love strikes one as more than a pure and honest act of honour. It is an act of rebellion. Cordelia refuses to put up with Lear's delusional tyranny, as well as with the hypocrisy of her sisters. But Goneril and Regan are given their complexity too. The evil sisters have to endure much from their father. And in what the aforementioned reviewer calls a "dubiously underdeveloped" moment, Lear even forces a kiss upon Goneril (Williams 2018). One must also note that when Lear wishes the gods to "convey sterility" upon his daughter's womb

(1.4.233) it is portrayed with such horror from Emma Thompson's Goneril that one has to wonder whether he is not, intentionally or not, alluding to some past event. Even elsewhere, it is made clear that the concerns of the sisters are not wholly without merit. Lear's "so disordered, so deboshed and bold" knights (1.4.197) are, indeed, jeering and disrespecting Goneril as she voices her concerns to her father. Unlike in Martin's interpretation, the sisters do not need to impose gerontophobic narratives onto their father. He gives them plenty of reasons to question his sanity, while no doubt testing theirs.

No, the sisters are no heroes, no redeemed martyrs in some sort of feminist rewriting meant to strip the text of its possible misogynistic interpretations. They remain scheming adulteresses who kill each other over a man and plot to strip their father of his rights and property. They are *viragos*, the manly and domineering women (Cox 1998, 144), arguably misogynistic caricatures. But they are extended a lot more sympathy than in many traditional portrayals. Goneril and Regan, for all their cruelty and unnaturalness, are dealing with a very modern problem. They are handling the burden of a demented, dying father. For dementia is, indeed, a form of death, a progressive mental annihilation of the individual that precedes their physical disappearance. Furthermore, the majority of the cases develop at age in which biological death is already necessarily close, and they seem to take the form of a terminal condition that slowly strips the individual of mental and physical autonomy until their final breath. At one point, the afflicted require support for even the most basic of functions, and depend on the kindness of others to endure comfortably until their heart and brain cease to function.

Yet, whereas the burden of caring for the dying was once shared by a whole little society of neighbours and friends,[3] it steadily contracted until it was limited to the closest relatives. But in the twentieth century, the pace of modern life hardly allows one to look after a terminal patient at home and

3 One must once again stress that there was never a golden age to be old, but it is true that the responsibility of caring for the old in early modern England was less focused on the family and further shared by the entire community. Indeed, "approximately one in three of elderly females lived either alone or with persons to whom they were not related" (Smith 1998, 65). For example, in Northern and Central Europe, if a peasant farmer had no living children in the area to whom he could leave his land in exchange for care, an "agreement was drawn with a relative or with non-kin" (57).

keep a job or an occupation at the same time. Death is confined to the hospital and to the decisions of bureaucrats. As Ariès claims:

> Death no longer belongs to the dying man, who is first irresponsible, later unconscious, nor to the family, who are convinced of their inadequacy. Death is regulated and organized by bureaucrats whose competence and humanity cannot prevent them from treating death as their "thing," a thing that must bother them as little as possible in the general interest. (Ariès 1981, 751)

In this context, the dying man is entirely lacking in agency. Though Ariès claims that the domination of the dying by the family began in the eighteenth century, with the will falling out of fashion as a legal document and the last wishes being relayed directly to the heirs, what one sees in the film is a step beyond that. Regan and Goneril, too, behave like bureaucrats in the face of their father's illness and decay. They want his death to be quick and clean, to be as little of a bother to them as possible. When Lear steps out into the storm in the scene that draws upon the text of act 2, scene 4, they seem eager to let him go and almost hopeful about the possibility of him causing harm to himself. Elsewhere, their attitude towards Lear is reminiscent of Kellehear's (2007) claim that "old people are frequently treated not as dying people, nor even more simply as adults, but as children" (211). "What need you five and twenty? ten? or five? / To follow in a house where twice so many / Have a command to tend you?" (2.4.254-256), Goneril asks her father in a scolding and condescending manner, laced with desperation.

But Lear does not cooperate. And it is at this point that one must recover Ariès's suggestion that our twenty-first-century notion of a "good death" is a sudden, peaceful one, a death in which one is docile and unaware that they are dying. Whereas Lear's original "crime," according to Martin, was to refuse the gerontophobic narratives imposed upon him, to want to cling to his authority and dignity in a world that would deny it to him, his transgression here is similar in some ways, but crucially different in others. Hopkins' Lear is, indeed, a degenerating old man, and he displays his decay in a way that shocks and frightens the other characters. He rages, he lives past his prime and confronts his daughters with his illness and madness.

Furthermore, dementia, and the aforementioned DLB in particular, cannot be reconciled with what one now understands or, indeed, with what anyone has ever understood, as a good death. For despite the general confusion that it brings, the patient is often restless, aggressive, even raging in a long process of dying, a dying of the self that they know will precede the death of the physical body. Indeed, "whatever other cognitive problems people living with dementia might experience, understanding that they are dying does not seem to be one of them" (Kellehear 2007, 208). The demented old man is neither docile enough for a seamless hospital death nor conscious enough to live out the deathbed scenes idealized in the nineteenth century. Lear's is "the bad death, the ugly death without elegance or delicacy, the disturbing death" (Ariès 1981, 750). In this light, the frustration and revulsion that his daughters feel towards Lear becomes the same that the modern society feels towards those who confront it with the obscene image of the enemies it has been unable to defeat: senescence and, ultimately, death.

Conclusion

Some might argue that reducing Lear's madness in the original text to a medical condition "stultifies the whole tragedy and cannot represent the author's intention" (Bennett 1962, 141). Others, like Martin, identify its cause as being the precise inability to accept the idea of redundancy, as well as the external perception of physical and cognitive decline, projected onto him. Indeed, one must concede that diagnosing Shakespeare's characters according to our modern medical criteria risks verging into anachronism. Yet, when placed in a modern setting, no adaptation can escape the echoes of the protagonist's dementia and the current cultural conception of the unsanitary and undignified death.

It would also be fair to point out that using a book written in the late twentieth century as a framework through which to discuss the cultural conceptions of death in the new millennium may not be entirely correct. One can only speculate on the kind of impact the Covid-19 global pandemic, coupled with the images of people dying under ventilators, which are constantly broadcast to people in lockdown, will have on our perception of death in the nearest future. But one might also argue that even the dismissive way in which some seem to react to the "unavoidable" deaths of the most fragile citizens, including the elderly, does reflect the invisible cultural conception of death that Ariès expanded upon. It is something too distasteful to be confronted, an ugly thing to be hidden and begrudgingly accepted. In fact, is there a better example of what Ariès calls our false indifference when dealing with technology and progress's inability to defeat death than the Brazilian president, Jair Bolsonaro's, reaction upon being told that the number of casualties in Brazil had surpassed five thousand? "So what," indeed (Phillips 2020).

One can, therefore, still argue that *King Lear* (2018) holds up a mirror to our modern inability to deal with the old and mad, echoing the dread of the sort of humiliating death and decline experienced by the titular character. In this light, the last sentence of the Folio version carries a new meaning. When Edgar states that "The oldest hath borne most; we that are young / Shall never see so much, nor live so long" (5.3.299-300) he is not speaking "as though the length of human life had been shortened as a result of the play's action" (Frye 2008, 299). He is echoing modern preoccupations with living too long, with dying aggressively and aware, after having outlived every reason to survive. Poor Lear, "he but usurped his life" (5.3.291). Indeed, the "theme that repeatedly emerges from doing the numbers game in ageing and dying is that timing is everything" (Kellehear 2007, 233). The threat of outliving one's health, sanity or purpose now looms closer than ever and no medical condition symbolizes it better than that of dementia. DLB seems particularly suited to the case, as "there is evidence to support the presence of all three [of its core features] in King Lear's case" (Matthews 2010, 223).

King Lear was once evoked as the play of the mid-twentieth century for the way its apocalypse echoed the horror of World War II and the anxieties of possible nuclear annihilation (Neill 2006, 1). Yet, it is doubtful that it has become any less relevant to the twenty-first century. The threat of annihilation is alive and well, after all, with the looming climate catastrophe adding to the forgotten, but still present threat of nuclear arms. Moreover, it gains an additional sting in the light of the current Western cultural attitude towards dying. The 2018 *King Lear* brings out the text's relevance to a society struggling with an increasing number of old people and with an inability to preserve their dignity in the face of what it sees as a dirty and shameful death.

References

Ariès, P. 1981. *The Hour of Our Death.* New York: Vintage Books.

Bennett, J.W. 1962. "The Storm Within: The Madness of Lear." *Shakespeare Quarterly* 13(2). 137-155.

"Cancer Survival Rates 'Continue to Improve.'" 2014. *BBC News.* https://www.bbc.com/news/health-29832237. Accessed 14 June 2020.

Cox, C.S. 1998. "'An Excellent Thing in Woman': Virgo and Viragos in *King Lear.*" *Modern Philology* 96(2). 143-157.

Cumming, E. 2018. "*King Lear* on BBC Two, Review: Anthony Hopkins Led a Seriously Starry Cast but the Modern-day Setting Let Them Down." https://www.telegraph.co.uk/tv/2018/05/28/king-lear-bbc-two-review-anthony-hopkins-led-seriously-starry/. Accessed 20 July 2018.

"Dementia with Lewy Bodies." n.d. Alzheimer's Association. https://www.alz.org/alzheimers-dementia/what-is-dementia/types-of-dementia/dementia-with-lewy-bodies. Accessed 20 July 2018.

Featherstone, M. 1982. "The Body in Consumer Culture." *Theory, Culture & Society* 1(2). 18-33.

Frye, N. 2008. "King Lear." In: H. Bloom (ed.), *Bloom's Shakespeare Through the Ages.* New York, NY: Infobase Publishing, 288-304.

Furness, H. 2014. "Could King Lear Have Suffered Lewy Body Dementia?" https://www.telegraph.co.uk/culture/theatre/williamshakespeare/10622547/Could-King-Lear-have-suffered-Lewy-bodydementia.html. Accessed 23 July 2018.

Halio, J.L. 1992. "Introduction." In: W. Shakespeare, *The Tragedy of King Lear.* Edited by J.L. Halio. Cambridge, UK: Cambridge University Press, 1-81.

"Health at a Glance: Europe 2016. State of Health in the EU Cycle." 2016. OECD. https://doi.org/10.1787/health_glance_eur-2016-20-en. Accessed 13 June 2020.

Hess, N. 1987. "King Lear and Some Anxieties of Old Age." *British Journal of Medical Psychology* 60. 209-215.

Kellehear, A. 2007. *A Social History of Dying.* New York, NY: Cambridge University Press.

King Lear. 2018. Dir. R. Eyre. BBC Two.

Lawson, M. 2018. "*King Lear* – Can the BBC's Starry Adaptation Avoid Bard Mistakes?" https://www.theguardian.com/tv-and-radio/2018/may/28/king-lear-bbc-anthony-hopkins. Accessed 25 July 2018.

Madavilli, A. 2020. "The 'London Patient' Cured of HIV Reveals His Identity." https://www.nytimes.com/2020/03/09/health/hiv-aids-london-patientcastillejo.html. Accessed 14 June 2020.

Martin, C. 2012. *Constituting Old Age in Early Modern English Literature, from Queen Elizabeth to King Lear.* Boston, MA: University of Massachusetts Press.

Matthews, B.R. 2010. "Portrayal of Neurological Illness and Physicians in the Works of Shakespeare." In: J. Bogousslavsky et al. (eds.), *Neurological Disorders in Famous Artists – Part 3*. Frontiers of Neurology and Neuroscience 27. Basel: Karger, 216-226.

Neill, M. 2006. "Introduction." In: M. Neill (ed.), *Othello, the Moor of Venice*. New York, NY: Oxford University Press, 1-179.

Phillips, T. 2020. "'So What?': Bolsonaro Shrugs Off Brazil's Rising Coronavirus Death Toll." https://www.theguardian.com/world/2020/apr/29/so-what-bolsonaro-shrugs-off-brazil-rising-coronavirus-death-toll. Accessed 14 June 2020.

"Proposed Working Definition of an Older Person in Africa for the MDS Project." 2012. WHO. https://www.who.int/healthinfo/survey/ageingdefnolder/en/. Accessed 14 June 2020.

Shahar, S. 1998. "Old Age in the High and Late Middle Ages: Image, Expectation and Status." In: P. Johnson and P. Thane (eds.), *Old Age from Antiquity to Post-Modernity*. London: Routledge, 43-63.

Shakespeare, W. 1992. *The Tragedy of King Lear*. Edited by J.L. Halio. Cambridge, UK: Cambridge University Press.

Smith, R.M. 1998. "Ageing and Well-being in Early Modern England: Pension Trends and Gender Preferences under the English Old Poor Law c. 1650-1800." In: P. Johnson and P. Thane (eds.), *Old Age from Antiquity to Post-Modernity*. London: Routledge, 64-95.

Sweeting, A. 2018. "*King Lear*, BBC Two Review – Modernised TV Adaptation is a Mixed Blessing." https://theartsdesk.com/tv/king-lear-bbc-two-review-modernised-tv-adaptation-mixed-blessing. Accessed 25 July 2018.

Williams, H. 2018. "*King Lear* Review: Anthony Hopkins Stars in a Murky Adaptation." https://www.independent.co.uk/arts-entertainment/tv/reviews/king-lear-reviewbbc-amazon-anthony-hopkins-andrew-scott-emma-thompson-shakespearea8373481.html. Accessed 25 July 2018.

TÂNIA CERQUEIRA

University of Porto

"O R, R! Wherefore art thou Zombie?" Death, Posthumanism and the Self in *Warm Bodies* (2013)

Abstract

Throughout the times, the perception of death has been changing. If once the eternal rest was accepted, even if feared, now, in societies where rituals, beliefs, and institutions that previously offered comfort have been questioned, and some even became obsolete to many, death has become a source of anxiety. In the post-modern Western society, death is a taboo, as Philippe Ariès famously claimed in the 1980s. Neither individuals nor society is willing to recognize the existence of death. Due to the desire to live eternally, humankind has turned to science and technology. Immortality, however, may be more appalling than death. Inside the Pandora's box, where immortality remains locked, there may be an apocalyptic world haunted by monsters. In this essay, through the analysis of the film *Warm Bodies* (2013), a retelling of William Shakespeare's play *Romeo and Juliet*, in which Romeo is a zombie, I will argue that, in the contemporary society, the zombie is not only a violent projection of human emotions regarding natural death, but it also represents the fear of what humankind could turn into if immortality were to be discovered. The film can be interpreted as a cautionary tale about the potential that human emotions have to lead people down a dark and dangerous path, as in *Romeo and Juliet*. Death will be analysed in light of Philippe Ariès's concepts discussed in *The Hour of Our Death* (1980). The monster and the cultural significance of the zombie will be explored through the essay "Monster Culture (Seven Thesis)" (1996), written by Jeffrey Jerome Cohen. Furthermore, the analysis of the zombie will take into consideration some key concepts, such as *Doppelgänger* and posthuman.

Keywords: monster studies, zombie, death, identity, posthumanism

Resumo

Ao longo dos tempos, a perceção que se tem da morte tem vindo a alterar-se. Se no passado o descanso eterno era aceite, apesar de receado, hoje, as sociedades em que as crenças e as instituições que anteriormente ofereciam conforto se tornaram obsoletas, a morte tornou-se motivo de ansiedade. Na sociedade pós-moderna ocidental, a morte é um tabu, como Philippe Ariès asseverou nos anos oitenta. Nem o indivíduo, nem a sociedade estão dispostos a reconhecer a sua existência. Devido ao desejo de viver eternamente, a Humanidade virou-se para a ciência e para a tecnologia. Contudo, a imortalidade pode ser mais aterradora do que a morte. Dentro da caixa de Pandora onde a imortalidade está fechada pode encontrar-se um mundo apocalíptico assombrado por monstros.

Neste ensaio, através da análise do filme *Warm Bodies* (2013), um reconto da peça de William Shakespeare *Romeo and Juliet*, em que Romeo é um zombie, irei argumentar que na sociedade contemporânea, o zombie não é só uma projeção violenta dos sentimentos do ser humano em relação à morte natural, mas também representa o medo daquilo em que a Humanidade se pode transformar se a imortalidade for descoberta. Este filme pode ser interpretado como um aviso sobre o potencial das emoções humanas para guiar o ser humano por caminhos obscuros e perigosos, tal como em *Romeo and Juliet*. O conceito de "morte" será analisado através das noções apresentadas por Philippe Ariès em *The Hour of Our Death* (1980). O conceito de "monstro" e o significado cultural da figura do zombie serão explorados tendo em conta as considerações de Jeffrey Jerome Cohen em "Monster Culture (Seven Thesis)" (1996). Além do mais, a análise do zombie terá também em consideração alguns conceitos chave, tais como *Doppelgänger* e pós-humano.

Palavras-chave: estudos sobre o monstro, zombie, morte, identidade, pós-humanismo

Ah, dear Juliet,
Why art thou yet so fair? Shall I believe
That unsubstantial death is amorous,
And that the lean abhorred monster keeps
Thee here in dark to be his paramour?

William Shakespeare, *Romeo and Juliet* (5.3)

Introduction

Death is universal and inevitable. Once, this reality was accepted by the Western society, which through rituals, religion and the support of the community was able to embrace the natural death of the body. Back then, death was tamed. However, by the middle of the twentieth century, according to Philippe Ariès, death has become invisible. In other words, death has turned into something that one keeps hidden from prying eyes. The final days are no longer spent with the community, but in a hospital bed, waiting for death to come. In the Western world, death "has become something ugly, and then it became medicalized" (Ariès 2013, 612). Death is no longer tamed. With the creation of a barrier between the community and the dying, death became something to be feared and the terror that surrounds the annihilation of the body has increased. If once the eternal rest was accepted, now, in a society where beliefs and institutions that previously offered comfort have been questioned, and some even have become obsolete to many, death has become a source of anxiety. A death-denying Western culture has emerged and neither individuals nor the society is willing to recognize its existence. In fact, nowadays people will do whatever they can to avoid the destruction of the body and to prolong their own lives and lives of their loved ones.

Due to the desire to live eternally, humankind has turned to science and technology in hopes of finding ways to extend life. This turn towards scientific and technological advances to transform and transcend the human body is intertwined with the philosophical perspective of posthumanism. Immortality, however, may be more appalling than death. After all, the Pandora's box, in which immortality remains locked, may contain an apocalyptic world inhabited by ruthless and deadly creatures. The postmodern society's fear of death is projected in the culture it produces, from painting and fiction to films. *Warm Bodies* (2013), directed by Jonathan Levine, an adaptation of the book under the same title by Isaac Marion, can be interpreted as a cultural representation of the dread of the annihilation of the self and of a posthumous non-existence. *Warm Bodies* portrays a world where death no longer means the extinction of the body. However, in this immortality, neither the body nor the mind are preserved. The dead, which are denominated "Corpses" by the humans, rise from their graves without cognitive functioning (the Corpses cannot learn, remember, reason, and so on) and roam in the realm of the living searching for nourishment, that is, searching for human flesh. The social structures have fallen and the world has been taken over by zombies.

Through the exploration of death, following Ariès's perspective, I will argue that in the contemporary Western society, as depicted in *Warm Bodies*, the zombie becomes a violent projection of human emotions regarding natural death, as well as represents the fear of what humanity could turn into if immortality were to be discovered. Due to the strong presence of the zombie in this film (after all R, the protagonist of *Warm Bodies*, is a zombie), I will, too, explore the zombie tradition, how this undead creature is interpreted as a monster and a cultural artefact and why it can be interpreted as a posthuman body. I will begin by mentioning some theoretical considerations, to which I will return in the article's conclusion that relates the perspectives discussed to how the zombie works in *Warm Bodies*, as well as how R connects to death and posthumanism. I am going to justify the statement that by using the zombie, *Warm Bodies* evokes the same premise about emotions and their destructive power as Shakespeare's *Romeo and Juliet*, the play that inspired both Marion's book and the film. My analysis leads to the conclusion that reading the past can reveal numerous insights about the present and help us understand the times we live in.

"Why can't I connect with people?": R

Warm Bodies, a contemporary-slash-apocalyptic film, begins by introducing the viewer to its hero, R, who is sauntering in an airport terminal infested by other undead creatures. The narrative is told from his perspective, that is, the story is told from the perspective of a zombie with hoarding tendencies, who has a tedious afterlife and wishes to connect with other beings. As for the zombie, this being is "a singular and important figure in American historical and cultural studies, as it is the only canonical movie monster to originate in the New World" (Bishop 2010, 31). The hosts of popular Western monsters have roots in the Old World: the vampire is strongly connected to the Eastern European legends of vampirism and the werewolf is part of the European folklore, having as its prototype Lycaon of Arcadia, who was transformed by Zeus into a wolf as a form of punishment. The zombie, an undead creature, emerged as part of Haitian folklore narratives, having its roots in colonialism.

According to the folk tales, "priests or shamans called 'bokors' possessed the power to resuscitate the dead so that, deprived of free will, they could work night and day for their master without food, drink, or rest" (Knickerbocker 2015, 62). Since its first appearance in folk tales, the zombie has evolved to something more dangerous. Today the discourse regarding

> zombie mythology is colored by George Romero's fusion of the zombie with the ghoul in his monumental film *Night of the Living Dead* in 1968. Nearly every film made after Romero's first sequel to *Night, Dawn of the Dead* (1978), can be linked back to Romero's characterization of the zombie. (Boon 2011, 5)

Since *Night of the Living Dead*, the zombie has turned into an undead creature, a being that is technically dead but still animated. Nowadays, the most commonly used zombie is the "zombie ghoul," a being that is a "fusion of the zombie and the ghoul [and] has lost volition and feeds on flesh" (Boon 2011, 8). The zombie has hence become a predatory creature without cognitive functioning that has a strong craving for human meat. These are the creatures that "leak disgusting fluids, parts of their bodies are often missing [...] [and that] don't even seem to know what's going on around them, beyond the fact that they're hungry / pissed off / both" (Greene and Mohammad 2010, 13).

Otherwise some of the most common monstrous creatures, the zombies have become one of the most unique members of "the monster pantheon" because, although "creatures such as ghosts, werewolves, vampires, and reanimated corpses were also born in the depths of folk tradition, the zombie is the only supernatural foe to have almost entirely skipped an initial literary manifestation" (Bishop 2010, 12-13). Unlike other monsters, the zombie is more often associated with the cinema than with Gothic literature. This being has been part of the motion picture industry since the early Hollywood films, with the release of titles such as *White Zombie* (1932) and *I Walked with a Zombie* (1943), but only with Romero's masterpiece did this creature move to the limelight. Nonetheless, subsequent to its popularization in the sixties, the zombie went through dormant periods, resurging every time the United States of America found themselves troubled by social and political issues. This can be seen, for example, with reference to Romero's filmography, as *Night of the Living Dead* is a condemnation of the violence of the Vietnam War and *Day of the Dead* (1985) manifests fears regarding the Cold War. After the tragic events of 9/11, the zombie returned, becoming once again popular and taking the cinema theatres and television screens by storm. The resurgence of the zombie in the twenty-first century, a period that Kyle William Bishop (2010) refers to as "Zombie Renaissance" (12), is closely related to mass death. Then, as in the past, traumatic events are the reason behind the return of this undead creature to the media, taking it by storm.

Warm Bodies is loosely based on one of the most well-known tragedies of William Shakespeare, *Romeo and Juliet*. In the world depicted in the film, due to an unknown event, hordes of zombies plague the land, ravaging the United States of America. Everywhere are the humans faced with death: walking corpses and decaying bodies hunt them for their flesh. Therefore, in this retelling, Romeo Montague becomes R, a zombie that constantly craves human brains because its consumption makes him feel human, and Juliet Capulet becomes Julie Grigio, a human who is part of a walled-off human enclave. After R rescues Julie from being devoured by other zombies through covering her in zombie blood, he takes her to the abandoned plane he calls home. Soon after, his heart starts beating and R finds himself helping Julie to get back home and saving the human race from extinction. As the frames go by, the two fall in love, as Romeo and Juliet did, and R ends up becoming human once again.

While in the famous play, the House of Capulet and the House of Montague are involved in a prolonged feud, in *Warm Bodies* humans (Julie's family) must fight for their survival in a world in which zombies (R's family) have no willpower to stop their desires of eating human flesh. The reason behind the feud between the House of Capulet and the House of Montague remains secret. The animosity between humans and zombies has its origin in the notion of kill or be killed and affects the whole planet, not just Verona. In this clash, R ends up eating Julie's boyfriend, Perry, killing her suitor, just as Romeo killed Paris. Another similarity the film's post-apocalyptic world shares with the Shakespearean tragedy is the presence of violence, death, and revenge (Julie's father's hatred towards zombies comes from wanting to avenge the death of his wife). Besides, it even features the iconic balcony scene and a final moment in which the destiny of R and

Juliet is put in jeopardy after they jump off a building to save themselves from their pursuers. Needless to say, as a zomedy, *Warm Bodies* does not end tragically and R and Julie have the chance to rebuild the world and live happily ever after. Not only does *Warm Bodies* make use of key scenes and elements of *Romeo and Juliet*, but it also has as its premise one of the play's major themes, love. In the Shakespearean tragedy, love is a cause of death and violence. By observing the play, one can perceive that this powerful emotion "leads to death from the start" (Dillon 2007, 14), culminating in the untimely death of Romeo and Juliet, who commit suicide to preserve their love. This tragic play reveals that love has the power to lead as much to destruction as to happiness. The same occurs in *Warm Bodies*, as I will discuss later on in this essay.

Throughout the times, changes can be perceived in zombie films, but the core of a zombie story stays the same in every representation: they are undead creatures that came back to life after an unknown event and feed on humans. A mindless cannibalistic monster that preys on humans, whose body is in the state of decomposition, and with the ability to destroy the social infrastructures, the zombie is a creature to be dreaded. Unsurprisingly, this undead being is part of the monster tradition. In the last decades, the representation of the zombie in the cinema has repeatedly tended to reveal a different side of this undead being. Some of these representations have added new characteristics or have changed what viewers have always thought to know about the zombie figure by highlighting their certain "humanness" which inspires empathy and compassion in spectators. In *28 Days Later* (2002), the infection takes only seconds to manifest after someone is bitten and the zombie must feed or die of starvation. In *Resident Evil* (2002-2017), loosely based on a video game series, zombies can evolve and they reveal body mutations. In the cinema adaptation of *World War Z* (2013), zombies move fast, exhibit animal behaviours and ignore any human being who is not healthy. *Warm Bodies* also introduces a zombie that breaks with the tradition since not only can the zombification process be reversed through the power of love, but also the Corpses display human behaviours (e.g. they are able to pronounce single words, even if they struggle to do so, and show remorse for eating human flesh). The film shows a humanized version of this cannibalistic creature.

Additionally, though *Warm Bodies* still represents the zombie ghoul created by Romero with human characteristics, it also creates a new kind of zombie: Boneys, skeletal zombies that have lost all of their humanity. Boneys were originally Corpses, but having lost all hope, they have shed their flesh, and now they prey on anything with a heartbeat. As R explains, "We all become them someday. At some point we just give up, I guess. We lose all hope. After that, there is no turning back" (*Warm Bodies* 2013, 00:02:52-00:02:58). In *Warm Bodies*, the zombie can evolve, or rather retrogress, into something worse.

"Corpses look human. They are not!": A Monster Among Humans

As mentioned previously, the zombie belongs to the monster tradition. To comprehend how this vicious creature can be interpreted as a representation of one of the deepest fears of our society, as *Warm Bodies* demonstrates through the representation of the Corpses and Boneys, it is important to reflect on the concept of "monster." The origin of the word is not clear. However, it derives from two Latin words: *monstra*, which means "to show," and *monstrum*, a derivate of the word *monere*, which signifies "a divine omen indicating misfortune" or "an evil omen." Therefore, etymologically, it can be said that a monster is a being that shows something, that is, a monster is a being that warns about something. When one is confronted with the word "monster," it usually

> conjures up [in the human mind] figures from gothic horror, such as Frankenstein or Dracula, classical images of exotic peoples with no heads or grotesquely exaggerated features, and the kinds of impossible chimerical beasts inhabiting the pages of medieval bestiaries. (Lawrence 2018)

Nevertheless, these are simplistic views of this being. Throughout the years, the meaning of this creature has been discussed in several study fields. For example, Timothy K. Beal (2002) argues that monsters are "threatening figures of anomaly within the well-established and accepted order of things" (4). For Sigmund Freud they are beings that represent the unknown, they are "representations of our id, our repressed impulses that are perceived as threatening by our superego which, due to a symbolic fear of castration, attempts to repress what is not accepted by society" (Forcen 2017, 247). Jeffrey Jerome Cohen (1996) claims in his seminal essay "Monster Culture (Seven Thesis)" that every monster is "a double narrative, two living stories: one that describes how the monster came to be and another, its testimony, detailing what cultural use the monster serves" (13). Hence, it can be stated that a monster is a creature that produces fear and torments the human being, either because of its terrifying appearance or unusual behaviour or because it challenges and forces the human being to confront its greatest fears. Born out of fantasies produced by the human, the monster is a primitive manifestation of the terrors of the subconscious, reflecting the fears and anxieties that haunt the human being. As Cohen (1996) declares, "Monsters are our children" (20).

As part of the human imagination, monsters end up having their origin in the culture that produces them, thus, being possible to be interpreted as a cultural artefact. By observing the monster and its roots, one can comprehend the worries and terrors of a certain historical period and its society. The monster becomes then a culture-bound projection of human anxieties: of the anxieties about the times in which one lives, about their own humanity, about their identity. In this sense, it can be said the monster shapes a collective identity, that is, the identity of a society. Moreover, if the fears of a person are mirrored by a monstrous creature, a fragment of the self is revealed to the outside world, which means that the monster also plays a part in shaping personal identity.

In their multitude of significances, monsters are also produced to warn the human being of the consequences of their actions. In the nineteenth century the modern prototypes of monstrosity emerged: the Creature of Frankenstein in *Frankenstein; or, The Modern Prometheus* (1818) by Mary Shelley, Mr. Hyde in *Strange Case of Dr. Jekyll and Mr. Hyde* (1896) by Robert Louis Stevenson, and Count Dracula in *Dracula* (1897) by Bram Stoker. By observing these Gothic monsters, it is possible to discern the anxieties that disturbed the society at the time of their creation. The Creature of Frankenstein expresses fears regarding the power of science and warns about what it can do to humanity. Count Dracula reveals concerns related to Otherness as well as to immigrant waves and contagious diseases that were difficult to be treated by the medicine of the time, such as the plague. Mr. Hyde exposes the concern that even the most respectable men and women have viciousness and evilness dormant inside of them and can be contaminated by immoral vices and perversity. Furthermore, two of these modern prototypes of monstrosity are manifestations of fears that are connected to death. In *Frankenstein*, Victor, who is horrified by death, obsessively chases its secrets. In his pursuit, Victor is able to bring back to life a creature made of human body parts he stole from the graveyard. The Creature is repudiated by society due to his horrendous appearance.[1] Victor may be able to unveil the secrets of death, but not without consequences. Horrified by what his hands created, he abandons the Creature that, after being despised and rejected by humankind, leaves a path of destruction and death behind him. Count Dracula is a living-dead creature that feeds on human blood and can live hundreds of years, unless someone drives a stake through his heart or decapitates him, or he is exposed to sunlight. Although Dracula can live forever and pass as human, his feeding habits, which end up turning humans into heartless vampires or killing them, and vicious behaviour turn him into a malicious revenant hunted by people.

As a monster and a cultural artefact, the zombie also comes to represent fears and anxieties that beset society. While in the past it represented the terror of slave uprisings and loss of white imperialist sovereignty,[2] nowadays, the zombie, as it can be interpreted through *Warm Bodies*, represents mostly the terror of death, may it be one's own death or the death of their loved ones. In fact, the zombie even "directly manifests the visual horrors of death: unlike most ghosts and vampires, zombies are in an active state of decay" (Bishop 2010, 21). In the post-modern Western societies, death is the unspeakable, a lingering presence that no matter how much the human tries to ignore, it is always there proclaiming their destruction. As Ariès declares, "our attitude toward death is defined by the impossible hypothesis of success" (Ariès 2013, 611). Therefore, the zombie becomes not only a personification of what the human being fears the most, but also a violent projection of human emotions regarding natural death. As a posthuman being, as I will discuss later in this essay, the zombie represents too the fear of what society can become if science and technology discover immortality. All things considered, thus, the zombie is a portent of the frightening future the human being tries to hide from, but cannot avoid. Death befalls upon everyone.

1 The Creature of Frankenstein is described as a being of huge proportions with yellow skin that "scarcely covered the work of muscles and arteries beneath." His hair was "of a lustrous black […] [and the] teeth of pearly whiteness." His watery eyes "seemed the dun-white sockets in which they were set" and he had a "shrivelled complexion and straight black lips" (Shelley 2012, 50).

2 In Haitian folk tales, the zombie is "a popular manifestation of the long-standing conflicts that have arisen from imperialism, oppression, and slavery […] the zombie worked as an allegorical figure, functioning as an oppressive ideological apparatus in Haiti and other colonial nations by instilling both black and white populations with fears regarding enslavement and the loss of individual sovereignty" (Bishop 2010, 32).

For the human to gaze at the zombie is like staring at themselves. It is like looking at their own reflection in a mirror, even if the body standing in front of their eyes is a decaying putrefied one. By staring at this reflection, consequently, the human further recognizes that there is something strangely familiar about the zombie. This strange familiarity provokes a diffuse sensation of anguish and terror in the human, a feeling that is associated with the *unheimlich*. In *Warm Bodies*, we can see it when Julie's father, Colonel Grigio, faces R, who sneaks into the human enclave to tell Julie about the growing humanity of the Corpses. Once Grigio looks at R, he is possessed by this sensation – leading him to want to shoot R – that is, to exterminate a being that feels so familiar and yet so strange.

Sigmund Freud in the essay "Das Unheimlich" (1919) explores in detail the titular concept that is also fundamental for this analysis. Etymologically, *unheimlich* comes from the word *heimlich*, which has several meanings: it might mean *häuslich* (something that is part of the house) or something "which is concealed or kept from sight, and hence sinister" (Tatar 1981, 169). Additionally, it might also be a synonym of "secret," "conceal," or "occult." If *heimlich* is related to something familiar, in other words, to something that is homely and makes one feel safe, then *unheimlich* refers to something that threatens "one's sense of 'at-homeness,' not from the outside but from *within* the house" (Beal 2002, 4-5, emphasis of the author). *Unheimlich* is hence the realization that something that is in a familiar place (may it be the home, the self, or the society) does not belong there. It is "an experience of otherness within sameness" (Beal 2002, 5) that happens when something familiar suddenly becomes unknown. In general terms, Freud describes the *unheimlich* as "that species of frightening that goes back to what was once well-known and had long been familiar" (Freud 2003, 124). It is a feeling of terror that arises from situations that are at the same time strange and familiar. This sensation usually emerges when the human being is confronted with "something that was long familiar to the psyche and was estranged from it only through being repressed" (Freud 2003, 148).

In his discussion, Freud also explores the ways how the *unheimlich* is represented and interpreted in literature. His considerations regarding literature and the *unheimlich* can be applied to cinematic works. Ultimately, as in literature, cinema "affords possibilities for a sense of the uncanny that would not be available in real life" (Freud 2003, 157). Through films, it is possible to diverge from the real and accept the existence of bizarre beings that are responsible for the terror provoked by the *unheimlich*. However, in imaginary worlds, "many things that would be bound to seem uncanny if they happened in real life are not in the realm of fiction" (Freud 2003, 156). For example, in fairy-tales, animism no longer has the power to cause this uncanny feeling because the existence of clocks and toy tin soldiers that speak and move is something common. Nonetheless, the *unheimlich* effect can still happen if the action takes place in a world that viewers identify as their own. *Warm Bodies* is set in a post-apocalyptic United States of America that eight years after a zombie outbreak still resembles the contemporary society the viewer lives in, which allows this diffuse sensation of dread to happen. Moreover, while talking and moving toy tin soldiers are regarded as an impossibility, a creature like the zombie is still a very real possibility to today's society due to its posthuman origins. At its peak, the *unheimlich* terror "is represented by anything to do with death, dead bodies, revenants, spirits and ghosts" (Freud 2003, 148). Figures such as ghosts, spirits and zombies are liminal beings, neither alive nor dead, and are found outside the systems of meaning (these beings are between life and death and because of such conditions one does not know how to categorize them). Liminal figures represent the chaos among order and their presence has the power to destroy values that rule society, as well as notions about the self, revealing the insecurities individuals have about themselves and the world that surrounds them.

Being on the threshold of the supernatural world, that is, amid life and death, creates in the human being this horror. That is to say, the presence of beings which are between life and death and should not have returned to the world of the living also evokes in the human being a feeling of restlessness. As I have mentioned previously, the relation of the Western society with death is one of uncertainty. After all, the structures that once offered comfort have now become outdated. As Ariès (2013) states, "neither the individual nor the community is strong enough to recognize the existence of death" (614). Everything that reminds the human race that it is not immortal has the power to cause the terror connected to the *unheimlich* since it compels the individual to confront something familiar (death is part of the human's life, may it be the individual's death or the death of those around), but at the same time unknown (what comes after death is uncertain). This relationship of uncertainty with death and dying can be perceived in R, too. As James Calderwood (1987) points out, "The simplest way to deny death is to stay alive, and the simplest way to stay alive is to eat" (17). Although R's inner voice expresses guilt and regret for feeding on humans, in other words, while he feels guilty for what he has to do to deny death, R still eats human flesh and brains to survive and not become an unemotional Boney. He "stand[s] for what endangers one's sense of at-homeness, that is, one's sense of security, stability, integrity, well-being, health and meaning" (Beal 2002, 5). As stated previously, the zombie is a monster and, consequently, it becomes a personification of the *unheimlich*.[3]

As a monster, the zombie also becomes a double of the human being, and as such, its power to provoke this uncanny feeling increases. In his research, Otto Rank explores the various types of doubles.[4] This study discusses the physical double, the double that shares the same body, as the duplicate, and "a likeness which has been detached from the ego and become an individual being" (Rank 1971, 20). The latter arises from the human's desire to become immortal. The double stands, then, as a form of preservation against extinction caused by death. Freud also shares this view, yet, the double is no longer a being that prevents the annihilation of the self. As he declares, "the meaning of the 'double' changes: having once been an assurance of immortality, it becomes the uncanny harbinger of death" (Freud 2003, 142). The double becomes a physical shadow of its creator. Its presence is a threat to the existence of the individual because, typically, this dark being wishes to destroy whoever gave it life. Ultimately, "the impulse to rid oneself of the uncanny opponent in a violent manner belongs [...] to the essential features of the motif" (Rank 1971, 16-17). As a double, the zombie is interpreted as a *Doppelgänger*,[5] a demon shadow of its creator, hunting and feeding off them.[6] Thus, in *Warm*

3 The zombie is also able to stir this unsettling feeling because its presence threatens the self, forcing humankind to confront the annihilation of the self.

4 Two common manifestations of the double are the alter ego and the *Doppelgänger*. The alter ego is viewed as a positive double while the *Doppelgänger* is interpreted as a negative one. The concept of *Doppelgänger*, which matters the most for this discussion, "refers to the twin shadow double, demon double and split personality" (Snodgrass 2005, 83).

5 As a *Doppelgänger*, the zombie becomes a manifestation of evil. Thus, once again, this being shatters notions about death that have been long part of the Western society. Death is no longer the last refuge of evil since once individuals die, they rise from their graves and become evil itself.

6 The zombie consumes the human. It feeds on its flesh, organs, everything meaty. Carolyn Daniel explains that "stories about monsters who threaten to consume, whether they are wolves, witches, sharks, or aliens continue to be mainstream of much grotesque-horror fiction aimed at both children and adults. Monsters such as these act outside cultural and social prohibitions and represent the antithesis of civilized humanity" (qtd. in Abbruscato 2014, 22). In light of the Western societies' values, cannibalism is seen as something monstrous. Cannibalism is something that is not mentioned. Thus, the zombie breaks another Western taboo with its appetite for human flesh and cannibalistic tendencies.

Bodies, R and his undead companions are nothing more than harbingers of death, a representation of death itself. They cannot be controlled and must be stopped by their creator before destroying the whole world. This is not the double nor the immortality humankind is looking for.

"O true apothecary, / Thy drugs are quick": Posthuman Death

As discussed throughout this essay, death has become something unspeakable in the post-modern contemporary Western societies. This happened because:

> Death [is] an emphatic denial of everything that the brave new world of modernity stood for, and above all of its arrogant promise of the indivisible sovereignty of reason. The moment it ceased to be "tame," death has become a guilty secret; literally, a skeleton in the cupboard left in the neat, orderly, functional and pleasing home modernity promised to build. (Bauman 1992, 134-135)

In the past, death was not a taboo among the community. Of course, it was "never experienced as a neutral phenomenon [...] remain[ing] a misfortune" (Ariès 2013, 605). Then, what happened to change the paradigm? How did death become such an embarrassing topic? How did death become a skeleton in the cupboard?

During the Renaissance a new vision emerged about the human: humanism. This new vision "affirmed values of the individual and the right to self-determination" and "enshrined 'Man' as unique, the origin of all meaning, protagonist of History, the hegemonic measure of all things" (Knickerbocker 2015, 67). Man was an individual being with agency, responsible for his own destiny, reigned by reason, and the centre of the universe. Renaissance was also a period marked by

> the discovery and exploration of new continents, the substitution of the Copernican for the Ptolemaic system of astronomy, the decline of the feudal system and the growth of commerce, and the invention or application of such potentially powerful innovations as paper, printing, the mariner's compass, and gunpowder. [...] It was primarily a time of the revival of Classical learning and wisdom after a long period of cultural decline and stagnation. ("Renaissance" 2020)

Hence, humanism, individualism, reason, and the scientific revolution contributed to the rediscovery of the fearfulness of death. As Carol Margaret Davison asserts,

> The advent of secular modernity, the putative triumph of Reason, and the unsettling of religious certainties during the Enlightenment about the existence of God, the soul, and the afterlife, constituted a type of cultural trauma that alienated us from an earlier familiarity with death while giving rise to greater anxieties and uncertainties about mortality, loss, and remembrance. (Davison 2017, 21)

It is no surprise that this fear that has overcome the West became manifested in a ferocious figure such as a zombie with its putrid body and ability to shatter taboos.

Death is the only thing that resists the power of human progress. However, the human being keeps trying to avoid or overcome natural death. There is an urge to prolong life endlessly, "almost as if we [humankind] have taken death as just another disease to be conquered" (Kübler-Ross 2009, 14). Posthumanism may fulfil the human wish of living eternally. This philosophical perspective defends that the human being can be transformed, transcended, or eliminated either by technological advances or evolutionary processes. As Victoria Flanagan (2014) explains, posthumanism "focus[es] on the impact of technology on human subjectivity and social relationships" (15). In *Posthumanism*, Pramod K. Nayar (2014) argues that this cosmovision can be discussed through two frameworks: on one side it refers to "a new *conceptualization* of the human," and on the other

> refers to an *ontological condition* in which many humans now, and increasingly will, live with chemically, surgically, technologically modified bodies and/or in close conjunction (networked) with machines and other organic forms (such as body parts from other life forms through xenotransplantation). (Nayar 2014, 13, emphasis of the author)

In the twenty-first century, to be posthuman signifies

> to be more than human or less than human, depending on one's perspective, but it always means being different from human. Thus posthumans can include cyborgs and artificial intelligences but also ghosts and vampires. However, as most people apply the term, posthuman incorporates some kind of biotechnological

> change in the human such as attaching cybernetic prostheses or transferring a human consciousness into an animal body or machine. (White 2018, 258)

It should be highlighted, then, that its condition as a monster already renders the zombie in *Warm Bodies* as posthuman. After all, monsters are decidedly different from what is considered to be human, even without cybernetic prostheses.

As observed, posthumanism offers countless possibilities. While some of these possibilities are embraced with enthusiasm and hope for a better future, others rouse in the human being an unparalleled terror. This philosophical perspective may open the door to immortality. However, opening this door may be like opening the infamous Pandora's box. A brain eater may rampage through those doors to exterminate humankind, as it might have happened in *Warm Bodies*. Although most books, television shows, and films do not explain the origin of the zombie (there is always fearfulness in the unknown and not knowing what is behind the birth of this creature intensifies the distress in the human being) since Romero's *Night of the Living Dead*, which only speculates on the reason for the zombie outbreak, the zombie has mostly become the result of a biological catastrophe. It may be a nuclear war or the creation of a vaccine to treat a pandemic infectious disease or to prolong the human's life-span. As the result of posthuman scientific and technological advancement,[7] the zombie has another cultural meaning: similar to the Creature of Frankenstein, the zombie represents the fear of science being taken too far. Besides, this creature is also a warning about what human life could turn into if posthuman progress discovered immortality. As depicted in the film under analysis, human beings could end up fighting in order not to be extinct at the hands of their own creation. After all, "from Romero forward, zombies offer the first truly apocalyptic monster, obsessed not only with the destruction of individuals but of human race as a whole" (Knickerbocker 2015, 72). In *Warm Bodies*, R does not know how the zombie apocalypse began. As he explains, "It could have been chemical warfare, or an airborne virus, or a radioactive outbreak monkey" (*WB* 00:01:49-00:01:52).

[7] This vision of posthumanism evokes another branch of this study field: transhumanism. Transhumanism "seeks to perfect the human species via life extension technologies, genetic manipulation, and biotechnological prostheses" (White 2018, 275). This branch focuses on enhancing human attributes and physical characteristics while still placing the human at the centre of the university. As Cary Wolfe (2009) explains, transhumanism is simply "an intensification of humanism" (xv).

Nevertheless, it appears that in this cinematic work the posthumanist advancement has led to the destruction of the society as it is known. The infrastructures that kept the society running are long extinct and the surviving humans built a walled city where they try to keep the last remains of humanity afloat and must scavenge for food, medication and other goods.

Posthumanism does promise a better version of the human, but R's body was not perfected. Instead of becoming a perfect specimen, R became a shell of a human, ruled by cravings and survival instincts, and whose body is rotting. Nevertheless, this rotting body is not easily destroyed and the Boneys have no desire to feed on it. R has the tools to live in a posthuman world, in which the human population is decreasing every day, even if having them meant losing everything that made him once an individual, from his living human body to his cognitive abilities. Even though tools to live in a post-apocalyptic world are offered, the overcoming of death is still represented as something grotesque. The body is decaying and sooner than later all Corpses become Boneys, eating their own skin until they are nothing more than skeletons.

"These violent delights have violent ends": Losing the Self

One of the terrors of death is the prospect of annihilation of one's self and the silencing of one's voice. After all, the human being cherishes the self, one's identity, above everything else – even above the body. The self represents who an individual is, being the result of a set of memories and experiences an individual goes through that construct their subjectivity and individuality. As Margaret MacMillan (2010) points out, "as individuals, we are all, at least in part, products of our own histories, which include our geographical places, our times, our social class, and our family backgrounds" (xi). If one cannot remember their own history nor their past, then they lose everything that made them who they are.

In *Warm Bodies*, R, who still has an inner voice, says to himself: "I wish I could introduce myself. But I don't know my name anymore. I mean, I think it started with an R, but that's all I've left. I can't remember my own name or my parents or my job" (*WB* 00:01:02-00:01:12). He does not even remember how he died and became a Corpse. Although R can still grunt single words, such as "eat," he cannot remember who he was before becoming an undead monster. When a human becomes this apocalyptic creature, something essential to the self is lost. As pointed out by Kevin Boon (2011), "The original self [...] [is] altered in a way that guts its essence. The person is no longer a person in either an existential or metaphysical sense" (7). Something is lost in the violent process of transformation from human to zombie. R does show signs of rationalization, but he rarely can express his thoughts. However, only after meeting Julie and being able to connect with someone, does R begin to articulate his feelings and thoughts (it happens because he is slowly becoming human again). When he became a Corpse, R lost everything that once made him human. Every zombie "experiences a loss of something essential that previous to zombification defined it as human" (Boon 2011, 7). The zombie may lack the soul, the mind, the will, or, in some cases, the personality. By losing what defined it as human, the zombie loses its own self. In other words, this being loses its identity, its subjectivity, and its individuality.

As Dale Knickerbocker (2015) claims, "In opposition to the free will and individualism held so dear by humanists, the zombie lacks autonomy and individual identity, each action exactly as its peers and thus functioning – literally unwittingly – as a collective" (68). There is no individuality in death. When one becomes part of a horde of mindless creatures who are all alike (they walk the same way, they grunt the same way, they crave to eat the same food, and so on), the self is erased. Therefore, the zombie shatters the notion of individualism not only because the memories that made it an individual are lost after the transformation, but also because this undead being is part of a collective that acts exactly the same way. This creature reminds and forces the post-modern Western society to face the fact that individuality may be lost in death, especially in mass death.

Conclusion

The zombie is a *memento mori*. With its decaying flesh, this undead being compels the human to confront one of the biggest taboos and fears of the post-modern contemporary Western society. In order to accept the extinction of the body, the human must face death, instead of keeping it a secret and treating it as something that should never be mentioned. The zombie clearly enables this confrontation and makes the human question if a mindless violent tedious existence is worth overcoming death. But has the zombie truly overcome death? After all, in order to live, these beings must first die. Indeed, the zombie has a second chance to be part of the realm of the living, even if it is an existence where everything that was part of it before is long gone. Even if it is an existence in which humanity lacks. Nonetheless, the zombie does not live endlessly. There is still a way to put an end to this second chance at living. In *Warm Bodies*, as well as other cinematic representations of this creature, once the brain is destroyed, there is no coming back. It still is possible to give these creatures an eternal rest.

As explored in this essay, the zombie brings to the surface the fear of death in a contemporary Western society that, as previously discussed, no longer accepts natural death. As Ariès (2013) argues, "Where death had once been immediate, familiar, and tame, it gradually began to be surreptitious, violent and savage" (608). This new aftermath of death, the zombie, is seen as something violent and savage. What better creature to represent this anxiety? Therefore, *Warm Bodies* makes use of the figure of the zombie, an apocalyptical and posthuman creature, to expose the contemporary anxieties related to the crisis of death. Or perhaps, to expose the anxieties related to the crisis of the quest for immortality. Inspired by Shakespeare's cautionary tragedy about the potential that human emotions have to be all-consuming and lead people astray, *Warm Bodies* and its zombies warn humankind of their potential for destruction, in the hope of preventing society from collapsing into a post-apocalyptic world inhabited by horrors of their own making. This film shows that the conflicted emotions death provokes in the human, especially when one is faced with the loss of a loved one, can cause the dismissal of the known world and turn those we most care about into monsters. The reality of death may be repressed, but it remains utterly ineradicable. Only when the human finally accepts this truth can death be once again tamed, as *Warm Bodies* demonstrates. After asking R if her boyfriend would come back as a Corpse and R shakes his head, Julie says: "It's just in my world people die all the time... so, you know, it's not like I'm... I'm not sad that he's gone. Cause I'm. But I think I've been preparing for it through a really long time" (*WB* 00:36.21-00:36.42). By living in a post-apocalyptic landscape where anyone (Corpse or human) can die at any moment and the aftermath of death is not hidden from sight, Julie has learned how to accept it (although accepting does not mean that losing someone will no longer hurt).

In the end, after watching the connection and love between R and Julie, the other Corpses slowly recover from their undead state, becoming human again. They even end up saving the human enclave, when it is attacked by Boneys. As in *Romeo and Juliet*, the same feeling that has the ability to evoke in the human the power for devastation "is seen to have had value, indeed [the] power to change the world" (Dillon 2007, 51). In the play, the love between Romeo and Juliet reconciled the Houses of the Montague and the Capulet. In the film, the love between R and Julie, which does not lead them to tragedy as is the case of the original star-crossed lovers, saved the enclave, reconciled zombies and humans, and teared down the walls that separated the humans from the rest of the world. Love has the power to destroy, but it also has the power to restore.

Warm Bodies ends up offering the viewer a happy ending. There is hope for humankind to thrive and the Corpses have the opportunity to experience life again. Naturally, those who go through death are never the same. After his time as a Corpse, R, who did not recover his memories from the time before the zombification process and still does not remember his name, will always be posthuman, even after reverting to his human self. R's body went through a process of zombification and then revivification, contesting everything that humanism defends, showing that being human "has never been a fixed state but always dynamic, still changing, always evolving" (Tarr and White 2018, 12). Moreover, R's transformation blurs the boundaries between the human and what is seen as the Other. The posthuman cosmovision "acknowledge[s] that we *are* others" (Nayar 2014, 47, emphasis of the author), questioning and dismantling the binary opposition of self/other defined by humanism. The finale of the film reveals that no one wants to experience a second life as an immortal undead corpse, whose day-to-day is nothing more than roaming through a zombie inhabited airport and hunting humans, without knowing who you are. Accepting that every living creature will have to face its annihilation one day will prevent humankind from losing itself and becoming zombies that ravish the world not in search of sustenance, but in search of immortality.

References

Abbruscato, J. 2014. "Introduction: The State of Modern Fairy Tales." In: J. Abbruscato and T. Jones (eds.), *The Gothic Fairy Tale in Young Adult Literature: Essays on Stories from Grimm to Gaiman*. Jefferson: McFarland, 6-33.

Ariès, P. 2013. *The Hour of Our Death*. New York: Vintage Books.

Bauman, Z. 1992. *Mortality, Immortality and Other Life Strategies.* Stanford: Stanford University Press.

Beal, T.K. 2002. *Religion and Its Monsters.* New York: Routledge.

Bishop, K.W. 2010. *American Zombie Gothic: The Rise and Fall (and Rise) of the Walking Dead in Popular Culture.* Jefferson: McFarland.

Boon, K. 2011. "And the Dead Shall Rise." In: D. Christie and S.J. Lauro (eds.), *Better Off Dead: The Evolution of the Zombie as Post-human.* New York: Fordham University Press, 5-8.

Calderwood, J. 1987. *Shakespeare and the Denial of Death.* Manchester: Manchester University Press.

Cohen, J.J. 1996. "Monster Culture (Seven Thesis)." In: J.J. Cohen (ed.), *Monster Theory: Reading Culture.* Minneapolis: University of Minnesota Press, 3-25.

Davison, C.M. 2017. "Introduction – The Corpse in the Closet: The Gothic, Death, and Modernity." In: C.M. Davison (ed.), *The Gothic and Death.* Manchester: Manchester University Press, 18-44.

Dillon, J. 2007. *The Cambridge Introduction to Shakespeare's Tragedies.* Cambridge: Cambridge University Press.

Flanagan, V. 2014. *Technology and Identity in Young Adult Fiction: The Posthuman Subject.* London: Palgrave Macmillan.

Forcen, F.E. 2017. *Monsters, Demons and Psychopaths: Psychiatry and Horror Film.* Florida: CRC Press.

Freud, S. 2003. *The Uncanny.* Translated by D. McLintock. London: Penguin Books.

Greene, R., and K.S. Mohammad. 2010. "A New Lease of Life for the Undead." In: R. Greene and K.S. Mohammad (eds.), *Zombies, Vampires, and Philosophy: New Life for the Undead.* Illinois: Open Court, 10-14.

Knickerbocker, D. 2015. "Why Zombies Matter: The Undead as Critical Posthumanism." *Bohemica Litteraria* 18(2). 59-82.

Kübler-Ross, E. 2009. *Death: The Final Stage of Growth.* New York: Touchstone.

Lawrence, N. 2018. "What Is a Monster?" https://www.cam.ac.uk/research2/discussion/what-is-a-monster. Accessed 7 May 2020.

MacMillan, M. 2010. *The Uses and Abuses of History.* London: Profile Books.

Nayar, P.K. 2014. *Posthumanism.* Cambridge: Polity.

Rank, O. 1971. *Double: A Psychoanalytic Study.* Translated by H. Tucker Jr. Chapel Hill, NC: The University of North Carolina Press.

"Renaissance." 2020. *Encyclopædia Britannica.* https://www.britannica.com/event/Renaissance/. Accessed 17 May 2020.

Shakespeare, W. 2000. *Romeo and Juliet.* Edited by C. Watts. Ware, Hertfordshire: Wordsworth Editions.

Shelley, M. 2012. *Frankenstein.* London: Penguin.

Snodgrass, M.E. 2005. *Encyclopedia of Gothic Literature.* New York: Facts On Life.

Tarr, A., and D.R. White. 2018. "Introduction." In: A. Tarr and D.R. White (eds.), *Posthumanism in Young Adult Fiction: Finding Humanity in a Posthuman World.* Jackson: University Press of Mississippi, 10-36.

Tatar, M.M. 1981. "The Houses of Fiction: Toward a Definition of the Uncanny." *Comparative Literature* 33. 167-182.

Warm Bodies. 2013. Dir. J. Levine. Mandeville Films.

White, D.R. 2018. "Posthumanism in *The House of the Scorpion* and *The Lord of Opium.*" In: A. Tarr and D.R. White (eds.), *Posthumanism in Young Adult Fiction: Finding Humanity in a Posthuman World.* Jackson: University Press of Mississippi, 253-288.

Wolfe, C. 2009. *What is Posthumanism?* Minneapolis: University of Minnesota Press.

KATARZYNA HÜBNER

Jagiellonian University

"We are such stuff as dreams are made on." The Ethics of Imitation in Shakespeare's *The Tempest*, Bacon's *New Atlantis* and Ridley Scott's *Blade Runner* (1982)

Abstract

René von Schomberg's article "A Vision of Responsible Research and Innovation" becomes a stimulus for my discussion about ethical implications of imitation. His main concerns are how a new invention is introduced to society, whether it is thoughtfully planned or constructed, and how will it be legally supervised. Imitation naturally can become an invention. It is also a frequent topic in literary and visual works. In my analysis I observe that three works of art, which vary in their genre, similarly alert to the aspects of irresponsible science, especially to imitation of nature which deceives the consumers, allows to take control over them or misuses products of imitation. In my opinion, Shakespeare deliberately gives Prospero the magical power to imitate the natural phenomena in order to present that imitation may become either a tool for entertaining the audience or a weapon to regain the control over the others. I focus on particular scenes in *The Tempest*, namely, scene 3 in act 3 about the banquet in the forest and scene 1, act 4 about Juno, Ceres and Iris's performance for the engaged couple. The methodology of close reading allows me to find clues in specific expressions or stage directions which prove my assumption that Prospero with his god-like features is both a director and a mad scientist. The first conducts fairies as his puppets to create a cathartic spectacle for the characters and the real-life audience; the second experiments on the characters with magic to satisfy his selfish needs. Additionally, I notice that Prospero can be also seen as a colonial force which misuses his labour: fairies and Caliban, and has a monopoly on the access to knowledge and information. As I observe, in Francis Bacon's *New Atlantis* imitation is understood dualistically: on the one hand, it is a creation "in the shape of something," on the other, it is a clone. Moreover, imitation is a way of learning the secrets of nature; science in *New Atlantis* is a language to communicate with and understand God's creation. Like Prospero, Bensalem is physically and mentally isolated from other civilisations; they withdraw from any kind of cooperation with other nations, simultaneously observing their progress. Presentism allows me to draw an analogy between them and people in the time of Covid-19 when the process of global alienation and scientific competition are present. Subsequently, I discuss *Blade Runner* which uses Baudrillard's concept of simulacrum in its representation of androids. Here, imitation combines features from Shakespeare and Bacon: androids are created "in the shape of" humans but they are unique works of art with distinct physical and mental traits – new humans. I also recognise the colonial motive from *The Tempest*: androids are treated as slaves despite the fact that they are almost undistinguishable. Sophia the Robot's example helps me to reflect upon ethical problems, which may appear while introducing AI to our society, and reach the conclusion that taking responsibility is fundamental to the modern science and solidity of ethical standards.

Keywords: responsible science, artificial intelligence, imitation in literature, simulacrum, *The Tempest*, *New Atlantis*, *Blade Runner*, ethical dilemma

Streszczenie

Inspiracją dla moich rozważań na temat etycznych konsekwencji imitacji była praca René von Schomberga pod tytułem *Wizja odpowiedzialnych badań i innowacji*. Główne kwestie, jakie porusza, to sposób, w jaki wynalazek zostaje wprowadzony do społeczeństwa; czy jest on dokładnie skonstruowany lub zaplanowany i jak jest nadzorowany przez prawo. Naturalnie imitacja może stać się wynalazkiem. Jest ona także częstym tematem utworów literackich i wizualnych. Analizuję trzy utwory, które różnią się gatunkowo, ale w podobny sposób ostrzegają przed skutkami nieodpowiedzialnej nauki, zwłaszcza przed imitacją natury, która oszukuje swoich konsumentów, pozwala ich kontrolować lub nadużywa produktów imitacji. Moim zdaniem Szekspir celowo obdarza Prospera magicznymi mocami imitowania zjawisk naturalnych po to, by pokazać, że imitacja może stać się zarówno narzędziem rozrywki, jak i sposobem przejęcia kontroli nad odbiorcami. Skupiam się na wybranych epizodach *Burzy*: scenie 3 aktu 3 oraz scenie 1 aktu 4. Metodologia *close reading* pozwala mi na odnalezienie w konkretnych wyrażeniach lub didaskaliach sugestii, które udowadniają, że Prospero z przypisanymi mu boskimi atrybutami jest jednocześnie reżyserem i szalonym naukowcem. Jako reżyser zarządza wróżkami jak marionetkami, by stworzyć katartyczne widowisko dla bohaterów sztuki i jej widowni. Jako szalony naukowiec eksperymentuje na bohaterach, używając magii, by zaspokoić swoje egoistyczne pobudki. Dodatkowo zauważam, że Prospero może być również rozumiany jako kolonialista, który eksploatuje swoją siłę roboczą, wróżki i Kalibana, oraz posiada monopol na dostęp do wiedzy i informacji. Natomiast w *Nowej Atlantydzie* Francisa Bacona imitacja jest rozumiana dwoiście: z jednej strony jest ona stworzeniem „na kształt czegoś", z drugiej strony jest klonem. Co więcej, imitacja jest sposobem poznawania sekretów natury; nauka w *Nowej Atlantydzie* jest językiem komunikacji z Bogiem i próbą zrozumienia jego stworzenia. Podobnie jak Prospero cywilizacja Bensalem jest fizycznie i mentalnie odizolowana od innych cywilizacji; jej mieszkańcy odcinają się od wszelkiej współpracy z innymi narodami, jednocześnie obserwując ich postępy. Prezentyzm pozwala mi na wykazanie podobieństw między nimi a społeczeństwem w czasach koronawirusa, które uwidaczniają proces globalnej alienacji oraz rywalizację. Następnie przechodzę do analizy *Łowcy Androidów* Ridleya Scotta, w którym została wykorzystana idea symulakrum Baudrillarda w kreacji androidów. Tutaj imitacja łączy elementy z Szekspira i Bacona: androidy są tworzone „na kształt (podobieństwo)" ludzi oraz są unikatowymi dziełami sztuki z charakterystycznymi dla siebie cechami fizycznymi i emocjonalnymi – są nowymi ludźmi. Rozpoznaję również motyw kolonializmu z *Burzy*: androidy są traktowane jak niewolnicy, mimo że prawie nie da się ich odróżnić od ludzi. Robot Sophia służy jako przykład w mojej refleksji nad etycznymi problemami, które mogą się pojawić przy wprowadzeniu tak zaawansowanej sztucznej inteligencji do społeczeństwa. Analiza przeprowadzona w artykule prowadzi do wniosku, że odpowiedzialność jest fundamentalną postawą we współczesnej nauce i filarem trwałości standardów etycznych.

Słowa kluczowe: odpowiedzialna nauka, sztuczna inteligencja, imitacja w literaturze, symulakrum, *Burza*, *Nowa Atlantyda*, *Blade Runner*, dylemat etyczny

Introduction: Research Methodology

According to the definition provided by René von Schomberg in his article "A Vision of Responsible Research and Innovation," an innovation is required to answer "the (ethical) acceptability, sustainability and societal desirability of the innovation process and its marketable products (in order to allow a proper embedding of scientific and technological advances in our society)" (von Schomberg 2013, 63). Otherwise, the innovation will violate a natural or legal law, and its implications may disturb the further development of society. Imitation as an innovation is ambiguous in the sense of its ethical legitimacy. Should humans imitate nature? If yes, where will it lead us? Such questions often arise in discussions about genetic modifications, cloning or artificial intelligence. Discovering secrets of nature fascinates not only scientists, but also writers. Imitation appears as one of major aspects in William Shakespeare's *The Tempest*, Francis Bacon's *New Atlantis* and in the contemporary film *Blade Runner* (1982) directed by Ridley Scott.

I will analyse these works as three different visions of imitation using the methodology of close reading and presentism. Close reading has its roots in Practical Criticism developed by I.A. Richards between 1920s and 1930s: it is a study of literature interested in the analysis of the text itself without taking into account the already established theories ("Introduction to Practical Criticism" 2016). This technique allows to "take particular passages out of context" to analyse their individual structure, rhythm, meaning and position in the text. As it is described on the website of University of York, close reading is "not reading between the lines, but reading further and further into the lines and seeing the multiple meanings a turn of phrase, a description, or a word can unlock" ("Close Reading" 2018). In my essay it is reflected by focusing on specific expressions, stage directions, terms and pieces of dialogues from analysed works of art whose individual meanings I will prove to be influential on the general understanding of the complete texts and the subject of imitation.

Whereas presentism is a theory which explores how contemporary readers interpret the literature of the past: it "understands a text through the context in which it is consumed" (Gajowski qtd. in Hansen 2020). It is commonly used in interpreting Shakespeare's plays, nevertheless, it may be employed in analysing other works of the past as well. Such a practice allows me to draw an analogy between the events of the past and the present and to discuss how former narratives and patterns may help to view contemporary phenomena. It is manifested by providing the examples of current affairs such as Sophia the Robot's role in our society or global reaction to the Covid-19 reality.

Imitation in Research Literature: Presentation

In *The Tempest* imitation is presented as an illusion in the performative scenes by Prospero and his fairies, mainly in misleading the crew of the drowned ship with a banquet set in the forest (act 3, scene 3) and introducing the goddesses Juno, Ceres, and Iris in the masque for Miranda and Ferdinand (act 4, scene 1). Here, imitation becomes a theatrical tool: it means directing, acting, and experiencing the play at the same time. Therefore, Prospero can be seen as a director conducting his actors (fairies) to influence the other characters (the protagonists of the play), as well as the audience.

In *New Atlantis* (Bacon 1960) imitation is presented as a device to manipulate human senses by copying the mechanisms of living creatures (making sounds, movements, smells, etc.). It is the first idea of simulacrum presented by Jean Baudrillard in *Simulacra and Simulations*; people are unable to distinguish reality from falsification. Imitation becomes a hyperreal experience of the world. The inventors of such mechanisms can be considered as gods of reconstruction, because, as in watchmaking, they analyse the structure of nature and repeat its patterns without actually creating anything new. In today's terms we could say that they clone nature.

Blade Runner (1982) is a combination of both. A device of imitation becomes the art of simulation. The creators know the secrets of nature, and are able to produce new life. They may be considered to be artists as well; they distinguish their creations by giving them extraordinary and unique features. Androids are more than artificial intelligence: they are hyperreal new Adams and original pieces of art.

These works present different trends in considering the topic throughout the time. The last one particularly expresses the increasing fear of artificial intelligence's presence in today's society. To what extent can we act as gods in our inventions? What consequences will the introduction of AI have for our attitude to nature and in our construction of law? Is, in view of such questions, imitation a responsible science? Finally, what does it mean to be human? In this paper I will consider these questions to provoke a discussion about proper means to be taken in further works on the technological advancement of a modern society.

Prospero's Scientific Profile: The Renaissance View of Magic and Natural Philosophy

Due to the appearance of fantastic elements, such as fairies, goblins or Prospero's grimoire, *The Tempest* may be seen as a fantasy drama about magician's revenge. Prospero possesses all the attributes which are associated with sorcery: a "magic garment" (Shakespeare 2015, 1.2.29; all subsequent references to this edition are by act, scene, and verse only), books of art mercifully smuggled by Gonzalo on Prospero's expulsion from Milan, and fairies under his command, especially Ariel who, as the reader is informed, was released by him from the power of the witch Sycorax. However, in my view, Prospero's magic is more theatrical than scientific. It is needleless to say that, in order to perform the events on the island, Prospero has to be educated. A thorough study of the natural science, observations, and magical practice allow him to use nature for his advantage, which is seen at the very beginning when the crew struggles with an unexpected storm. It also corresponds with the Renaissance view of magician as a scientist of the natural philosophy trying to discover the secrets of nature. As Marie Boas Hall (1994) argues, the scientists of various fields were often undistinguishable from magicians due to their uniforms and they themselves could not tell at which point their field becomes mystic (166-171). The aura of mysticism was also enhanced by the fact that only the adepts could have an insight into the secrets of science (166-171). The procedures taken by Prospero are fastidiously planned, reminding one of a scientist preparing for an experiment. Nevertheless, his trials are non-recurring, extraordinary in the objects of study and the results.

Therefore, Prospero should be seen as a stage director who engages the other characters on the island in his interactive experimental play in which fairies have a leading part. This view is shared by Jakob H. Mortensen, as well as Amir Hossain and Arburim Iseni, although approached from different perspectives. Mortensen (2019) claims that "a magician is an artisan," whose knowledge is an art of "an objective creative force" (2). He assumes that Prospero gains authority due to the other characters' loss of control which results in his god-like ability to "create cosmos out of chaos" (Mortensen 2019, 4). It is visible especially in the third scene of act 3 in which Alonso, Sebastian, Antonio, Gonzalo and others are witnessing a mysterious banquet of an unidentified group of people. The stage directions inform the reader that Prospero is present on the stage. Moreover, his position is highlighted: "enter Prospero on the top invisible" (3.3.22-23). In the Elizabethan theatre the position of actors had a great, often symbolic, significance. The stage in its form created a vertical model of the world where the lower level referred to the underworld inhabited by ghosts and demons, the middle part was the real and present world of the characters, and the higher part (on the balconies) was the position of God or other controlling forces. Here, Prospero's location on the stage suggests that he is equal to God in his authority: he is observing, judging, and supervising the proceedings of his actors as if he was a puppet master. His puppets are not only the fairies, but also members of the crew who are engaged as actors in the performance devised by him. Thanks to the fact that they are tired with the island's exploration, their guard is lowered, which makes them more susceptible to deceit. Prospero's show is divided into three parts: the first is the creation of the atmosphere by "solemn and strange music" (3.3.22) which makes them curious and attentive. The second is a mysterious company of unidentified beings dancing and inviting them to feast at the banquet to gain their trust and provoke their reaction, which reaches its climax in the third part when Ariel enters "like a harpy," destroying the happy vision with "thunder and lightning" (3.3.69-70). Ariel seems to be very much aware of his function on the stage; he "breaks the fourth wall" and addresses the spectators directly with the words: "I have made you mad" (3.3.75), and then informs them of his and other fairies' role: "I and my fellows / Are ministers of Fate" (3.3.78-79), which means that they are trying to fill the men with remorse. Remorse becomes possible only by the experience of catharsis evoked by Ariel's monologue. Gonzalo's expression, indeed, proves that the characters start to think their sinful past over: "All three of them are desperate. Their great guilt, / Like poison given to work a great time after, / Now 'gins to bite the spirits" (3.3.127-129).

In the first scene of act 4 Prospero is no longer above; he stays on the same level as Ferdinand and Miranda during the play, which means that he does not direct them to feel or think in a specific way, but rather entertains them, which is his gift for their engagement: "Bestow upon the eyes of this young couple / Some vanity of mine art. It is my promise, / And they expect it from me" (4.1.43-45). Here Prospero can be seen as a magical entertainer. This scene also presents a professional relationship between the director and his audience: the audience chooses to be entertained by a particular show, and the task of the director is to meet the expectations. Again, the performance is thoughtfully conducted by Prospero: the choice of the goddesses is not coincidental. Iris in the Greek mythology is described as "the messenger of gods" and personifies the rainbow, a symbol of peace and reconciliation ("Iris" 2007), and she in fact introduces the other two goddesses in this scene; Ceres and Juno are both in Roman mythology concerned with marriage: the first blesses the betrothed with fertility of any kind: in plants and in offspring, the second with happiness ("Ceres" n.d.; "Juno" n.d.). The masque is Prospero's way to express his blessing for Miranda and Ferdinand's marriage. Nevertheless, he is still in charge by marking the beginning and the end of the play to the audience and actors as well. He also answers Ferdinand's question about the nature of the spirits, by which he proves that his magic has a directional quality: "Spirits, which by mine art / I have from their confines called to enact / My present fancies" (4.1.134-136).

Fusion of multiple realities: Dangers of Prospero's reckless illusion

Ferdinand's question: "May I be bold / To think these spirits?" (4.1.132-133) reveals that Prospero's theatrical imitation blurs the division between reality and falsification. The characters stimulated by his magical interference often question their sanity. As Hossain and Iseni (2014) argue, the audience in the play and the audience of real-life spectators or readers cannot always succumb to the suspension of disbelief, because Prospero himself is questioning the world's construction (84). To combine this with Mortensen's view, Prospero is in fact the creator of a new cosmic chaos or chaotic cosmos. The fantastic elements add to the "disorientation and uncertainty" of the characters (Hossain and Iseni 2014, 84).

The Tempest employs the metaphor of life as a theatre. This can be concluded from the epilogue in which Prospero asks the real-life audience to release him from the play. It suggests that there are more realities than only the one described in the plot and the one of theatrical performances; there is at least one more which signifies the reality of imprisoned Prospero, the dethroned and banished ruler, forced to perform his art of imitation all over again in order to survive and maintain control of what is left to him.

However, Prospero's conduct may entail many dangerous implications for those who are deceived by him. Ariel's monologue, which interrupts the banquet, reassures Alonso in his belief that his son Ferdinand has died in the storm, which almost results in his mental breakdown. Prospero also allows Sebastian and Antonio to plot against Alonso to usurp the throne of Naples, which endangers the king's life. The magician literally fakes the reality to make characters behave according to his plan, which is known only to himself, and he never answers for his misuse. Prospero irresponsibly uses the characters' ignorance and their weak mental and physical condition due to the catastrophe to obscure their perception of reality. The characters are lost and cannot trust their senses anymore, and thanks to this Prospero may easily trap them in his plotting. He also uses his parental authority over Miranda and torments her via limiting the lovers' encounters as long as it is suitable for him. Therefore, he may appear as a mad scientist who will use his subjects (in this case, both fairies and people) to the maximum to increase the chances of his experiment's success.

Prospero as the personification of colonialism and the intellectual gap

Prospero may be also seen as a colonial force which outsources its labour, especially Ariel and Caliban. The first is obliged to serve because the service is an expression of gratitude towards Prospero for freeing him from the witch Sycorax, the mother of Caliban. Ariel's loyalty is rooted mainly in Prospero's promise to free him forever after he will have managed all the tasks assigned by the magician. The second represents a slave worker being deprived of his right to the island and his personal freedom. Caliban is a native inhabitant of the island which Prospero colonised as soon as he reached it. Initially, Prospero seemed to share his basic knowledge with Caliban, but after having discovered that Caliban was seeking the opportunity to rape his daughter Miranda, he took the monopole over the whole island, closed Caliban in a stone cell and forced him to serve, at the same time using the supplies provided by the native. It may seem a fair punishment, but Prospero in fact admits to his superiority which he has held from the very beginning: "But thy vile race […], had that in't which good / natures / Could not abide to be with" (1.2.430-434).

The conflict between Prospero and Caliban reflects also the intellectual gap between the educated and the uneducated (the primitive, the analphabetic, the narrow-minded). The gap is broadened by the pretentiousness of intelligence: Prospero feels powerful due to censoring information to the laymen. He is the only one skilled to read the magical books and does not intend to allow the others to learn from them. Caliban was taught only the basic skills of communication (language) and handwork. His uncivil behaviour towards Miranda was the result of Prospero's bias and reserve towards teaching anyone. The magician's monopolised education is the reason for his superior attitude towards his creation and towards the tools he uses. The word "tools" is used here deliberately to convey the people and fairies engaged in his performances, because the magician does not take into account their attitudes and abilities to meet the challenges he creates for them. From the scientific perspective, he violates the ethical law by outsourcing people and the island only to satisfy his own egoistic purpose, which is to revenge and to retrieve his dukedom of Milan. As an artist, he creates a controversial, yet highly cathartic piece of art, which stimulates the mind of every character in the play.

Bacon's *New Atlantis*: Angelical Science of Salomon's House

The premise of Salomon's House in *New Atlantis* is to acquire the "knowledge of causes, and secret motions of things; and the enlarging of the bonds of human empire, to the effecting of all things possible" (Bacon 1960, 265). Baconian scientists are natural philosophers or, as Richard Serjeantson (2002) suggests, natural magicians who are concerned with "practical knowledge," which means "to change and to use the natural world" (84). Due to their insightful experiments, they are acquainted with the secrets written in the Book of Nature. It is given with the Bible by God to enable people to seek him or, as Krishan Kumar (1991) puts it, "to lead to man's recovery of his original command over creation" lost in Paradise (29). Science of Salomon's House does not contradict religion; in fact, it confirms God's presence. It is a channel of communication with him and the way to understand the phenomena of his creation. People of Bensalem were particularly motivated to devote their work and discoveries to God after having been gifted the arc containing "books of the Old and New Testament [...], the Apocalypse itself; and some other books of the New Testament, which were not at that time written" (Bacon 1960, 247), including also the letter of Bartholomew, who was obliged by an angel to provide the scriptures to people of the island. This miracle has a great significance in the development of the island's society by the fact that people received "the original gift of tongues" (248). Therefore, in spite of their cultural and linguistic differences, everyone was able to understand the books. As the Governor relates, the island was "saved from infidelity by an ark, through the apostolic and miraculous evangelism of St. Bartholomew" (248). It is the reason why Bensalem's science should be considered "as (more) angelical than magical" (249) contrary to Prospero's vision of science.

Duality of imitation: resembling and deceiving

Imitation is one of the methods to learn the secrets of nature. In *New Atlantis* it is treated as a device, an innovation which may stimulate other inventions. Christopher Kendrick (2003) proposes that imitating is rewritten possessing: as long as Salomon's House has imitations of animals or plants, it is able to imitate other beings or substances (1024-1025). On the other hand, Richard Serjeantson (2002) claims that imitating is only part of Bacon's interest, which is conquering nature itself (86).

In *New Atlantis* there are in fact two different types of imitation. One of them is imitating as creating "in the shape of something" or "on the basis of something," for instance the caves used "for the imitation of natural mines" or "artificial wells and fountains in imitation of the natural sources" (Bacon 1960, 266-267), which may help to acquire new substances or possibilities. The imitation of various sounds helps to create new instruments or ways of passing the sound information (271-272). The perfume-houses and their imitated smells may enhance the production of new confiture flavours (272). Imitating "flights of birds" allows men to fly by a vehicle (272). These examples seem to prove Kendrick's view.

There is also the other type of imitation which means "to deceive" or "to pretend." Salomon's House governs "the houses of deceits of the senses, where we represent all manner of feats of juggling, false apparition, impostures and illusions, and their fallacies" (Bacon 1960, 273). They are controversial in the sense of the obscurity of their purpose. Bacon does not provide an explanation for the existence of such houses. Nevertheless, one may presume that they are for the inhabitants to learn about possible dangers which may appear due to the wrong use of imitation. He warns against it by highlighting the importance of punishing such misconducts ("ignominy and fines") and presenting the work "only pure as it is" (273).

All of those instances require a thorough examination of the thing imitated. The scientists of Salomon's House have to work as watchmakers: in order to imitate faithfully, without a danger of misconduct, they need to analyse a thing's structure and copy it atom by atom. The result of their work should be an ideal copy of the thing; in a modern terminology they in fact invent a clone. It is one of the first literary descriptions of almost a perfect simulacrum (Baudrillard 1988). The users of such clones or inventions should not be able to distinguish the original from the copy. Baconian scientists can be described as gods of reconstruction; they mainly clone an object without introducing original features into it. Only possessing a clone and knowing the structure of nature allows them to manipulate things.

Controversies around Bensalem's legal restrictions concerning outsiders

As it was mentioned, the scientists of Salomon's House are to obey strictly the law of the island. Otherwise, they will be punished for their misconduct. The new inventions cannot violate nature or harm the people of Bensalem, who are their main receivers or consumers. They cannot misuse subjects of the examination for their own purposes; general public is not allowed to use objects against their destiny. All people of Bensalem are expected to work on God's service. Yet, the most striking and controversial law considers the way of sharing their discoveries with other nations – "strangers." The people of Bensalem are required to obey "the laws of secrecy" (Bacon 1960, 245). Those who are travelling across the ocean need to hide their true nationality and specific facts about their place of living, especially the location of Bensalem. Their task is to relate the situation of the countries where they are sent (256). They need to gather information about other countries' discoveries, inventions, arts and science, and purchase materials and goods for inspiration (256). Strangers who happen to appear on the island experience hospitality from the inhabitants, but they are obliged to follow the protocol as well. During their stay they are accommodated in the Strangers' House and the area where they may move or visit alone without official permission is limited.

Such a practice may arouse suspicion about the intentions of the islanders. Similarly to Prospero, they guard the dissemination of their knowledge, but while Prospero is focused mainly on satisfying his needs, the people of Bensalem share knowledge within their society. The ethical question is whether or not it is appropriate for them to spy on other nations and take what is beneficial for them without any attempt of cooperating. They have their justification for their unwillingness, for instance losing ships in some excursions and the flood which almost swept the island into the ocean. Additionally, when the island was regenerating from the catastrophe, other nations resigned from long sea travels and, as a result, navigation lost its importance (Bacon 1960, 253). Thanks to such events, the inhabitants of the island created perfect conditions for a utopian society being undisturbed by other nations' claims, problems, and interference: "free from all pollution or foulness [...] the virgin of the world" (262). Nevertheless, due to their distrust, they are not able to take risks and cooperate with other nations, which could benefit not only the greater good of the entire human civilisation, but also them as a nation. In truth, they avoid being confronted by other ideas and visions, which may be against their assumption of science as a recognition of God, the Almighty Creator.

Reality of Covid-19 pandemic and Bensalem's social alienation and competition

Unfortunately, we are now experiencing global physical and mental distancing since Covid-19 began to spread. Reasonably, countries around the world have decided sooner or later to close their borders and limit the trade transport to prevent the infection as much as it is possible. Yet, such a prolonged alienation endangers the economic situation of less-prosperous states and contributes to prejudices against foreigners seen now as potential virus bearers. One of the most disadvantaged groups of people are the Chinese, because of the fact that they fell victim to a new disease first. People of Asian origin are experiencing racial discrimination. In January 2020, the BBC reported that French Asians were discriminated not only by the non-Asian people in public areas, but also by the French media, which used racist expressions in their news' reports. Due to this incident a new hashtag "*JeNeSuisPasUnVirus*" (I am not a virus) became the way of protesting against racial prejudice against the people who are the most affected by the virus ("Coronavirus: French Asians" 2020).

A similar situation could be observed in Poland with the group of Silesian miners and the Silesians in general during the first wave in spring 2020. The number of infected people has dramatically risen there because, for one thing, works in mining companies have not been suspended early enough. For another, Silesia is one of the most populated regions in Poland. Nevertheless, we learn from the MEP Łukasz Kohut's report for *Gazeta Wyborcza* that unaffected people were publishing hateful tweets about the Silesians and the miners (Bednarek 2020). The worst fact about such "virus" prejudices is that they are often based on long-held prejudices about certain groups, and the fear for the new reality is stimulating them.

In the context of Bacon's work we can somehow link Bensalem's accommodation of strangers to the situation of the most affected by Covid-19 or travellers in general. Although strangers are treated with kindness on the island, their visit is organised in accordance with Bensalem's laws which restrict their space of motion or the durance of their visit. In the pandemic reality many countries have introduced new rules concerning the migration of people. In some of them international travelling has been inhibited or the medical test is required to cross the border. Often travellers are enforced to quarantine in their place of declaration which can be associated with the Strangers' House in Bensalem. The presence of international groups has become concerning since it poses a potential threat to health of both – the migrants and the inhabitants. Yet, such a threat may result in an irrational racist behaviour towards ethnic groups as we have already established.

Hostile behaviours are also provoked by the irresponsible use of mass media: professional journalists are prone to relate the most negative and controversial events concerning the pandemic, because such emotionally-engaging news have the highest viewership, whereas the majority of people has an access to the Internet, which results in spreading fake news or conspiracy theories worldwide. Such a flow of information adds to the global frustration when people are forced to obey the restrictions of "a new reality." Undoubtedly, politicians together with healthcare institutions are trying to find safe solutions for reviving their countries' economy. Yet, as the BBC reports about opening the European boarders for the Americans, such decisions are often "political and economic" ("Coronavirus: EU" 2020). Again, it resembles Bensalem's policy of self-isolation. As we know, the island's economy is thriving since the society decided to withdraw from any kind of cooperation with other nations. In this way, Bensalem remains independent from various political or cultural influences. Nevertheless, it maintains a minimum of contact with the outside world by sending expeditions to examine its achievements; it is actually a one-way communication. In reality, it is impossible to resign from any sort of cooperation since we all live in the global village created by the net of international exchange of goods and services. In the long run, it would affect the economy of the countries which are relying on the international trade the most. Thus, one of the priorities in the Covid-19 crisis is to contain the spread of the disease while maintaining the cooperation with the essential associates.

Therefore, the countries around the world have high hopes of the quick distribution of the vaccine. Yet, another question arises: can we also consider the Covid-19 vaccine distribution as a political and economic issue? On 12 January 2021 WHO states on its official website that the COVAX Facility (The Covid-19 Vaccines Global Access) has been founded to "ensure the procurement and equitable distribution of Covid-19 vaccines" ("Access and Allocation" 2021). WHO ensures that all member states of COVAX Facility will be provided with enough vaccines for the most endangered groups of people, that is, health care employees, the elderly and people with serious conditions ("Access and Allocation" 2021). However, we may already witness some aberrations from these suggestions, like, for example, the controversy around vaccinating people from the cultural or political sector out of their turn. Such practice leads to the division into the privileged and unprivileged. Referring to Bacon, people of Bensalem can be regarded as the privileged, particularly the scientists of Salomon's House, because they have a full access to information and knowledge of which the other nations or strangers are devoid. Similarly, Prospero is definitely on the superior position since he does not teach nor allow anyone to read his books which gives him the advantage over Caliban, the fairies, the crew or even his own daughter Miranda. Provided with the literary context, the question is: can the authorities, that is the world's governments and institutions, be trusted with the fair distribution of the vaccine?

Ridley Scott's Replicants: Simulated Human Beings

In *Blade Runner* (1982) directed by Ridley Scott, imitation comes up on a higher level. In fact, imitation is replaced by simulation defined by Giuliana Bruno (1987) as the production in oneself of the selected features (68). Tyrell Corporation, which manufactures the replicants in the movie, provides the humanoids with original characteristics, such as a physical body and appearance, skills needed in every-day life and their labour in the colonies, or memories; they can also simulate other people's behaviours. This makes them extraordinary, one and only of their kind, which results in people's confusion whether the androids are human or not. Moreover, they cannot even be recognised in normal social situations. Tyrell Company proudly announces that their replicants are "more human than human" (*Blade Runner* 1982, 0:22:00); "hyperreal," using Baudrillard's reference (1988, 166).

Additionally, their human-like anatomy is emphasised several times in the film, especially in the scenes of the eye manufacture and of Zhora's retirement. The first gives an insight into the methods and policy of Tyrell's company. It is understood that the company divides the production into several sectors concerned with different parts of body, which resembles the organisation of the "discipline houses" in *New Atlantis*. It signifies how detailed the creation is and to what extent the producers are acquainted with natural philosophy. The second conveys, for the first time in the film, the fact how vulnerable the androids' bodies are. Similarly to humans, the androids are prone to be injured or die; their injuries bleed and make them suffer. This proves that they experience life in its physical and mental form.

Too human for a simulation: A threatening challenge for humanness

Rachael – the new Nexus-6 model – serves as an illustration of a perfect simulacrum in flesh and mind. Equipped with photographs from her childhood, she is certain of her authenticity as a human being. She almost finishes the Voigt-Kampff Empathy Test with such confirmation. As Nigel Wheale (1991) observes, she also withstands Deckard's objectification by evoking in him a sexual attraction (300). She even puts his humanness into question by pointing out his "instrumental" attitude towards her (300) and suggesting that he himself should be tested in order to confirm his right to be a human being or to testify the Empathy Test's credibility. I agree with Bruno's (1987) view that Rachael's phenomenon lies in the meaning of her simulation: she in fact "realizes" and "experiences" features of her identity without being aware that she is a replicant too (68).

What is interesting, some of the androids seem to be aware of their simulation potential, and even a man can be regarded as a simulation of an android. The scenes in J.F. Sebastian's apartment prove this assumption.

J.F. Sebastian is one of the producers at Tyrell Corporation. Next to the replicants, he also creates minor robots, mechanical dolls, and toys for his own pleasure and in the simulation of other people: "I make friends. They're toys. My friends are toys. I make them" (*BR* 0:40:26). He also suffers from a genetic disease of hastened ageing. Therefore, he has a confined life-span, similarly to the replicants. When they come to his studio, they bond as if he was one of them. In another scene, Pris uses her extravagant appearance and total mechanical control over her body to pretend that she is a doll. She freezes and waits for Deckard to attack him. A simulation of a human simulates an inanimate object. These two instances present how the distinction between men and robots is blurred. In Bensalem such imitation would be forbidden according to the law. On the one hand, in Salomon's House the scientists are only reconstructing the structure or mechanisms of an organism or phenomenon without changing them. On the other hand, such imitations cannot be used against people, tested on them or used in every-day life by the non-scientists. In other words, *Blade Runner*'s androids would be considered as a danger, because they cause chaos in nature and challenge the concept of humanness.

As it was suggested earlier, photographs have a great importance in androids' perception of themselves. It is the evidence to claim their right to exist on the same conditions as humans. The photographs, which originally belonged to Tyrell's workers, give the replicants a sense of their origin; they create an artificial sentimental bond between the replicants and the places where they believe to have been or people considered as their relatives. Their bodies are given a physical meaning of being born, not produced in a laboratory, thanks to the idea of having a mother. Implanting memories was introduced as a way to gain more control over the replicants, but in fact they start to exhibit affection and desires previously denied to them.

Tracing memories becomes one of the replicants' obsessions; the other one is to extend their lives. It is the wish of the rebel group commanded by the charismatic Roy Batty, who comes to Earth to meet Tyrell and asks him to "repair" them. The androids are given a limited life-span of four years. As Bruno (1987) writes, they are "condemned to a present tense," but their life is "an extremely intense experience," because their desperation allows them to see "more things than anybody else would even be able to imagine" (70). They appreciate life in a way human beings could. What is more, they seem to enjoy it more than the people confined to their routine, which adds to their hyperreal nature. In addition, Roy cannot be easily classified, because "he stands on the border between dangerous and playful, beauty and terminability, masculine and transvestite, machine and agency" (Bertek 2014, 8). He is, indeed, a mockery of "distinctions between the authentic and the artificial" (Bukatman qtd. in Bertek 2014, 8) and his originality is highlighted by killing Tyrell: "he becomes an ultimately free subject, a copy without original" (Bertek 2014, 8).

Androids' rebellion: An attack on colonialism, hierarchism, and technology's reliability

The replicants' presence on Earth is not only dangerous to people's monopoly on humanity, but also to class distinctions, as Bertek observes. They are the products to serve the higher classes who can afford living in the colonies: they cannot leave them in the same way as the poor cannot leave Earth (Bertek 2014, 4). Furthermore, the distinction into poor and rich classes results in a technological and intellectual gap between them, similar to the conflict between the educated Prospero and the primitive Caliban and the isolation of Bensalem from other nations. The androids are indeed robot slaves – the American Calibans – devoid of human privileges, who, again, cause chaos in an established world order. Blade runners, such as Deckard, are responsible for suppressing any act of rebellion by tracing the replicants and "retiring" them. In other words, "retiring" means "killing," but, because of the replicants' status as machines, they are denied the right for a legal process or a humanitarian punishment. Rachael's words "Have you ever retired a man by mistake?" (*BR* 0:17:50) echo loudly when we remember that men and replicants are almost undistinguishable. The Voigt-Kampff Empathy Test is to avoid mistaking a man with a robot by examining the physical response of eye pupils to the questions, but, as Bertek (2014) notices, this test is conducted by another machine which is claimed to be objective in its judgement (5). The test also empowers the authorities to judge who is and who is not human, analogically to Prospero who is empowered by his books of magic to conduct the people on the island as he pleases. It is essential to observe that no one seems to challenge the test's results except for Rachael; people believe in one machine's validity and discriminate the authenticity of other "more human than human" machines at the same time (*BR* 0:22:00).

Currently, we are challenged to find an effective solution to prevent further spreading of the coronavirus. Most of these solutions are based on technological inventions. The BBC relates that the UK is cooperating with the biggest IT companies, such as Goggle and Apple, in creating a tracing application for mobile phones which will investigate the way how the virus is transmitted and warn the users if someone is ill or had contact with a virus bearer via Bluetooth (Cellan-Jones 2020). This app will require the user's agreement for publishing medical data which are to be collected and supervised by the NHS (Cellan-Jones 2020). However, the government and the companies cannot achieve a consensus about the form of the app: there are some controversies around privacy and technical issues concerning the usage of mobile batteries (Cellan-Jones 2020). In this perspective, the performance of the application does not differ from the one of the Voigt-Kampff Empathy Test in terms of reliability. It will be entrusted with similarly sensitive personal information which in fact may endanger the safety of its users. It may result in either the misuse of the provided medical data or encouragement of hostile behaviour towards the affected. For androids, the privilege of the testing machine over the new species of human beings is a cruel act of injustice which ends in the "retirement" of the second.

Blade Runner: The posthumanist vision of science and manifestation of fears

In the film, imitation equals creation. The producers of the replicants can be considered as gods of creation in its full meaning: not only do they know the secrets of nature, but they also produce new secrets by a mechanical creation of a human being made of flesh and able to think abstractly. The androids are in fact more than artificial intelligence: they are new Adams who change the definition of humanity. They are also original pieces of art distinguished with extraordinary features given by their creators. In *Blade Runner* science meets the art.

Scott's film is a posthuman vision of the world in 2019. It expresses all the fears and suspicions connected with a rapid technological development at the time of its making: the dominance of Asian companies and culture in the West, the environmental pollution and decay of natural areas, an excessive use of raw materials (therefore the colonies on other planets are created), overpopulation, high level of consumption, and dependence on machines. Does this vision apply to the present time? Unfortunately, most of these predictions have actually come true – the greenhouse gas emission, climate change, all sorts of pollution of the environment, just to mention a few. What about the androids then? Is this problem relevant to a modern society?

It occurs that this question requires a careful examination in the process of creation of artificial intelligence and definition of its role in the society. One of the best examples is Sophia the Robot created by Hanson Robotics. As it is written on the official website of the company about Sophia, she is able to process language to give "responses unique to any given situation or interaction," "recognize human faces, see emotional expressions, and recognize various hand gestures" ("Sophia" 2019). Moreover, Sophia can "estimate one's feelings during a conversation," and she has her "own emotions too," because she "simulates human evolutionary psychology and various regions of the brain" ("Sophia" 2019). She responds not only in an audible way, but also via face expression thanks to her synthetic face. She resembles a woman in appearance (inspired by Audrey Hepburn) and posture; her motor skills are being improved.

David Hanson, the founder and CEO of Hanson Robotics, said at the DLD conference in Bayreuth that Sophia's purpose is a "therapeutic and service application," such as examining "how people model emotions," helping to connect them even if they are remote, "unlocking the mysteries of intelligence," and – the most essential – "provoking the discussion about rights" for various species: all humans, animals, and robots (DLDconference 2019). He claims that if the robots like Sophia were commercialised, people should be their legal guardians and he disagrees with some ethics' suggestions that those machines cannot be humanized and they should only be at the service of people; he observes that this would create "intelligent sentient slaves." His goal is to make machines compassionate to bring them closer to people. Hanson concludes that "we have to dream, we have to speculate" in order to find answers and solutions for ethical questions to develop as human beings (DLDconference 2019).

In his essay, von Schomberg (2013) writes that the innovators should collaborate in their work and take "a collective responsibility both for the right impacts and negative consequences" (60). He suggests that the research groups should have "a multidisciplinary approach" meaning that the teams should gather the specialists from various fields (von Schomberg 2013, 65). Hanson Robotics seems to answer this requirement by implementing Sophia Intelligence Collective: "The humans in my [Sophia's] intelligence collective comprise widely diverse expert AI scientists, philosophers, artists, writers, and psychologists, from diverse cultures, ethnicities, gender orientations, working together towards the ideal of humanizing AI for the greater good" ("Sophia" 2019). Yet, there is still an unanswered question: will the right policy of the company prevent some of the problems concerning AI presence in society?

In 2017 Sophia evoked many controversies due to the fact that she, as the first robot, received a citizenship of Saudi Arabia, where women's rights are violated. She appears publicly without covering her head and a male guardian obligatory for assisting women there, which met with a harsh critique (Gittleson 2017). What was the purpose of giving a female robot a citizenship of a country dominated by patriarchal ideology?

Conclusion

What I would like to emphasise is that our society cannot define what it means to be a human: is it the vulnerable physical body, is it the conscious and abstract-thinking mind, is it the ungraspable soul or the essence which gives us a meaning, or do our deeds alone define who we really are? We still rely on some easy-to-be-confronted assumptions of humanity, trying to confirm our view from different religious perspectives which are not always applicable for people of various ethnic backgrounds. The problem is that our society is so diverse and divided that we cannot give an unequivocal answer. Is it possible for mechanic humanoids to be accepted as a new species in a society which cannot accept the diversity of religions, genders, sexual orientations, cultures or ethnic origins?

The other aspect is that we are choking with capitalistic ideas which shape our attitude toward money, goods, and possession. There is a likelihood that such robots as Sophia would be distributed worldwide to various institutions or governments which may misuse them in military service or in scientific experiments. Another problem is whether those robots should be accessible for the public and how people would acquire them; if sold, then the robots would be regarded as products. Therefore, it is very important to seek for solutions which may help to prevent such situations and provide safety not only for people, but also for the robots.

I hope that this essay may contribute to the general discussion about the AI future and raise new questions to be taken into consideration. I was trying to prove that even in the Elizabethan time the issues concerning the imitation of nature were discussed by presenting all of its implications and forms. Shakespeare is one of the first authors who observed that imitation may be dangerous when it is used solely in the control of and for the advantage of the person who imitates; that individual's powers may be insufficient and sometimes require a collaboration of skilful agents, and that imitation may also serve for artistic purposes to entertain. Bacon presents how it is important to divide science into compartments and fields to make it more approachable and efficient in the exploration of the secrets of nature. He also draws attention to the fact that science should be guarded by legal regulations to bring positive outcomes to the society. Finally, *Blade Runner* makes us aware of the scale of damages in the environment and suffering of various beings caused by irresponsible decisions and the attitude focused on financial profit. It also reminds us that we still need to rethink what it means to be a human being.

References

"Access and Allocation: How Will There Be Fair and Equitable Allocation of Limited Supplies?" 2021. WHO. https://www.who.int/news-room/feature-stories/detail/access-and-allocation-how-will-there-be-fair-and-equitable-allocation-of-limited-supplies. Accessed 21 January 2021.

Bacon, F. 1960. *New Atlantis. Advancement of Learning.* Oxford: Oxford University Press.

Baudrillard, J. 1988. "Simulacra and Simulations." In: M. Poster (ed.), *Jean Baudrillard: Selected Writings.* Stanford: Stanford University Press, 166-184.

Bednarek, M. 2020. "Europoseł o fali koronawirusa: Zamiast zamykać kopalnie, rząd zamknął lasy." https://katowice.wyborcza.pl/katowice/7,35063,25934982,koronawirus-w-woj-slaskim-hejt-na-mieszkancow-wojewodztwa.html. Accessed 27 June 2020.

Bertek, T. 2014. "The Authenticity of the Replica: A Post-Human Reading of Blade Runner." *[sic] – A Journal of Literature, Culture and Literary Translation* 5(1). 1-12.

Blade Runner. 1982. Dir. R. Scott. Warner Bros.

Bruno, G. 1987. "Ramble City: Postmodernism and Blade Runner." *October* 41. 61-74.

Cellan-Jones, R. 2020. "Coronavirus: What Went Wrong with the UK's Contact Tracing App?" https://www.bbc.com/news/technology-53114251. Accessed 29 June 2020.

"Ceres (mythology)." n.d. *Wikipedia, The Free Encyclopedia.* https://en.wikipedia.org/wiki/Ceres_(mythology). Accessed 22 July 2019.

"Close Reading." 2018. University of York website. https://www.york.ac.uk/english/writing-at-york/writing-resources/close-reading/. Accessed 25 June 2020.

"Coronavirus: EU Considers Barring Americans from Travel List." 2020. *BBC News.* https://www.bbc.com/news/world-europe-53161447. Accessed 27 June 2020.

"Coronavirus: French Asians Hit Back at Racism with 'I'm Not a Virus.'" 2020. *BBC News*. https://www.bbc.com/news/world-europe-51294305. Accessed 27 June 2020.

DLDconference. 2019. "On the Future of Robotics (David Hanson & Jennifer Schenker) | DLD Campus 19." https://www.youtube.com/watch?v=S_duUwJCgEY. Accessed 26 July 2019.

Gittleson, B. 2017. "Saudi Arabia Criticized for Giving Female Robot Citizenship, While It Restricts Women's Rights." https://abcnews.go.com/International/saudi-arabia-criticized-giving-female-robot-citizenship-restricts/story?id=50741109. Accessed 26 July 2019.

Hall, M.B. 1994. *The Scientific Renaissance: 1450-1630*. New York, NY: Dover Publications.

Hansen, C. 2020. "Introduction to Presentism." http://shakespearereloaded.edu.au/introduction-presentism. Accessed 25 June 2020.

Hossain, A., and A. Iseni. 2014. "Perception of the Supernatural Worlds in Shakespeare's *The Tempest*." *Anglisticum: International Journal of Literature, Linguistics & Interdisciplinary Studies* 3(6). 78-89.

"Introduction to Practical Criticism." 2016. University of Cambridge website. https://www.english.cam.ac.uk/classroom/pracrit.htm. Accessed 25 June 2020.

"Iris." n.d. *Encyclopædia Britannica*. https://www.britannica.com/topic/Iris-Greek-mythology. Accessed 22 July 2019.

"Juno (mythology)." n.d. *Wikipedia, The Free Encyclopedia*. https://en.wikipedia.org/wiki/Juno_(mythology). Accessed 22 July 2019.

Kendrick, C. 2003. "The Imperial Laboratory: Discovering Forms in *The New Atlantis*." *ELH* 70(4). 1022-1028.

Kumar, K. 1991. *Utopia and Anti-Utopia in Modern Times*. Oxford: Blackwell Publishers.

Mortensen, J.H. 2019. "Modes of Consciousness and Reality in *The Tempest*." https://www.academia.edu/13235099/Modes_of_Consciousness_and_Reality_in_The_Tempest. Accessed 15 July 2019.

von Schomberg, R. 2013. "A Vision of Responsible Research and Innovation." In: R. Owen, J. Bessant, and M. Heintz (eds.), *Responsible Innovation: Managing the Responsible Emergence of Science and Innovation in Society*. Chichester: John Wiley & Sons, 51-74.

Serjeantson, R. 2002. "Natural Knowledge in the *New Atlantis*." In: B. Price (ed.), *Francis Bacon's New Atlantis: New Interdisciplinary Essays*. Manchester: Manchester University Press, 82-105.

Shakespeare, W. 2015. *The Tempest*. Edited by B.A. Mowat and P. Werstine. https://shakespeare.folger.edu/downloads/pdf/the-tempest_PDF_FolgerShakespeare.pdf. Accessed 15 September 2020.

"Sophia." 2019. *Hanson Robotics*. https://www.hansonrobotics.com/sophia/. Accessed 26 July 2019.

Wheale, N. 1991. "Recognising a 'Human-Thing': Cyborgs, Robots and Replicants in Philip K. Dick's *Do Androids Dream of Electric Sheep?* and Ridley Scott's *Blade Runner.*" *Critical Survey* 3(3). 297-304.

PART III

The Theatre of Politics

AGNIESZKA ORSZULAK

Jagiellonian University

Different Types of Authority in William Shakespeare's History Plays

Abstract

William Shakespeare's history plays illustrate interesting examples of various forms of authority, the leaders' and the subjects' attitude towards it, and its political significance. In her analysis, the author follows the classification of types of authority proposed by Max Weber (traditional, charismatic, and legal) and Claudia Rapp (pragmatic). She then applies these notions to the portrayals of power as presented in the plays *Richard II*, *Henry IV* part 1 and 2, and *Richard III* and distinguishes a pattern in the subsequent representations of authority. Richard II exercises traditional authority of an anointed king, yet he lacks control in other aspects. Henry IV demonstrates his pragmatic and charismatic authority by managing to overthrow an inadequate monarch, however, this triumph deprives him of any hope for achieving the divine status of his predecessor. Prince Hal exerts charismatic and pragmatic authority and represents a change in the attitudes towards power, believing that acting as a legitimate king is more important than actually acquiring traditional authority. Richard III, following the shift in the modern understanding of power, does not respect the traditional authority of a divinely sanctioned king and establishes his rule on charismatic authority, which withers shortly after his ascension to the throne. Subsequently, the author examines the contemporary representations of power, using Polish President Andrzej Duda and American President Donald Trump as examples. In the times of democracy, legal authority has prevailed and although it may seem the most just and appropriate to our current value system, it still proves fallible.

Keywords: William Shakespeare, history plays, Max Weber, types of authority, contemporary politics

Streszczenie

Kroniki historyczne Williama Szekspira prezentują interesujące przykłady podejścia do władzy, sposobów jej sprawowania oraz konsekwencji politycznych, które ze sobą niosą. Analiza przeprowadzona w artykule opiera się na typologii władzy opracowanej przez Maxa Webera (tradycyjna, charyzmatyczna i legalna) oraz Claudię Rapp (pragmatyczna). Wyróżnione źródła legitymizacji władzy wykorzystane są następnie do analizy metod panowania przedstawionych w *Ryszardzie II*, *Henryku IV* część 1 i 2 oraz *Ryszardzie III*, co prowadzi do wyróżnienia schematu kolejnych przedstawień władzy. Ryszard II posiada władzę tradycyjną, jednak w jego sposobie panowania wyraźnie brakuje pozostałych cech charakteryzujących dobrego władcę. Henryk IV, za pomocą władzy pragmatycznej i charyzmatycznej, obala nieudolnego króla i zajmuje jego miejsce, jednak tym samym pozbawia się możliwości osiągnięcia tradycyjnego źródła władzy. Książę Hal reprezentuje nowe pokolenie władców, którzy dostrzegają różnicę pomiędzy odgrywaniem roli a byciem prawowitym królem, dlatego władza pragmatyczna i charyzmatyczna stanowi dla niego wystarczające potwierdzenie legitymizacji jego panowania. Ryszard III, zgodnie z nowym nurtem w rozumieniu władzy, nie uważa władzy tradycyjnej za władzę uświęconą i opiera swoje rządy na charyzmie, która jednak zanika niedługo po objęciu przez niego tronu. Autorka porównuje także renesansowe przedstawienia władzy do sposobu, w jaki prezentowane są osoby sprawujące władzę na współczesnej scenie politycznej – na przykładzie Prezydenta Andrzeja Dudy i Prezydenta Donalda Trumpa. Ten zabieg ma na celu udowodnienie istnienia więzi pomiędzy postrzeganiem władzy i wiarą w jej zasadność w XVI wieku i obecnie.

Słowa kluczowe: William Szekspir, kroniki królewskie, Max Weber, typy władzy, współczesna scena polityczna

Introduction

Power and authority have been desired and sought from the beginning of the human civilization. The allure of having dominance over other people has not diminished over the centuries, although its form has been changing with the development of the human race, from pharaohs through kings to presidents. The history plays by William Shakespeare display a variety of different types of authority, the leaders' attitudes towards it, and its political significance. Four plays, *Richard II*, *Henry IV* part 1 and 2, and *Richard III*, were chosen for their depiction of the crisis of authority and the crisis of representation in early modern England. By juxtaposing the portrayals of Richard II, Henry IV, Prince Hal and Richard III with the current political situation in Poland and the United States, this paper attempts to demonstrate a connection between the representation of authority in the past and in the contemporary world.

The Concept of Authority

Authority, understood as "the power to influence others" ("Authority" n.d.), has always been a subject of discussion and theoretical debate. Many philosophers and sociologists proposed their own explanations and classifications of the concept, however, the most prominent one was devised by a German thinker, Max Weber. He based his categorisation on the source of the legitimacy of power, distinguishing three types of authority: traditional, charismatic, and legal.

Traditional authority (also called "substantial") relies on "an established belief in the sanctity of immemorial traditions" (Weber 1964, 328). As Kendall (2010) explains, its legitimacy is based on a long-standing custom, often connected to religion and deeply-rooted in the community's culture, which is accepted and respected by the society (432). The source of traditional authority is located outside of the individual wielding power and is self-sufficient. This authority of being, most frequently depending on the blood right or the divine right, is enough to sanction the individual's position to rule, independently of his personality or abilities.

Charismatic authority is based on the individual's exceptional character and personal qualities or his heroism and extraordinary accomplishments that inspire support and loyalty from followers (Kendall 2010, 432). It is not restricted to a specific social group and is accessible to all, as far as they exhibit desired "charismatic" abilities. This type of authority tends to be temporary and relatively unstable. Weber (1964) notes that it depends greatly on the leader's individual nature and the ability to excite devotion, as well as on the public recognition (363). By the virtue of its source, it cannot be hereditary and it cannot establish a succession of power. This often leads to the "routinization of charisma," which is succeeded by a rationally established authority (Weber 1964, 363).

According to Weber (1964), legal authority depends on "a belief in the 'legality' of patterns of normative rules" (328). Its legitimacy lies in law and written regulations, where established procedures guarantee order and obedience. Therefore, the authority belongs to the office itself, not to the individuals who hold it. Kendall (2010) observes that the leaders have the right to exercise power only when they obtain their position in a "procedurally correct manner," for example through election or appointment, and only within the scope of the office's jurisdiction (432). Thus, with this type of authority, a person enjoys control only temporarily and in a limited way, being subjected to the legal and temporal constrains of the position.

Claudia Rapp, in her categorisation of the notion, proposes yet another type of authority, pragmatic authority or authority of acting. It relies on the individual's actions and their behaviour in relation to holding power. However, in distinction from charismatic authority, these actions are not meant to illustrate the leader's heroic accomplishments, but they are executed to the benefit of the public. It is not universally accessible, for "its achievement depends on the individual's wherewithal, in terms of social position and wealth," to perform these actions (Rapp 2013, 17). If completed successfully, they secure the public's recognition of the person striving for power, which is necessary for the legitimisation of this type of authority.

Figures of Authority in Shakespeare's History Plays

Almost all of Shakespeare's history plays were written during the reign of Queen Elizabeth I, at a time crucial for developing and reinventing the sense of national identity. Henry VIII's rule put England in a radical and isolated position in Europe, leaving the country in a state of uncertainty and threat of social and political unrest. The Elizabethan era brought stability and relative peace, infused people with a new sense of power, which awakened the national self-awareness and pride (Bevington 1999). Meeting the audience's demand, Shakespeare joined other contemporary writers and turned his focus to the country's history.

In the late sixteenth and early seventeenth centuries, the term "history" did not yet refer to a factual account of the events of the past. The stories described as "histories" often combined historical and mythical figures and tales, prioritising moral instruction over authenticity and truthful representation (Parvini 2012, 87). Therefore, while reading Shakespeare's history plays, it is important to remember that the playwright did not intend to recreate on stage the way things really happened, which would be difficult in itself, given the inevitable bias of the early historiographers, rather, he appropriated historical figures and events in order to address the present. Hence, many anachronisms are present within the plays, such as introducing fictional characters, placing people in the incorrect times and generations, or attributing them with features characteristic of contemporary individuals. Shakespeare offered "not reflections *of* the past but reflections *on* the past," inextricably intertwining dramatization with commentary (Hattaway 2002, 16). His works are concerned with historical process and change, matters of statehood and nationality, difficulties of governance and court politics, ceaselessly questioning the role of monarchy in the emerging English state.

E.M.W. Tillyard believed that Shakespeare's history plays endorsed the propaganda of "the Tudor myth" and were aimed at justifying and reinforcing the Tudors' claim to the English throne (qtd. in Hattaway 2002, 20). Although Shakespeare did mythicize his account of the past – he shaped history into ordered stories with beginning, middle, and end, identified individual characters as villains and heroes, it is more accurate to say that his approach was exploratory, not prescriptive (Leggatt 2003, viii). He examined power and its implications realistically, focusing his depiction on people, their personalities and actions. Such a treatment of history allows us to see how much is often determined by decisions made by the few and their potential to affect thousands, and exposes the fragility and insecurity of their privileged positions (Parvini 2012, 106).

Richard II

Richard II's authority as a king originates from his position as "God's vicegerent" (Mabillard 2000). He is believed to possess a divine right to rule over England, assured by his royal bloodline, which is affirmed by his anointment. Therefore, he exercises traditional authority, being divinely sanctioned to be a king. The importance of this status is emphasised on numerous occasions not only by Richard himself, but also by his subjects: "our sacred blood" (*R2* 1.1.119[1]), "thy anointed body" (*R2* 2.1.98), "that Power that made you king / Hath power to keep you king in spite of all" (*R2* 3.2.27-28). The power of the crown is so absolute that John of Gaunt remains loyal to the king, despite acknowledging his faults and misdeeds. He confesses that:

> God's is the quarrel – for God's substitute,
> His deputy anointed in His sight,
> Hath caus'd his death; the which if wrongfully,
> Let heaven revenge, for I may never lift
> An angry arm against His minister. (*R2* 1.2.37-41)

Gaunt believes that even if Richard's actions are wrong, it is not people's responsibility to judge him, for this privilege belongs only to God. The king is above his subjects and any worldly jurisdiction, thus he deserves indisputable trust. Similarly, for Richard his divine right is equal to his kingly position. It does not mean that he "conceives of himself as the right king but that he conceives of himself simply as *the* king" (Calderwood 1979, 17). He does not merely assume the position of a king and all the functions that it encompasses, but he believes that he is inherently entitled to them, as his blood right, the fact which he often refers to, accentuating that "Not all the water in the rough rude sea / Can wash the balm off from an anointed king" (*R2* 3.2.54-55).

Richard, installed at an early age into the kingship, puts complete trust in his status as a divinely-ordained king and lacks authority in other aspects, which proves his inadequacy and irresponsibility (Bevington 1999). Most notably, he does not possess pragmatic authority, the deficiency that renders him unfit to be a good ruler. His incompetency at managing the affairs of the kingdom is visible already at the beginning of the play in act 1, scene 3, when he decides to stop the duel between Bolingbroke and Mowbray and sentences them to banishment. Apart from illustrating his

1 All in-text references to William Shakespeare's works are to editions listed in the Reference section at the end of this paper. The abbreviations used are as follows: 1H4 for *King Henry IV, Part 1*; 2H4 for *King Henry IV, Part 2*; R2 for *King Richard II*; R3 for *King Richard III*.

indecisiveness, this scene also demonstrates his lack of understanding and respect for long-established traditions. In the medieval England, a duel constituted a natural way of settling disputes, since the outcome of the fight was left in the hands of God (Amt and Smith 2018, 160). By interfering with the ritual, Richard challenges divine authority, therefore, undermining his own right to rule. This incident illustrates also that he allows his emotions to shape his decisions instead of employing cool judgement of what is the best for the country (Mabillard 2000). He is self-absorbed and naïve and does not display any interest in gaining people's sympathy and support, the flaw that is fatal to his attempt at governing. By neglecting his subjects and failing to establish an effective interaction with them, he soon loses their loyalty. Richard is also susceptible to greed and flattery and prefers to listen to self-interested noblemen rather than to a sound council of faithful servants. He confiscates the nobles' land and properties, acting more like a "Landlord of England" (*R2* 2.1.113) than a king. He betrays the trust that people put in him as their God's chosen sovereign, putting his own needs and desires before theirs. His unkingly manner, political incompetency, and negligence lead to unrest in the kingdom and threaten the traditional order of affairs.

Henry IV

Henry Bolingbroke establishes his reign in an untraditional way. He rebels against Richard II and comes to power as a usurper, thus, as an illegitimate monarch without the support of substantial authority. However, his claim to the throne is based on his pragmatic and charismatic authority, which he demonstrates from the beginning of *Richard II*, when he is young and does not yet consider an open insurgency. Bolingbroke is far better versed in the art of politics than his predecessor, the quality which is significant enough to carry out a successful rebellion and overthrow an inadequate king. He understands the importance and necessity of people's support and dedication, which allow him to influence the masses. However, Henry believes that all his actions and political decisions are based on what he deems the best for the nation and performed in the name of the well-being of his subjects (Mabillard 2000). He establishes his social position and recognition through gaining the public's trust and affection:

> How he did seem to dive into their hearts
> With humble and familiar courtesy;
> What reverence he did throw away on slaves,

> Wooing poor craftsmen with the craft of smiles
> And patient underbearing of his fortune,
> As 'twere to banish their affects with him. (*R2* 1.4.25-30)

Bolingbroke is a shrewd politician and he understands the mechanics of ruling over people. Apart from getting into their good graces, he also exhibits great leadership qualities. He pays attention to what is happening around him and to the constantly changing dynamics between the nobles in the kingdom. He then uses his observations and people's adoration to manipulate them into following him, so that he even manages to convince them to oppose the divinely anointed monarch: "I did pluck allegiance from men's hearts, / Loud shouts and salutations from their mouths, / Even in the presence of the crowned king" (*1H4* 3.2.52-54). His charisma and mastery with words are especially visible in act 3, scene 3 during his speech to the lords gathered before Flint Castle. He is able to confidently answer the nobles' doubts and insecurities over the blasphemous act and quench their fear of God's retribution. Henry's political tact and resolution are also visible after his victorious battle with Richard, when he proves his ability to control the situation and effectively handle the two antagonised lords. This instance illustrates Bolingbroke's competence and knowledge of the human nature, the qualities befitting a good king.

For Henry, those personal values are sufficient recommendation to be worthy of becoming a king. He believes that common acceptance, rather than divine support, lends him authority to seize the throne. He promises to "Redeem from broking pawn the blemish'd crown" (*R2* 2.1.293), however, by overthrowing a lawful king, he only further demeans the royal status. As Calderwood (1979) points out: "This 'debasement' of kingship involves the secularizing of language as well, the surrender of a sacramental language to a utilitarian one in which the relation between words and things is arbitrary, unsure, and ephemeral" (6). By becoming Henry IV, Bolingbroke deprives the crown of its divine status, undermining his position on the throne and paving the way for unrest in the kingdom.

Despite his political deftness, Henry's reign proves to be tumultuous and troubled, by some considered to be God's punishment for his betrayal of the natural, divine order. As a usurper without any legitimate claim to the throne, he suffers the consequences of his actions both personally and publicly. By obtaining the power in an unlawful way, he opens up the doors for further opposition and rebellion, causing disorder in the kingdom. Constant resistance, doubt, and uneasy conscience hurt the nation, continually crippling his potential and noble wishes for the better future, as well as taking a toll on the king's psyche, exhausting him mentally. Henry experiences guilt and distress over his crime of usurpation, lamenting that "Uneasy lies the head that wears a crown" (*2H4* 3.1.32). He is depressed, afraid, and suspicious of everyone, slowly losing the charisma of his youth. The awareness that his crown is hollow, that he has no traditional authority to support his reign makes him particularly concerned with public opinion and appearance, knowing that the favour of the common people is what legitimises his rule. Unfortunately, pragmatic authority and sophistication are not enough to ensure him a peaceful and secure rule and he eventually dies a disappointed man (Bevington 1999).

Prince Hal

When we meet Prince Hal at the beginning of *Henry IV, Part 1*, he is presented as a disreputable idler who does not care for the matters of the kingdom nor for the decorum, spending his time with thieves, truants, and drunkards. His reckless and mischievous behaviour provokes his father and his opponents to condemn him as a disgrace, as an unsuitable candidate for a king, "The nimble-footed madcap Prince of Wales, / [...] that daft the world aside / And bid it pass" (*1H4* 4.1.95-97). At the same time, due to his unprincely manners, Hal is regarded by the common people as "one of them," a nobleman who does not think of himself as better than his future subjects. However, we soon realise the true motif behind the prince's dishonourable attitude:

> So when this loose behaviour I throw off,
> And pay the debt I never promised,
> By how much better than my word I am,
> By so much shall I falsify men's hopes;
> And like bright metal on a sullen ground,
> My reformation, glitt'ring o'er my fault,
> Shall show more goodly, and attract more eyes
> Than that which hath no foil to set it off.
> I'll so offend, to make offence a skill,
> Redeeming time when men think least I will. (*1H4* 1.2.203-212)

Hal confesses that his bawdy behaviour and friendship with wastrels are part of a carefully-constructed act, a brilliant political manoeuvre. He intentionally creates a displeasing, disreputable image of himself as an unruly princeling in order to lower the expectations that surround him. In this way, once he reveals his true self, Hal plans to look as good as possible, appearing as a strong and valiant hero, especially in comparison with his previous endeavours. He wants to surprise and shock the country, gaining people's support and admiration, which he knows he needs in order to become an accomplished king. Thus, he seeks a way to achieve popularity among them and establish a favourable connection with his subjects even before his rule. His charm endears him to both the common people and the nobility and inspires them to follow the prince and put their faith in him as their leader, proving his ability to exact charismatic authority.

Hal's plan has yet another objective – he wishes to "redeem time." He is a young politician who is aware of the precarious and unstable situation in the kingdom. He knows his family's history and how they came to power, however, unlike his father, he does not feel remorse over the unlawful seizing of the crown. For Hal, what is fundamental to gaining and maintaining authority is not the divine right, but strength, competence, and people's support. He knows that he needs to establish his position in the kingdom as a rightful heir to the throne and is "determined to direct the forces of history and bend them to his will" (Cohen 2002, 303). He devises a plan to take control of the narrative and create a new future, one in which he will be perceived as a legitimate king and his rule will be unchallenged. He believes that by acting the part of a lawful monarch, by shaping a certain image of himself and maintaining the illusion of power, he will be able to feign traditional authority as well.

Yet, in order to do what is required of him, he cannot dwell on the past. For King Henry, his past deeds are the source of shame and regret that hinder and undermine his kingship. Hal does not intend to repeat his father's mistakes and adapts a new approach – it is as if he purposefully "[does not] contend any thought of his father's guilt" (Dickinson 1961, 38). Acknowledging the responsibility would mean letting the past affect his present and his future, raising scruples about his right of succession both in his and the public's mind. Instead, Hal recognises the uncertainty of his position and vows to do what is necessary to improve it, even if it encompasses deceiving and manipulating others. The fact that he is able to accomplish his cunning design is the testament to his charisma and political astuteness. He realises what needs to be done and he does not hesitate to see it through. For this reason, as a young king, Hal must publicly renounce his former companions, notwithstanding his personal affections: "I know thee not, old man [...] / Presume not that I am the thing I was, / For God doth know, so shall the world perceive, / That I have turn'd away my former self; / So will I those that kept me company" (*2H4* 5.5.43-55). He is not concerned with who may suffer on his journey to the throne, for he does not do it for the benefit of his subjects, but for his own merit, to intensify the greatness of his achievements.

It seems that King Henry also realises Hal's potential to amend for his sins and restore the legitimacy of kingship, "for what in me was purchas'd / Falls upon thee in a more fairer sort; / So thou the garland wear'st successively" (*2H4* 4.5.199-201). He believes that his son is the one who will unite traditional authority of divine anointment and charismatic authority of their political sophistication, reinstating the glory of their name (Mabillard 2000).

Richard III

Richard III is an ambitious and brilliant, yet ruthless man. He is portrayed as an epitome of vice, depravity, and wickedness, someone who will stop at nothing to achieve his goal. In the opening lines of *Richard III*, he confesses that he repulses the peaceful times, which are so at odds with his inner turmoil. He believes that he has been wrongfully punished with physical deformity; therefore, he feels that he deserves more from life, he requires compensation for his pain and suffering. He decides to shape his own fate and uses every means at his disposal. Richard arrogantly presumes that he has earned the crown and devises a vicious plan to get it: "Plots have I laid, inductions dangerous, / [...] To set my brother Clarence and the King / In deadly hate, the one against the other" (*R3* 1.1.32-35). He does not experience any remorse over scheming to murder not only the head of the country, but also his own family members, he is concerned only with pursuing his own agenda and increasing his power.

Richard is a master manipulator, clever, suave, and politically savvy. He uses his physical impairment to gain sympathy from others and create a favourable image of himself, deceiving people into believing in his good intentions. His charismatic persona, dazzling wordplay, and the ability to transform and adopt different characters at will enable him to pretend to be modest and moral on the outside, while mercilessly sacrificing human life to satisfy his selfish desires. His "apparent loyalty and piety that mask treachery" are so effective that he is able to convince even those who know his true nature (Colley 1986, 452). His carefully prepared appearance, skilful argumentation, and adept command of words aid him to seduce even such a woman as Lady Anne, who is aware that Richard orchestrated the death of her husband and father-in-law.

Paradoxically, the moment when Richard obtains the throne of England marks the turning point in his political career. Up until this point, he is sure of what he wants and what he needs to do in order to achieve it, but once he becomes a king, he is lost, he no longer knows how to behave. It is evident that Richard is not prepared to lead a country, he is short-sighted in his strategy and focuses only on his immediate future, disregarding the consequences of his actions. He has spent so much time and energy trying to seize the crown that when he accomplishes this goal, he realises that he does not actually understand what it means to be a leader. As a result, he is unable to present himself as a figure of authority, for a king needs faithful subjects and their ensured support for his reign, the assets which Richard is gravely lacking. In the course of his rise to power, he manages to estrange his friends and effectively reject potential allies, underestimating his opposition (Kingsbury 2016, 6). His charisma diminishes gradually, unravelling his control over the public and the events happening around him. His wit and oratory skills become progressively less convincing and alluring, allowing people to see behind his mask.

Richard's control deteriorates even further when Richmond begins his uprising. The elaborate manipulation, the mental strain of being constantly alert, and having to endure such rapid and dramatic changes in his behaviour to maintain the appearance, "the predilection to morph and fluctuate" finally take a toll on the king (Donkor 2016). The shifts in his personality start to manifest not only on the outside, but they become internalised as well, affecting his psyche. Act 5, scene 3 illustrates the culmination of his inner chaos and confusion when, after witnessing the procession of vengeful ghosts of his victims, Richard engages in a feverish speech, which represents the inner conflict of the character. His discourse breaks down, offering splintered phrases and oppositions:

> Is there a murderer here? No. Yes, I am!
> Then fly. What, from myself? Great reason why,
> Lest I revenge? What, myself upon myself?
> Alack, I love myself. Wherefore? For any good

That I myself have done unto myself?
O no, alas, I rather hate myself
For hateful deeds committed by myself. (*R3* 5.3.185-190)

It is as if Richard leads a dialogue with himself, shifting between "confidence and cowardice, resolve and ruefulness, defiance and despair" (Donkor 2016). He experiences an identity split, a complete dissociation of personality. It is the first time in the play that he expresses concern about moral issues and he does not know what to think anymore. The interplay of self-loathing and self-defence suggests that, when forced to acknowledge the monstrosity of his sins, even Richard's will and strength of character begin to crumble. He is a man without scruples, who resorts to murder in order to obtain traditional authority of blood right and divine anointment and who subsequently forfeits his charismatic authority, having not anticipated that his long-awaited kingship would come at the expense of his sanity. He undergoes a dramatic degradation of personality, transforming from a charismatic, ingenious, and ambitious puppet-master into a cowardly tyrant who is unable to exert discipline.

Authority in the Contemporary World

After examining Shakespeare's portrayal of the four kings, we may infer that an ideal ruler must wield both traditional and pragmatic or charismatic authority. His rule, in order to be successful and enduring, needs to be established on the divine right of succession as well as on the individual's political astuteness and leadership skills. However, none of the monarchs analysed above embodies this perfect model. We can observe a gradual decline in the significance of traditional authority as a guarantee of power and the rise of authority based on the individual qualities of a ruler. This pattern can be also applied to the contemporary world. Nowadays, power is temporal and depends on the candidate's ability to display a strong set of leadership skills in order to attract voters to elect him as their representative, hence obtaining legal authority. This type of authority is characteristic of the democratic system, where it is the institution itself that holds power, not the individual who resides in the office for a limited period of time.

It is a common belief that "under democracy governments are representative because they are elected" and therefore they will act in the best interest of the people, to support their welfare (Manin 1999, 29). Yet, this view proves problematic when we consider the individual goals, concerns, and values of politicians. Even if their intentions are noble and they aim to serve the public, they first need to be elected. In order to achieve it, candidates need to persuade people to vote for them, to present themselves in the most favourable light. Sometimes this may entail deceiving the voters by creating a sympathetic image of the aspirant and his political ambitions, manipulating information or making empty promises just to meet the public's expectations. Furthermore, the triumphant candidates, once they are elected, may want to pursue their own agenda or an objective that differs from that of the citizens (Manin 1999, 29). Therefore, even though they came to power in a legal and publicly-approved way, such politicians do not represent the interests of their voters, betraying the trust people put in them.

It is also worth remembering that none of the electoral systems is truly authoritative and infallible. For instance, the plurality or majority systems, the most frequently used voting systems, require a candidate to poll more votes than the opponent(s) or to receive an absolute majority of votes (over 50 percent) respectively ("Plurality Electoral Systems" n.d.). Voter turnout, which is currently in decline, is another issue affecting the elections. Consequently, the winner often does not actually possess the support of the majority of the society, a flaw inherent to the contemporary polity.

Andrzej Duda

During the presidential elections in Poland in 2015, Andrzej Duda was praised for his "American-style" campaign that secured him the victory (Kołodziej 2015, 233). His presidency was promoted as being open and dynamic, focusing on the traditional values, such as family and religion, and, most importantly, aimed at restoring order and justice on the Polish political scene. Despite being a candidate of the right-wing Law and Justice Party (PiS), he was presented as a politician with central views, aiming to attract a wide range of voters (Kołodziej 2015, 240). His campaign promises included a monthly subsidy for families with children, the resolution of the so-called "Swiss franc borrowers' crisis," and lowering the retiring age (Michalski 2016). Although the reforms sound encouraging, they were aimed at the welfare of the specific groups, not the whole society. Accumulating funds needed for the additional endowment led to withdrawal of funding for medications and health care for the disabled children, causing a public uproar. The illusion of political neutrality faded already within six months after the elections, when Duda signed into law the constitutional tribunal bill, granting his former party the majority in the judiciary (Duval Smith 2015). His subsequent actions and political dependency on PiS's chairman, Jarosław Kaczyński, resulted in the conflict with the European Union and severing ties with other European countries. The Polish government was labelled "a threat to the rule of law" and was threatened with preventative measures executed by the EU (Boffey 2018).

With time, many of Duda's voters felt betrayed, when they reached the conclusion that he did not fulfil his promises and that the authority in the country did not represent their interests. They placed their trust in a candidate with great charm and conviction, who understood their needs and wishes. Unfortunately, once he obtained the position of power, he became more concerned with following the objective of the conservative party than doing what is right and beneficial for the citizens, whom he was elected to represent and protect. The situation escalated during the 2020 presidential campaign when Duda, seeking re-election, adopted anti-LGBTQ rhetoric and declared "the promotion of LGBT rights an 'ideology' more destructive than communism" ("Polish Election" 2020). This statement, propagated by government officials and state media, led to nationwide protests, with many protesters getting injured or detained in what some say was "an unprecedented level of police aggression against an LGBTQ demonstration" (Roache and Haynes 2020). Duda's close win in the second round election and continuous rallies prove that a considerable part of the society does not believe that their interests are being properly represented and they do not lend their support to the head of state.

Donald Trump

Similarly, when Donald Trump became the president of the United States, many Americans protested to having such a controversial figure as their representative. Despite vowing to "make America great again," his actions and decisions angered the citizens, who felt that his efforts had an opposite effect (Tumulty 2017). His nationalist foreign policy and "no tolerance" approach led to an immigration crisis after Trump declared his wish to build a wall separating the American-Mexican border. He also issued an executive order denying entry into the United States to citizens from several Muslim-majority countries, losing the support of the traditionally allied states (Shear and Cooper 2017). Trump's behaviour proved repeatedly that he had no concept of presidential function, disregarding the principles of legal authority and giving prominence to the individual, not the institution itself. He was known for notoriously using official social media accounts to express his personal views as well as often controversial and false statements, such as the infamous "Despite the constant negative press covfefe" tweet (LaFrance 2019).

Trump in the role of the president did not encourage respect or support, being several times accused of rape and engaging with prostitutes. As his presidency progressed, the sign "Not my president" became a slogan for those dissatisfied with the outcome of the elections of 2016, signalling their refusal to identify with the elected representative and his opinions. "Donald Trump does not represent our values, and therefore we refuse to honour him on Presidents Day," said one of the organisers of an anti-Trump rally in Chicago, aptly called Not My President Day protest (Hansler 2017). In 2020, the United States witnessed the rise of Black Lives Matter demonstrations, following the deaths of Breonna Taylor and George Floyd due to police's brutality. The Trump administration presented the country as "being overrun by violent leftwing protesters and 'domestic terrorists'" and encouraged violent interventions from government forces, stoking racial tensions (Beckett 2020). Trump's refusal to acknowledge and repudiate the wrongs of his supporters, as well as the demonization of his political opponents led to outrage within the nation and diminished America's standing worldwide.

However, with such a strong personality, Trump continued to draw admiration from his followers, despite the evident abuse of power entrusted to him by the people. His confidence and radical judgement lured them with the suggestion of authority and the elusive "better future." Although being branded as "the most deliberately divisive president of the past 100 years," the race to the White House in the 2020 presidential elections was very close (Bryant 2020). Even weeks after Joe Biden's victory had been confirmed, many of Trump's ardent supporters did not believe in the legitimacy of the voting and suspect falsification of the ballots.

Conclusion

As we have observed, even though we have progressed and evolved, overcome many obstacles, our present system of governance still has many flaws. Shakespeare's history plays illustrate that some of the shortcomings of exercising political power have been present for far longer than we would think and that, unfortunately, even after four hundred years we are unable to overpower them. Richard II exercises authority due to his royal bloodline despite his apparent inadequacy, Henry IV rebels against a rightful ruler, Prince Hal does not believe in the sanctity of traditional authority and deceives his subjects, Richard III adapts Machiavellian theory that the end justifies the means and claws his way to the throne. Even though the premise of democracy differs substantially from the monarchy described by the Bard, it is evident that neither of the systems works perfectly outside the theory. Their major flaw lies in the human factor and the universally known truth – power corrupts.

As presented in the history plays, it is not enough to be charismatic in order to become a successful leader, one needs also the support of people and the law. Similarly, holding the position of power without being able to perform it properly hinders the authority's responsibility to care for its subjects and always act in their best interest. Hence, it is frequently noticed that the democratic system operates on the performance, the appearance rather than on the contender's competence, a phenomenon observed already in Shakespeare's works. This leads to decline in public trust towards authority, manifested by the rise of social activity and protests against the ruling powers. The 2020 presidential elections revealed a deep divide within the nation, both in Poland and the United States. The slight difference in the number of votes between the two opposing candidates demonstrates how polarised the society truly is and that an agreement between the two parties is not feasible. This situation exposes the crisis of representation when, no matter the outcome, a great part of the citizens believes that the authority is no longer representative of its subjects.

References

Amt, E., and K.A. Smith. 2018. *Medieval England, 500-1500: A Reader.* 2nd ed. Toronto, ON: University of Toronto Press.

"Authority." n.d. *Oxford English Dictionary Online.* https://en.oxforddictionaries.com/definition/authority. Accessed 12 July 2019.

Beckett, L. 2020. "Nearly All Black Lives Matter Protests Are Peaceful Despite Trump Narrative, Report Finds." https://www.theguardian.com/world/2020/sep/05/nearly-all-black-lives-matter-protests-are-peaceful-despite-trump-narrative-report-finds. Accessed 16 September 2020.

Bevington, D. 1999. "William Shakespeare – Shakespeare's Plays and Poems." https://www.britannica.com/biography/William-Shakespeare/The-early-histories. Accessed 12 July 2019.

Boffey, D. 2018. "EU Demands Action by Poland's Government to Protect Rule of Law." https://www.theguardian.com/world/2018/may/14/eu-demands-action-by-poland-government-to-protect-rule-of-law. Accessed 22 July 2019.

Bryant, N. 2020. "US Election 2020: Why Donald Trump Lost." https://www.bbc.com/news/election-us-2020-54788636. Accessed 27 January 2021.

Calderwood, J.L. 1979. *Metadrama in Shakespeare's Henriad: Richard II to Henry V.* Berkeley, CA: University of California Press.

Cohen, D. 2002. "History and the Nation in *Richard II* and *Henry IV.*" *Studies in English Literature, 1500-1900* 42(2). 293-315. https://www.jstor.org/stable/1556116. Accessed 15 July 2019.

Colley, S. 1986. "Richard III and Herod." *Shakespeare Quarterly* 37(4). 451-458. https://www.jstor.org/stable/2870676?seq=1. Accessed 15 July 2019.

Dickinson, H. 1961. "The Reformation of Prince Hal." *Shakespeare Quarterly* 12(1). 33-46. https://www.jstor.org/stable/2867269?seq=1. Accessed 15 July 2019.

Donkor, M. 2016. "*Richard III* and Machiavelli." https://www.bl.uk/shakespeare/articles/richard-iii-and-machiavelli. Accessed 25 July 2019.

Duval Smith, A. 2015. "Law to Curb Power of Top Court 'Is End of Democracy in Poland.'" https://www.theguardian.com/world/2015/dec/28/poland-law-curb-power-top-court-end-democracy-andrzej-duda. Accessed 22 July 2019.

Hansler, J. 2017. "Thousands Gather for Not My President Day Protests." https://abcnews.go.com/US/thousands-gather-presidents-day-protests/story?id=45610079. Accessed 22 July 2019.

Hattaway, M. 2002. "The Shakespearean History Play." In: M. Hattaway (ed.), *The Cambridge Companion to Shakespeare's History Plays*. Cambridge, UK: Cambridge University Press, 3-24.

Kendall, D. 2010. *Sociology in Our Times: The Essentials*. 7th ed. Belmont, CA: Wadsworth, Cengage Learning.

Kingsbury, K. 2016. "Shakespeare's Richard III: Physiognomy, Physiology and Destiny in Syzygy: Villainy as a Cosmogony of Consequences." https://www.academia.edu/25732384/Shakespeares_Richard_III_Physiognomy_Physiology_and_Destiny_in_Syzygy_Villainy_as_a_Cosmogony_of_Consequences. Accessed 26 July 2019.

Kołodziej, S. 2015. "Wizerunek polityczny Andrzeja Dudy w prezydenckiej kampanii wyborczej Prawa i Sprawiedliwości w 2015 roku." *Studia Politicae Universitatis Silesiensis* 15. 233-265.

LaFrance, A. 2019. "Covfefe: The Real Meaning of a Trump Typo Turned Meme." https://www.theatlantic.com/politics/archive/2019/01/covfefe-trump-typo-turned-meme/579763/. Accessed 22 July 2019.

Leggatt, A. 2003. *Shakespeare's Political Drama: The History Plays and the Roman Plays*. London–New York: Routledge.

Mabillard, A. 2000. "Representations of Kingship and Power in Shakespeare's Second Tetralogy." http://www.shakespeare-online.com/essays/Power.html. Accessed 12 July 2019.

Manin, B., et al. 1999. "Elections and Representation." In: A. Przeworski et al. (eds.), *Democracy, Accountability, and Representation*. Cambridge, UK: Cambridge University Press, 29-54.

Michalski, P. 2016. "Mija rok od zaprzysiężenia Andrzeja Dudy na prezydenta. Oto bilans najważniejszych obietnic." https://www.rmf24.pl/fakty/polska/news-mija-rok-od-zaprzysiezenia-andrzeja-dudy-na-prezydenta-oto-b,nId,2246753. Accessed 22 July 2019.

Parvini, N. 2012. *Shakespeare's History Plays. Rethinking Historicism*. Edinburgh, UK: Edinburgh University Press.

"Plurality Electoral Systems." n.d. *ACE Electoral Knowledge Network*. https://aceproject.org/main/english/bd/bda01b.htm. Accessed 16 September 2020.

"Polish Election: Andrzej Duda Says LGBT 'Ideology' Worse Than Communism." 2020. *BBC News*. https://www.bbc.com/news/world-europe-53039864. Accessed 16 September 2020.

Rapp, C. 2013. *Holy Bishops in Late Antiquity: The Nature of Christian Leadership in an Age of Transition*. Berkeley, CA: University of California Press.

Roache, M., and S. Haynes. 2020. "Poland LGBTQ Protests: What's Next in Fight for LGBTQ Rights." https://time.com/5878424/poland-lgbt-protests-police-brutality/. Accessed 16 September 2020.

Shakespeare, W. 2011. *King Henry IV, Part 1*. In: R. Proudfoot et al. (eds.), *The Arden Shakespeare Complete Works*. London: Bloomsbury, 361-392.

——. *King Henry IV, Part 2*. In: R. Proudfoot et al. (eds.), *The Arden Shakespeare Complete Works*. London: Bloomsbury, 393-428.

——. *King Richard II*. In: R. Proudfoot et al. (eds.), *The Arden Shakespeare Complete Works*. London: Bloomsbury, 671-700.

——. *King Richard III*. In: R. Proudfoot et al. (eds.), *The Arden Shakespeare Complete Works*. London: Bloomsbury, 701-742.

Shear, M.D., and H. Cooper. 2017. "Trump Bars Refugees and Citizens of 7 Muslim Countries." https://www.nytimes.com/2017/01/27/us/politics/trump-syrian-refugees.html. Accessed 22 July 2019.

Tumulty, K. 2017. "How Donald Trump Came Up with 'Make America Great Again.'" https://www.washingtonpost.com/politics/how-donald-trump-came-up-with-make-america-great-again/2017/01/17/fb6acf5e-dbf7-11e6-ad42-f3375f271c9c_story.html. Accessed 22 June 2019.

Weber, M. 1964. *Theory of Social and Economic Organization*. Translated by A.M. Henderson and T. Parsons. New York: The Free Press.

EWELINA SZALECKA
Jagiellonian University

Jacek Woszczerowicz's Appropriation of Shakespeare's *Richard III* in Communist Poland

Abstract

In the aftermath of World War II, Polish theatregoers witnessed a cultural revival in which Shakespeare and his works held a significant place. In 1947, two years after the end of the Nazi occupation and the large-scale destruction of Poland, the Ministry of Culture and Art organized the Shakespeare Festival that manifested the extent to which his works were processed by the nation's new political power. Although the 1947 Festival was sometimes associated with extreme bravery and subversion, it was dominated by ideologically and politically selected interpretations. In the same year, communists took control of the government in Poland by winning blatantly falsified elections. In this context of new oppression, many theatre artists used allusions and metaphors to express the prevailing view on the contemporary situation and to surpass the imposed censorship. One of the most significant theatrical productions of the period, which manifested dissatisfaction with the communist leadership, was Shakespeare's *Richard III* directed by Jacek Woszczerowicz in 1960 and performed at Warsaw's Ateneum Theatre. Woszczerowicz, who also played the leading role, appropriated contemporary social concerns as the context of his staging. His bold interpretation, which became known worldwide through Jan Kott's seminal paper *Shakespeare, Our Contemporary*, conjured the image of what the eminent Polish critic called the "Grand Mechanism" of history. Kott's view of Shakespeare's history play in relation to the twentieth-century violent political changes confirmed its historical contemporaneity and universality. His readings of Shakespeare's plays, as well as the effort to update his dramas in the specific historical and political setting, were common and hugely influenced Polish audiences' approach to the Bard's works. The 1960 performance indirectly commented upon the turbulent situation and effectively communicated the topical message to all theatregoers. Woszczerowicz's ingenious reading of *Richard III* turned out to be extremely popular with Polish theatre critics and audiences alike. He used Richard's role to demonstrate his personal and artistic discontent with the current situation and redefined the character in contemporary terms, presenting his audience with a fascinating study of a man who was a product of a totalitarian regime. In this way, Woszczerowicz's innovative rendering served as a mirror to the political problems of his time.

Keywords: Shakespeare, World War II, communism, Poland, Woszczerowicz, theatre

Streszczenie

Po zakończeniu II wojny światowej polska publiczność teatralna stała się świadkiem odbudowy kulturowej struktury kraju, w której twórczość Szekspira odegrała znaczącą rolę. W 1947 roku, dwa lata po okupacji i zniszczeniu Polski przez nazistowskie Niemcy, Ministerstwo Kultury i Sztuki zorganizowało Festiwal Szekspirowski, który pokazał, w jaki sposób nowa siła polityczna narodu przetwarzała dzieła dramaturga. Pomimo że festiwal uznawano za symbol odwagi i kojarzono z działalnością wywrotową, przeważały w nim interpretacje ideologicznie narzucone przez ówczesne władze. W tym samym roku komuniści wygrali bowiem jawnie sfałszowane wybory i przejęli kontrolę nad polskim rządem. Kraj stracił swoją suwerenność, a jego obywatele walczyli przez całe dziesięciolecia, by odzyskać wolność słowa. W kontekście nowego ucisku politycznego wielu artystów teatralnych zaczęło posługiwać się aluzjami i metaforami, aby wyrazić sprzeciw wobec ówczesnej sytuacji i aby zwalczać narzuconą cenzurę. Jedną z najważniejszych inscenizacji teatralnych tego okresu, która wyrażała głębokie niezadowolenie z rządów partii komunistycznej, był Szekspirowski *Ryszard III* w reżyserii Jacka Woszczerowicza, wystawiony w warszawskim Teatrze Ateneum w 1960 roku. Woszczerowicz, który był również odtwórcą głównej roli, wykorzystał ówczesne obawy społeczne jako kontekst swojego przedstawienia. Jego śmiała interpretacja, która zdobyła światową sławę dzięki przełomowej pracy Jana Kotta pt. *Szekspir Współczesny*, przywołuje opisany przez krytyka obraz działania Wielkiego Mechanizmu. Stanowisko Kotta wyrażające jego stosunek do sztuki historycznej w odniesieniu do gwałtownych przemian politycznych XX wieku potwierdziło jej historyczną uniwersalność i współczesność. Odczytanie tekstu dramatycznego Szekspira w ten oto sposób, a także próba zaktualizowania jego sztuk poprzez umieszczenie ich w konkretnym kontekście historycznym i politycznym były częstą praktyką, która miała ogromny wpływ na to, jak polska publiczność rozumiała twórczość angielskiego dramaturga. Widzowie z łatwością podążali za narzuconą interpretacją i potrafili patrzeć na spektakl przez pryzmat totalitarnych doświadczeń własnego kraju. Przedstawienie z 1960 roku, które zostało dostosowane do ówczesnych realiów w Polsce, pośrednio komentowało burzliwą sytuację i skutecznie komunikowało aktualne przesłanie wszystkim odbiorcom. Niekonwencjonalne odczytanie Woszczerowicza cieszyło się ogromnym zainteresowaniem zarówno wśród krytyków teatralnych, jak i publiczności. Reżyser i aktor użył roli Ryszarda do uzewnętrznienia osobistego i artystycznego niezadowolenia z sytuacji politycznej i przedefiniował główną postać, wykorzystując współczesne odniesienia, aby zaprezentować swojej publiczności fascynujące studium człowieka – produktu totalitaryzmu. Nowatorska realizacja *Ryszarda III* posłużyła za zwierciadło, w którym odbiły się problemy polityczne tamtych czasów.

Słowa kluczowe: Szekspir, II wojna światowa, komunizm, Polska, Woszczerowicz, teatr

> *Many from my theatrical milieu, and not only, do not want to realize that theatre and acting is a fight, or at least a protest against everything that is irreversible, or what wants to appear as irreversible. Against everything that is evil.* [...] *Chaplin was an excellent representative of art understood in this way. And he excellently followed the beautiful tradition of his craft. He used to be a buffoon, which also meant to be the representative of the opposition, so well paid by the Mighty, just like in Shakespeare.*
>
> (a letter of J. Woszczerowicz to Z. Kliszko, qtd. in Kompel 2004, 169)[1]

Theatrical Interpretations – The Play's Universality

Shakespeare's *Richard III* has inspired a variety of interpretations over the centuries. Whether staged as a moral history, tyrant tragedy, religious or political satire or a combination of all of the above, the play does not only enter academic survey, but also people's lives and everyday culture.

1 All translations from Polish are provided by the author.

Its worldwide heritage as one of the most timeless and most frequently adapted of the playwright's histories continues to have a significant effect on contemporary audiences.

Although the play went through an enormous number of stage adaptations, there is no agreement on how to render its villainous protagonist. Each literary period or movement brought different criticism and placed him among distinct literary or theatrical options. The early Shakespearean critic, Charles Gildon, writing in 1725 argued that Richard "is not a fit Character for the Stage, being shocking in all he does; and we think [...] that Providence is too flow, and too mild in his Punishment" (Gildon 1725, 383). When compared to Atreus and Medea, whom he pronounced "passionate sinners," Richard is "a calm Villain" who "murders deliberately" (383). He called Shakespeare's histories "Draugths of the Lives of Princes, brought into Dialogue" and the "mixture of furious and comical Characters," which "cannot be placed under Tragedy, because they contain no Tragic Imitation" (372). In his *Observations on King Richard III*, Samuel Johnson (1825) called some parts of the play "trifling," "shocking" and "improbable" (168). In his view, Shakespeare's history plays are neither comedies nor tragedies, but

> compositions of a distinct kind; exhibiting the real state of sublunary nature, which partakes of good and evil, joy and sorrow, mingled with endless variety of proportion and innumerable modes of combination; and expressing the course of the world, in which the loss of one is the gain of another; in which, at the same time, the reveller is hasting to his wine, and the mourner burying his friend; in which the malignity of one is sometimes defeated by the frolick of another; and many mischiefs and many benefits are done and hindered without design. (Johnson 1825, 109)

And so Richard has been associated with the dramatic character of Vice from medieval morality plays, with a scheming "murderous Machiavel" (*Henry VI, Part 3*, 3.2.193), or with a deceptive actor or tragedian whose public performances have been considered highly theatrical. There have also been stage adaptations which attempted to humanize his villainy. Sigmund Freud famously commented on the play's opening passage that "we feel that we ourselves might become like Richard, that on a small scale, indeed, we are already like him" and goes on to call Shakespeare's creation "an enormous magnification of something we find in ourselves" (qtd. in Hillman 2012, 160). It can be assumed that from the very beginning the character and his twisted body dominate the text and performance, and so his deformity has been employed in a variety of similar contexts. Richard's solitude, to a certain extent, makes him a wicked human being, or can be perceived as something purely symbolic. Some critics stress the importance of Richard's violation of "fair proportion" and argue that there is a link between an individual's self-division or alienation, in this particular case the king who is the head of the body politics, and the society's disintegration (Shakespeare 2015, 1.1.18, all further references to this edition of *King Richard III* are by act, scene and verse number only). This may throw the kingdom into a state of disorder, which, in its most extreme form, leads to the outbreak of civil war. Richard's commonwealth is divided against itself analogically to his self-consuming dissembling nature.

In his universality, Richard makes his audience identify with him for political, moral or ideological reasons and provokes extreme responses. Not only is he a participant of dramatic action, but also a commentator of his appearance, the events and the "Plots [he] have laid" (1.1.32). His opening phrase, "Now is the winter of our discontent" (1.1.1), resonates quite often with "our discontent" with contemporary political environments. These and other points led some critics to discuss the continued importance of this particular play, its universality and the timelessness of its themes. The relevance of such studies for Shakespearian theatre today and its immediate impact on stage and film productions and reception merits meticulous attention. What follows here is a brief survey on an unconventional theatrical performance of *Richard III* by Jacek Woszczerowicz, popularised by Jan Kott's seminal commentary on Shakespeare's universalism, and on its role in making the audiences politically aware at an inauspicious moment of Polish history.

The Appropriation of Shakespeare in Post-war Poland

Shakespeare has been a living influence in Poland ever since his dramatic art reached its borders. One of the great paradoxes that can be observed, however, is that the significant period of flourishing of his *Richard III* in the Polish culture is to be traced back to the years after World War II, to the communist and post-communist era. During the Nazi occupation, the country's multicultural artistic life was brutally destroyed. Theatres were shut, many intellectuals, including university professors, artists, or writers were arrested or transported to concentration camps. Despite severe restrictions, Poland cultivated a range of underground cultural activities, including theatrical productions. The Nazi's plan to suppress the Polish culture met with a strong and spirited resistance from the theatre artists and enthusiasts. During this seemingly infertile period, many poets and artists derived their artistic inspiration from Shakespeare and searched for political and literary meanings in his works. Jacek Woszczerowicz, whose treatment of Shakespeare's *Richard III* is commonly considered the most significant and unconventional appropriation of the play in Poland under the communist regime, belongs to this group. Krystyna Kujawińska Courtney (2002, section 7, para. 2) notes that during the years of global conflict Woszczerowicz became "obsessed" with the text. In those difficult times of mass interrogations, numerous arrests and persecution, he would hide in his family village of Siedlce, located in eastern Poland, for five years (Kujawińska Courtney 2002, section 7, para. 2). Shakespeare's works accompanied him all the way and helped to endure those endless days (Kompel 2004, 64). It was then that he started to formulate his future theatre plans of staging *Richard III*. He had to wait twenty years to fulfil his ambitious undertaking.

Woszczerowicz's acting career was abruptly interrupted when the Nazi German forces invaded Poland and it is difficult to say how his development as an actor would have gone if it had not been for the war. One thing is certain: the outbreak of World War II had a negative effect on the artistic career of Woszczerowicz who, at that time, was a thirty-five-year-old aspiring theatre star undergoing the process of change from a skilled craftsman to a distinguished artist. He was forced to leave the stage at a time when he started to be entrusted with more demanding roles and tasks. When the war had come to an end, Woszczerowicz moved to Łódź, which temporarily functioned as Poland's capital at that time and which, after the years of forced artistic inactivity, offered good working and living conditions (Kompel 2004, 68). The exultation over the experience of freedom after the period of occupation awakened in the Polish theatre artists the feelings of courage and the growing sense of national individualism. Theatre people were striving to help the Polish theatre to recover from the devastation caused by the war, and to regain its high global standing.

Two years after the war, the Ministry of Culture and Art organized the national Shakespeare Festival, with the finale held in Warsaw, which revealed the Bard's crucial role in the revival of Polish cultural life (Kujawińska

Courtney 2016, 7). In the exact same year, Poland became the communist Polish People's Republic under the Stalinist rule. Thousands of voters were disqualified, many members of the Polish opposition party were locked in prisons and the official election results were falsified, giving the communists the overwhelming majority of the votes. The 1947 election was a mere formality that marked the establishment of the communist regime. In view of this new tense political situation, the 1947 Shakespeare Festival was sometimes perceived as a condemnation of the Soviet state and Marxist ideology for their subversion of Polish nation and culture (Kujawińska Courtney 2016, 24). It was the first great demonstration of performing art after the war, in which almost all scenes in Poland competed for the title of the best staging of the Shakespearean play. Kazimierz Braun claims that the notoriety and tumult which surrounded the competition were generated and controlled by the communist party in power to hide the ban of the classics of Polish literature (qtd. in Romanowska 2017, 24). The freedom of speech was non-existent at that time and the regime often exercised power to impose limitations, be it formal or ideological, on the theatre or on any other form of public expression and to use art for its own purposes (Romanowska 2017, 24). The struggle between the communist regime and Polish society could have been observed in the theatre, in which Shakespeare's political allusions and metaphors were appropriated both to praise and to criticise the new system. In this way Shakespeare's plays accompanied Polish theatre in taking an active part in the forthcoming fight against the new authorities.

The Grand Mechanism of *Richard III*

Joanna Godlewska notes that the competing playwrights underwent censorial control and the plays which did not follow the established interpretation or which were influenced by Jan Kott's collection of essays *Shakespeare, Our Contemporary* were not allowed to take part in theatrical rivalry (qtd. in Kujawińska Courtney 2002, section 7, para. 4). Kott's provocative and original study effectively challenged the traditional views and revolutionised Shakespeare's literary criticism and theatrical reception. His seminal work could offer, in a sense, consolation to those who experienced the post-war extreme political situation, showing that those times were merely a repeated mechanism. In his opening essay entitled "The Kings," he argues that the twentieth-century Polish readers of Shakespeare must have understood his universality and contemporariness, or at least must have identified their current political situation and experiences with what is presented on stage (Kott 1966, 5). Jean-Jacques Gautier, commenting on Woszczerowicz's production of *Richard III*, made similar observations. It is his contention that one may find some well-known current facts in the play text, which is about political upheavals, arrests, prisons, murders, intrigues, changing sides, building and resolving alliances. It shows the times marked by fear, which contemporary audience may identify with. He says that "we live in times of Shakespeare's drama, surrounded by fumes of hate and blood. Not Julius Caesar, but the world of Richard III, which is full of danger and growing fear, is closer to us" (qtd. in Kompel 2004, 144).

Kott maintains that the contemporary audience can find these parallels mainly in the Bard's histories and can perceive the deaths of their characters as a historical and political necessity (Kott 1966, 5). In Shakespeare, history does not change with time. Each of his history plays begins with the struggle for the throne and ends with the death of the usurping king. Each legitimate monarch marks his reign with mischiefs and is eventually overthrown, murdered and replaced by the new ruler, who also becomes an abuser of power. Kott observes that after reading all of Shakespeare's history plays, one may realize that they blur into one story that continuously repeats itself (7). He compares this mechanism of history to a grand staircase and depicts the way the kings walk up these grand stairs to gain the throne. When they reach the final step, they can only fall into the abyss (7).

In *Richard III*, Shakespeare for the first time allows us to see the human face of this Grand Mechanism and gives us the protagonist who is its "mastermind," its "will" and "awareness" (Kott 1966, 41). To Kott, Richard is a prince who understands the essence of Machiavellian power politics. He is a practical politician with an ambitious aim to acquire ultimate power. His machinations, scheming and manipulations are all amoral. He shapes the surrounding world in his hands as if it was made of clay and he creates history himself (41). The critic also observes that, paradoxically, the higher Richard steps, the smaller he becomes. The Grand Mechanism is stronger than the king. It absorbs him and makes him one of the wheels it puts into motion. Richard is no longer a murderer, but a victim. At the end of the play, he is frightened and weak, trying to escape and to save his life. The realm he struggled to win is now worth less than a horse.

When asked about aspects that fascinated him in the play, Woszczerowicz answered:

> It is the same that fascinates people in all Shakespeare for over 350 years. The work is about kings, murders, wars, hypocrisy, love, ambition, and most of all, about the mechanism of power. It is a commentary upon this mechanism. It places next to each other the backstage of theatre and the backstage of politics, the glamour of theatre and the glamour of politics, acting in theatre and acting in politics. What fascinates me in this play [...] if Balzac defined his work as human comedy, Shakespeare hanged over the entrance to his theatre the motto: *Totus mundus agit histrionem.* [...] This time it is a bloody comedy. Marked by humour. There are many people there. The closer we get to the end, the less characters from the previous acts we see. The reason for this is high mortality. These are the times we live in. The action moves fast. Sometimes it is accompanied by jest, and sometimes by the sound of a head rolling on the scaffold wood. (Woszczerowicz qtd. in Kompel 2004, 125-126)

In an interview for *Kurier Polski*, Woszczerowicz said:

> The character of Richard has something which, in my opinion, is very contemporary. This man, who is fascinated by wrongdoing, who is intelligent and stands above the rest is an example of an individual who overcomes certain human barriers, and while doing so, he must lose because he ceases to take people into account. (Woszczerowicz qtd. in Kompel 2004, 126)

Woszczerowicz was generally known as a meticulous and conscious actor who closely studied his play texts and secondary literature. His innovative, fresh and bold interpretations were praised by many critics. His roles, which were devised with the support of his vast knowledge, skills and in-depth reading of each text always helped the audience to see new shades of a character and to perceive a well-known play in a new light. Grażyna Kompel (2004) claims that the actor had a strong respect for literature and that he was aware of the ways in which language changes and evolves with time (152). That is why Woszczerowicz was always passionate about and preoccupied with finding the right word in his film and theatre productions and also with removing obsolete words from the texts he used. In this way, he would become an editor of any dramatic text he staged, including his *Richard III* in Józef Paszkowski's translation (Kompel 2004, 152).

It is significant that Woszczerowicz appears as the translator of the play on the first page of the 1997 theatre programme. In all probability the amount of textual modifications and engagement on the actor's part were so intense that later directors almost identified him with the author of the Polish text. Kompel (2004) notes that close and detailed language analyses, so characteristic of Woszczerowicz's style of working on a role, contributed to the fact that he was often referred to as "maniac" or "weirdo" (152). In truth, he was a "maniac" and a "weirdo," a "buffoon" and a "tragedian" at the same time.

His physical conditions made him very characteristic, and so when he appeared on stage, he was always in the centre of attention, just like his Richard. Henryk Szeletyński writes that he was perhaps "the most characteristic among the most characteristic actors," and also claims that he was "fascinated by the colouring and disproportions of the inner and outer physiognomy of characters, that one may discover during the process of staging" ("Jacek Woszczerowicz" 2016, para. 3). Woszczerowicz was a short and stocky man with long arms and hoarse voice. While playing Richard, he had to look up in order to see people's faces and this made him comic and hilarious (Kott 1966, 72). Juliusz Osterwa, a famous Polish actor and director, once even called him a person physically incapable of practising an acting profession ("Urodził się Jacek Woszczerowicz" 1989). The actor put a lot of work and effort to overcome his bodily limitations, to make his vocal register lower and to improve his physical prowess. After many years of training he became as athletic as an acrobat and he learned how to control the force of his look. He changed the proportions of his face exercising his facial muscles and he mastered flexibility and expressiveness of his hand movement ("Urodził się Jacek Woszczerowicz" 1989). Zofia Jasińska (qtd. in Kompel 2004, 131) pays attention to details, such as a characteristic grimace that appeared on his face, the odd gestures and poses he took, and the incredible costumes which always completed his characterisation. His renditions were always consistent, innovative, peculiar, memorable, and marked by a strong tendency towards comedy and grotesque. They were "realistically human" and "fantastically demonic" at the same time.

In the interwar theatrical milieu, Woszczerowicz had an opinion of being exclusively a comic actor. This assessment appears to be partially fair, considering the fact that most of his roles were rendered in a comic way. On the surface, his renditions contained many comic elements, but the type of humour he consciously employed allowed the audience to perceive the depth of each character. The choice of the comedic means was partially dictated by his physical condition. Woszczerowicz provoked laughter among audiences and he could not have been able to achieve a similarly strong response if he had implemented methods and techniques specific to a tragic actor. In an interview for *Głos Poranny*, he admitted that he felt like a comedian, not only professionally, but also personally, and that, because it was extremely difficult to differentiate between the comic and the serious, one ought to take Stanisławski's approach that a comedian should strive to bring out from a performance "the deepest and the most valuable aspects of all things and of all manifestations of life" (qtd. in Kompel 2004, 44). Here Woszczerowicz takes up his ideological stance, which offers a view on his own perspective on acting. He argues that behind a comedic role there is a deeper meaning, which is about more than raising a meaningless laugh among audiences. It can also be observed that some ten years before the war began, theatre critics had changed their focus from the description of the external form of the characters he played to the discussion of their psychological profiles. They attempted to find a connection between his characters' personalities and the emotional and mental processes that they underwent. In the roles he created the outward appearance always defined the inside. It could have been one of the reasons why the actor did not hesitate to render his future Richard with the use of exclusively comedic means.

Woszczerowicz's rendition of Richard met with an unprecedented success. Newspapers would compare the role to an earthquake which changed the theatre forever or would call the production "a big victory of the old writer and contemporary actor." Some would even encourage viewers to organize trips to Warsaw's Ateneum Theatre to see the real contemporary Shakespeare (Kompel 2004, 126). No other play directed by Woszczerowicz was so acclaimed and no other play received so many reviews. The number of its productions exceeded all the previous ones. It was staged for over two years, with ninety eight performances given at the Ateneum Theatre in the Warsaw's district, Powiśle, and one in Paris, only two times a week due to Woszczerowicz's failing health (Kompel 2004, 128). Audiences would come to Warsaw from all over the country to admire the actor's role and some would literally beg for admission. The auditorium was always full. Getting a theatre ticket well before the scheduled performance became almost impossible (127).

The 1960 Performance

In 1960 in the Ateneum Theatre in Warsaw, Woszczerowicz entered the stage as Richard III. Jan Kott admits that he had never seen such a "dense" Shakespeare before, and since he had watched the play for the first time in the Warsaw's House of Culture, he could not wait to see the performance again (Kott 1966, 71). While creating the role, Woszczerowicz studied the Tudor and the Plantagenet royal family history, his rendition, however, was hardly historical. Just like Shakespeare's (Kompel 2004, 129). He broke away with the Romantic tradition and rendered the character with comedic means. The critics generally agree that his rendition intellectually surpassed the achievements of his most acclaimed predecessors. Jan Kott commented on the performance:

> The room was full and the tiny platform was almost covered by the crowd. No special lightning and no props were used. Woszczerowicz took off his coat and remained dressed in a thick black pull-over with a high collar. He rolled up his left sleeve exposing a withered hand. On the forefinger of his right hand there was a large ring. Lady Anne wore an ordinary dress. The man in the black pull-over had murdered her father and husband. Now he asked her to sleep with him. The black pull-over, with a collar covering the lower part of his chin, looked like armour. But does one need armour to commit a murder? [...] He walks in briskly, dragging one of his feet slightly. He stops and begins to laugh. He says that the war is over, that peace has come, and jagged swords can be laid aside. From above, rows of iron bars are lowered down to the stage, one after the other, forming the background. Richard talks to himself, not to us. He laughs again, not at himself, but at us. He has a broad face, untidy hair, and wears a soiled and torn tunic. (Kott 1966, 52)

In his essay, Kott praises Jacek Woszczerowicz's stage adaptation of *Richard III*, whose independent interpretation of the play coincides with the ideas expressed by the critic in the first chapter of the book. The 1960 production was an unconventional undertaking marked by a non-traditional approach to politics and history. Having been both the director and the actor who played the leading role, Woszczerowicz gave a performance which the Polish audience, which not so long ago had witnessed the tragic consequences of the cult of the Nazi leader, understood, sympathized with and could relate to. It was one of the most awaited contemporary productions, advertised in advance, and a work of exceptional importance. In 1960, writing for *Przegląd Kulturalny*, Kott placed *Richard III* on the third position on the list of Shakespeare's plays numbered accordingly to the date of their last production in Warsaw (qtd. in Kompel 2004, 125). He based his survey on Wiktor Hahn's bibliography, and marked that it had been then sixty years since the last play, with Bolesław Ładnowski as Richard, was staged. Kott's publication and newspaper interviews with the actor served as a great support for Woszczerowicz's struggle to remind Poland about this rare theatre repertory position.

Following the common tradition of Renaissance writing about the body as reflecting the soul, Shakespeare made his character "rudely stamped" (1.1.16), "cheated of feature by dissembling Nature / Deformed, unfinished, sent before [his] time / into this breathing world, scarce half made up, / And that so lamely and unfashionable / That dogs bark at [him] as [he] halt by them" (1.1.19-23). Woszczerowicz emphasised Richard's disability and consciously made him smaller, or even dwarf-like, to show the audience that all his murders were not determined by fate. His Richard was a jester who laughed at peacetime and mocked it. Does it mean that one has to be a clown to become a tyrant?

Kott (1966) claims that buffoonery is "the highest form of contempt" (54). It is a philosophy of the most dangerous tyrants. Those who consider themselves buffoons, and who hold the whole world in contempt should be feared the most (54). Shakespeare's Richard is a great orchestrator of events and a great actor, even greater than Woszczerowicz, and he does not feel any shame to act as a buffoon. Just like many manipulative tyrants, he does not feel any shame at all. He stopped being a buffoon only when the performance came to an end. Until then, he was putting on a mask, manipulating, feigning pity, prayer and even his own fear. In the scene of the battle of Bosworth, he asked for a light armour. It seemed to be an unintended request of a man in fear, which made him appear more human. Woszczerowicz followed such interpretation and effectively communicated the meaning to the audience. Kott argues that his understanding of Shakespeare's protagonist has "a mark a genius" (54). His character was a self-conscious clown who lived in a world of buffoonery and this made him "the most terrifying kind of tyrant" (54). During the coronation, Woszczerowicz's Richard climbed the throne with his back towards the audience, dragging his leg behind. He looked heavy and decrepit, and he stopped before he reached the final steps (Kompel 2004, 130). The "royal robe" he was attired in was made hastily in a few hours. The action moved fast. There was no time for celebrations. His throne was put on an empty stage, and Jan Kott claims it resembled the gallows made of wooden boards. The small man sat on his thrown, holding the sceptre in his hand. The critic compares Richard's royal insignia to the gold stick carried by a man, who knew well its actual value (Kott 1966, 54).

A reviewer from *Współczesność* comments that in the final act, the audience witnessed the collapse of the tyrant, who fell into the abyss from the last step of the grand staircase. He became a weak human being, full of fear, who sensed that his life was threatened (Kompel 2004, 130). No longer a tyrant, nor a king, he would run at the centre of the stage and scream with a voice of an ordinary man: "A horse a horse, my kingdom for a horse!" (5.4.7). At that moment the boundary between performance and real life was crossed and Woszczerowicz's calling resonated on the Warsaw's streets, outside the theatre building (Kompel 2004, 130). Soon, Richard was replaced by a new, young king, who closed the play uttering a prayer for England's lasting peace. The bars fell on the stage, one after another, in the same way as they did in the opening scene. Unexpectedly, Henry VII made a "crowing sound," twisted his face in a grimace, and this reminded the audience of the previous tyrant. When all of the bars fell, the man's face returned to its original look (Kott 1966, 55).

The 1960 performance is sometimes perceived as Woszczerowicz's commentary on the contemporary political situation rendered on stage. Richard's role was a manifestation of his personal and artistic dissatisfaction with Poland's communist leadership marked by the mixture of cunning, duplicity, arrogance, brutality and cruelty. It served as a medium for his political self-expression. The contemporary Polish audience, who had been taught how to read and respond to political implications and allusions in the theatre, easily recognized Woszczerowicz's message, which made the production very popular. Behind Woszczerowicz's Richard they could see any communist leader who was making all kinds of big false promises with little intention of keeping them. This adaptation was also a study of a self-interested ruler of a modern tyrannical realm, a product of totalitarianism. The actor and director addressed the issue of the banality of evil and turned Richard's physical appearance into a grotesque parody. According to Zofia Jasińska, he made the character both "hideous and ugly" and "plain and funny." He took away from the evil "the wedges of pathos and heroism," and left it with its "ugliness and ordinariness" (qtd. in Kompel 2004, 131). Leopold Kielanowski, in his detailed study of Woszczerowicz's creation, adds that:

> The actor attempted to show that a tyrant does not have to be attired in Caesar's robes, or display the traits of highness. Neither does he need to hide his monstrosity. The animal fear makes people believe in everything he says, against logic. A strong contempt for everything that surrounds him is the most fundamental feature of Richard in Woszczerowicz's interpretation. No one even tries to stand against his mischiefs. Everyone becomes his partner [...]. He proves that one can be the smallest person on earth and the biggest criminal at the same time. We may easily identify Woszczerowicz's Richard with any other evil dictator of the period. [...] He creates in front of our eyes a terrifying vision of the world marked by crime [...] in which he is both an actor and a keen observer. (Kielanowski qtd. in Kompel 2004, 141)

Kielanowski also comments on the significance of the stage design. As was mentioned before, there were absolutely no props besides the movable bars, designed by Wojciech Sieciński, which constituted the background of this dark tragedy. Sometimes they were used as prison bars and sometimes as a gateway to the castle (Kompel 2004, 139). The reviewer argues that they conveyed the message that "the world is, and will remain, a prison" (143). In the final act, in which the young Henry gives a speech about peace, the end of fighting, and the end of torments in prisons, they would fall onto the stage, after each sentence he pronounced, to symbolize his cynicism and to visually contradict his words (143). One tyrant has died, the other will replace him.

This interpretation provoked a bit of controversy. The Polish Theatre in Warsaw refused to stage Woszczerowicz's plays. Rumour also has it that during the performance of *Richard III* at the 1962 Paris Festival, the actor replaced the word "England" with the word "Poland." When he came back, he had to face the authorities and defend himself against the attacks. The leading communist party was angered by the supposed "treason" and the artist experienced great difficulties. The implication that Poland is a prison was very dangerous at the time of Cold War and could cost him a lot. As a matter of fact, the performance itself was a way to present his ideological stance. Woszczerowicz never expressed his views directly. He did it as an artist, for the theatre and for his audience. He understood the text and attempted to make it the means to transmit its universal values. While constructing the role of a tyrant, he also wanted to show its childish and cruel side. When he was asked about the main issues associated with building a role, he replied:

> The topic is always the same: a man – death – freedom – truth – a man. [...] It can be Joseph K., a man without a surname in Kafka's *The Trial* [...] or Socrates in the Cave of philosophers. These are all different characters, from different works, and written by different authors. One may say that they talk about the same, but in a different way. So different that we do not realize that they talk about the same, and we become fascinated by how they do it. The way they talk about this is the core of each text. (Woszczerowicz qtd. in Kompel 2004, 168)

Conclusion

Jacek Woszczerowicz died on 22 August 1970 and was buried at the Powązki Cemetery in Warsaw with a copy of Stanisław Wyspiański's essay "Studium o *Hamlecie*." This text, highly significant for the reception of Shakespeare in Poland, which served as an inspiration to many actors and directors, encouraged theatre artists to read Shakespeare carefully and to appropriate his plays in order to inspire thinking among the Polish audience. Krystyna Kujawińska Courtney (2016) states that "never in Polish history was the relationship between culture and politics as strong as under the communist regime" (30). And never before was the relationship between Shakespeare and Polish culture as strong as during the times of the post-war oppression. In the second half of the twentieth century, Polish theatre artists appropriated Shakespeare's plays to make the audience politically aware and to encourage them to think about the nature of tyranny. Woszczerowicz's adaptation, which served contemporary purposes and was used as a lens for viewing contemporary times, was not an exception. It was a common practise employed, for instance, by directors such as Kazimierz Braun or Andrzej Wajda (Kujawińska Courtney 2016, 34-35). Although this brief survey presents exciting results, there are still many aspects of Shakespeare's appropriation in the extreme circumstances of political oppression that require further study. Allusions to the then current situation introduced by modifications of the text, the implications created and the metaphors employed in this and a number of similar stage adaptations at that time were interpreted as a message by the Polish audience who in Shakespeare's universalism could find solace and some answers to contemporary problems.

Gildon, Ch. 1725. "Remarks on the Life and Death of *Richard III* and *Henry VIII.*" In: Dr. Sewell (ed.), *The Works of Mr. William Shakespeare*, vol. 7. London: J. Darby, 372-383.

Hillman, D. 2012. "Shakespeare and Freud." In: C. Bartolovich et al. (eds.), *Marx and Freud*. London: Continuum, 136-177.

"Jacek Woszczerowicz." 2016. *Encyklopedia Teatru Polskiego*. http://www.encyklopediateatru.pl/osoby/6219/jacek-woszczerowicz. Accessed 2 March 2020.

Johnson, S. 1825. "Preface to Shakespeare." In: F.P. Walesby (ed.), *The Works of Samuel Johnson LL.D.* London: Talboys and Wheeler, 109-168.

Kompel, G. 2004. *Jacek Woszczerowicz: Geniusz? Błazen? Mag?* Łódź: Biblioteka "Tygla Kultury."

Kott, J. 1966. *Shakespeare, Our Contemporary*. Translated by B. Taborski. New York: Doubleday Anchor Book.

Kujawińska Courtney, K. 2002. "Shakespeare in Poland: Selected Issues." https://www.academia.edu/8848677/Shakespeare_in_Poland. Accessed 8 February 2020.

——. 2016. "Celebrating Shakespeare under the Communist Regime in Poland." In: E. Sheen and I. Karremann (eds.), *Shakespeare in Cold War Europe: Conflict, Commemoration, Celebration*. London: Palgrave Macmillan, 23-36.

Romanowska, A. 2017. *Za głosem tłumacza: Szekspir Iwaszkiewicza, Miłosza i Gałczyńskiego*. Kraków: Wydawnictwo Uniwersytetu Jagiellońskiego.

Shakespeare, W. 2001. *King Henry VI Part 3*. Edited by John D. Cox, Eric Rasmussen. London: Bloomsbury.

——. 2015. *King Richard III*. Edited by J.R. Siemon. London: Bloomsbury.

"Urodził się Jacek Woszczerowicz." 1989. *Kalendarz Teatralny*. http://www.e-teatr.pl/pl/artykuly/3958,druk.html. Accessed 2 March 2020.

Afterword

AGNIESZKA ROMANOWSKA
Jagiellonian University

Strategic Partnership Project as Academic Training Ground

Abstract

The article presents the Erasmus Plus Strategic Partnership international project "NEW FACES: Facing Europe in Crisis: Shakespeare's World and Present Challenges" (2016-2019), which was granted to and realised by a consortium of nine European universities, including the Jagiellonian University. In each of the three subsequent academic years two to four teachers from the involved universities and about sixty students participated in a high-level collaborative programme which included seminars, lectures, panels and other academic and non-academic events. The article describes the origin of the project, its main aims and objectives, as well as the achieved results. It presents the participating institutions' fields of expertise and their contribution to the content of the teaching and research programme. It reports on the rules and requirements of students' participation and on the tasks and activities the students were expected to undertake. It also summarises the seminar offer and some of the academic events that were organised in the course of the project years, as well as presents some teaching methods and procedures, referring to an example of one of the seminars. It is argued that a Strategic Partnership project can be an effective academic training ground that enables students to actively acquire and develop a range of academic, social and international competences and skills vital for their involvement in shaping the future of Europe as prospective scholars and as citizens.

Keywords: Strategic Partnership, international project, education, Shakespeare, European crisis

Streszczenie

Artykuł jest poświęcony międzynarodowemu projektowi naukowo-dydaktycznemu „NEW FACES: Facing Europe in Crisis: Shakespeare's World and Present Challenges", zrealizowanemu w latach 2016-2019 przez konsorcjum dziewięciu europejskich uniwersytetów w ramach Partnerstwa Strategicznego Erasmus Plus. W ciągu trzech kolejnych lat projekt skupiał od dwóch do czterech wykładowców oraz około sześćdziesięcioro studentów z uczelni partnerskich wokół ambitnego programu dydaktycznego oferującego seminaria, wykłady, panele oraz inne wydarzenia naukowe i pozanaukowe. W artykule zostały omówione założenia i koncepcje naukowo-dydaktyczne, które legły u podstaw ubiegania się o omawiany projekt, jego główne cele i osiągnięte efekty kształcenia. Zostały przedstawione pola badawcze reprezentowane przez uczelnie partnerskie oraz ich wkład w kształt programu naukowo-dydaktycznego, zasady rekrutacji studentów oraz wymagania i zadania stawiane przed nimi w ramach realizacji projektu. Artykuł streszcza ofertę seminaryjną oraz najważniejsze wydarzenia naukowo-dydaktyczne projektu, a także prezentuje niektóre metody i techniki uczenia na przykładzie jednego z seminariów. Omówiony projekt udowadnia, że inicjatywy naukowo-dydaktyczne realizowane w ramach Partnerstwa Strategicznego są skutecznym poligonem akademickim, umożliwiającym studentom wykształcenie i rozwój naukowych, społecznych i międzynarodowych kompetencji i umiejętności niezbędnych do ich zaangażowania w kształtowanie losów Europy jako przyszłych naukowców i obywateli.

Słowa kluczowe: Partnerstwo Strategiczne, projekt międzynarodowy, edukacja, Szekspir, kryzys europejski

Introduction

"Facing Europe in Crisis: Shakespeare's World and Present Challenges" (NEW FACES) was an Erasmus+ Strategic Partnership project realised by a consortium of nine European universities between 2016 and 2019. In the academic years 2016/17, 2017/18 and 2018/19, it enabled three international groups of students to participate in a high-level collaborative research-oriented teaching programme which included seminars, lectures, panels and workshops. Some of the results of the programme are presented in this volume and testify to a successful contribution of the youngest academics to the development of the humanities. While the students' essays reflect some of the topics discussed in the seminar sessions and during other activities of the project, the purpose of this closing article is to report on the project itself, its main objectives and the structure of its programme. Reaching beyond a general description of the NEW FACES Strategic Partnership, I wish to offer insight into some of the project's more practical aspects to illustrate the ways in which an undertakings of this kind may be a perfect academic training ground.

What Was It All About? Description of the Project's Objectives

The project's main aim was to promote historical understanding of the complexities of cultural, political, social, religious, economic, and other crises faced by contemporary Europe. A multidisciplinary approach applied by the members of the consortium helped to trace similarities of the present developments to, and their differences from, the dynamics of the early modern period (16th-17th centuries). Hence the focus of the NEW FACES Strategic Partnership on the cultural, political and economic functions of early modern theatre and its wider historical and literary context as global values and principal agents of cultural communication in relation to Europe in crisis.

This principal aim of the NEW FACES was achieved by designing a high-level collaborative research-oriented teaching programme, with the following partner universities having contributed their expertise in a variety of disciplines: University Paul-Valéry in Montpellier (the consortium's coordinator) in history of reading, rhetorical analysis, theatre studies, reception studies; Charles University in Prague in literary and cultural theory, rhetoric, comparative literature, theatre, film and performance studies; University of Porto in comparative literature, utopian studies and translation; Utrecht University in war studies, European studies, memory studies, musicology and word and image studies; Free University Berlin in cultural memory, literary and cultural theories, popular culture, women, gender and adaptation studies; University of Ferrara in literary criticism, aesthetics, inter-art studies, linguistics, sociolinguistics; University of Murcia in cultural anthropology, critical theory, commemoration studies, European literature, translation, film theory, intermedia studies, reception studies; University of Szeged in semiography, multimediality and cultural studies, and cultural iconology in state agencies, corporations and organisations; Jagiellonian University in reception studies, drama studies, early modern poetry and translation.

Through a close cooperation of its partners, the project contributed to improving the quality and relevance of higher education, having successfully realised the main objective of a Strategic Partnership, which, as can be learned from the official website of the European Commission, is designed to develop and share innovative practices and promote cooperation, peer learning, and exchanges of experiences in the fields of education, training, and youth. In the course of three academic years, the NEW FACES project gathered twenty scholars and one hundred eighty MA and PhD students (sixty per year, selected for their excellence) from nine European universities. The considerable diversity of the partner institutions, both with regard to their defining characteristics, and with regard to their local history, was from the very beginning seen as a great advantage. Teaching and learning space of this kind definitely helped to establish and develop intercultural competences and skills of the students taking part in the programme, including language skills and methods of transnational cooperation.

To meet the requirements of a partnership aimed at supporting the exchange of good practices, teachers and students worked together and shared their research and teaching/learning practices by participating in intensive teaching programmes (one per year) and virtual mobility (in the periods between the subsequent Intensive Programmes via the project's Moodle platform). The use of e-learning and teaching technologies contributed to promoting high-standard digital humanities and to improving the participants' academic practices on a European scale. Apart from seminars and lectures, the main activities included student power-point presentations of the results of individual seminars and student electronic discussion and publication platforms, as well as workshops introducing students to business-related skills. The unique nature of the programme resulted from the combination of high-level multidisciplinary expertise and the emphasis on management of crisis, subject-specific professional and entrepreneurial skills and employability.

The main target group were second cycle and doctoral students in English literature and cultural studies. A wider target group included non-academic institutions with which the project created interactions, as well as political officials, professionals in cultural business, cultural mediators and artists, representatives of secondary education, and researchers in economics and socio-political sciences who conducted workshops and round tables and participated in monitoring the programme. The teaching programme offered each year was validated through ECTS credits by the partner universities, while in the long run the project, having facilitated collaborative work among several institutions, heightened the interest in other transnational partnerships (joint MA, international research programmes) both among teachers and students. The outputs, which constitute a sustainable NEW FACES corpus (teaching materials, videos, panels, students' best essays and teachers' conference volume), are available in open access on the official website of the project: http://www.new-faces-erasmusplus.fr/.

A more general, yet by no means less vital, aim of the NEW FACES Partnership was to create a space in which academic and non-academic partners would have a chance to create a multidisciplinary transnational think-tank on the ways European crises on all levels can be faced and tackled. To meet this aim, the project encouraged participants and partners to share opinions and to engage in a long-term dialogue on different approaches to the subject. The understanding of the crises of the past was pursued in close interaction with cultural and socio-political actors and complemented with teaching entrepreneurial skills. Round tables on culture and/in crisis gathered a wide range of participants: academics, political officials, cultural mediators and artists. NEW FACES, as a high-quality teaching programme, strived at increasing the much-needed European civic awareness of culture being tightly interwoven with social issues and economy, as well as of the place and function of culture in times of crisis. The enhanced interaction with non-academic partner-institutions that had to deal with crises of various kinds helped to build bridges between society and the academia at a time when many of Europe's foundational concepts are questioned and when public opinion sees Europe as the source of economic and socio-political strife. The project, aimed at an in-depth exploration of the very concept of crisis, had an ambition of providing future decision-makers with tools to contextualise and rethink some of the predicaments of Europe, to explore the mechanisms that crises trigger, as well as to devise means that can be put in place to face critical situations by building bridges between literature, history and the arts and socio-political sciences, as well as institutions. Thanks to a transnational multidisciplinary focus and by fostering a dialogue with organisations that are currently on the ground facing various types of crises, the project put theatre, literature and the humanities at the heart of a political reflection on crisis, and aimed to show that they have a part to play locally as much as on a European scale.

The consortium's application for the grant highlighted that the NEW FACES project answered pressing societal needs. It focused on crisis as a unifying issue, common to all the partners, that needed to be tackled transnationally. The last ten years called for a project that would answer the need for a historicised understanding of precedents and parallels to current crises, to mention only the refugee crisis, terrorism and the rise of extremist movements. Writing this report in 2020, I cannot but add to this list the global pandemic, a crisis which was foreshadowed in some discussions on the global spread of deadly viruses, as illustrated by the outline of the seminar on death and dying in the section describing our work in seminar groups. Another important need underlying the project was to have the voice of the humanities heard by highlighting the role of literature and the arts in education and in the socio-political well-being of communities. Literature and theatre do help to foster cohesion, tolerance and resilience, which can be illustrated by the presence of Shakespeare's plays (both on page and on stage) in prisons, war camps or refugee camps. Last but not least, the project was designed in a way that increased the students' employability. The socio-historical insights made possible by a scholarly study of the past – specifically, early modern theatre and literature – were applied in the teaching of specific skills required by today's cultural industries. This was done with the purpose of helping students prepare for the world of business (the languages of advertising, publishing, management strategies), the needs of cultural institutions (theatre, dramaturgy, cultural journalism) and the challenges and opportunities of free-lance work (translating, editing).

How Do Students Get Creative? Requirements, Tasks and Challenges

The selection requirements for students included having interest in the culture of early modern Europe, excellent study results and proficient command of English. Although the project's focal period each year was the two-week Intensive Programme held in one of the partner universities (Szeged in 2017, Montpellier in 2018 and Porto in 2019), the pre-IP activities, realised in the period between December and May, were equally important.

The following sample timeline of activities gives an idea of the range of tasks and challenges that were to be tackled by the recruited teams under the supervision of their home university teachers:

October-November – selection of students by partner universities (individual motivational letters),

December-April – recording a presentation clip (group work),

January-February – communicating with home teachers about how to prepare for the IP (group/individual work),

January-April – visiting the non-academic partner institution co-operating with the home university and preparing a presentation/poster (group work),

January-March – selecting two seminars, one for each week of the IP (individual work),

March-May – getting acquainted with the Moodle platform, communicating with seminar teachers and students through the platform, reading the assigned texts, preparing research questions (individual work, virtual mobility),

June – participating in the two-week Intensive Programme (group and individual work: seminar participation, preparation of power point presentations and abstracts of final essays),

June-July – writing and submitting of the final essay (individual work).

The earliest stage of the selection included submitting a motivational letter which was to make students link their current research and academic interests to the topics of the project and to encourage them to think how the study of the humanities, through Shakespeare's culture, can contribute to the comprehension of current crises. In their motivational letters students highlighted their fields of interests that they saw as relevant to the project's topic and enumerated issues they would be ready to explore during the programme. Candidates would, for example, declare their interests in the study of early modern political writers and, referring especially to the current situation and future of the European Union, would ask a number of questions, like: Is the idea of a united Europe an unsustainable utopia? Can Europe truly create and maintain a sense of unity and solidarity under the weight of historical grievances, the diversity of its peoples and economies, and the constant pressure of political crises? Which direction should the European Union take? Other candidates, interested in linguistics or translation, would be eager to learn more about the early modern period's rapid rise of the importance of vernacular languages and compare this to what was happening to regional languages today. What is the situation, role and function of regional languages nowadays? In face of the growing globalisation? In the situation of refugee crisis? As it is evident from these examples, sometimes the immediately declared interests of students were not connected with Shakespeare's plays, or any particular literary text of the period, yet in the course of the project, they became successfully integrated within its scope.

Once the groups of students in each of the partner institutions were selected, in order to launch the program in a dynamic and intercultural way, they were required to record a short presentation video clip to be uploaded on the project's website several weeks before the IP. In the clip the students would introduce themselves, their home universities, their academic and other interests and speak about expectations regarding their participation in the project. The clip was to be as inventive and informative as possible and, according to the project's philosophy of celebrating unity in diversity, was to be recorded in the local language of the university's country with subtitles in English. Some really ingenious presentation clips can be enjoyed on the NEW FACES website, including an almost six-minute full-fledged film by the 2019 Kraków team who superbly blended their self-presentation with performing an episode from *Macbeth*.

Another original and challenging task was to develop cooperation with non-academic partners working on or active in the situation of crises. The project's associate partners included several local organisations currently tackling the issue or confronted with the effects of crises, especially refugee crisis, among others The Consortium of Migrant Assisting Organizations in the Czech Republic, Metanoia Artopedia Group, and MigSzol Szeged. The students were asked to interact with such local organisations (e.g. the Red Cross) and to report on this interaction during the IP meetings, in form of a group presentation (2017) and poster sessions (2018 and 2019), thus sharing their experience on a European scale. In Kraków, the institution that agreed to cooperate in the NEW FACES project was the Halina Nieć Legal Aid Center. It is a non-profit non-governmental organisation established in Kraków in 2002 whose main aim is to provide free legal aid for the poor, victims of social discrimination and domestic violence, foreigners, refugees and asylum seekers. The Center's legal experts, collaborating with specialists and volunteers, are involved in protecting human rights, monitoring human rights standards, legal interventions and preventing human trafficking. In each year the Kraków students visited the Center for a session on the current problems connected with the refugee crisis in our part of Europe and on the Center's activities undertaken to tackle it. They were also invited to participate in the Center's various activities (film projections, discussions and workshops). They learned about the voluntary work done on the borders and in the refugee camps, about the engagement in the paperwork connected with the applications for the refugee status, as well as in the very basic acts of human compassion.

Strategic Partnership or How to Teach Transnationally?

The assumption behind the project was that the humanities offer tools that can help to comprehend current crises and provide society with some intellectual resources to face them. The partners of the project see knowledge of the past, and especially of the literature and history of the past, as vital in tackling and overcoming the current tensions and conflicts. The project was initiated in 2016, the year that celebrated the 400th anniversary of the death of William Shakespeare, the author whose transnational relevance should be seen as a unifying cultural force. That is why the focus was put on Shakespeare and his world, the early modern period, but also on Shakespeare in our world today. Some of the pivotal questions of the NEW FACES were: What can Shakespeare do for Europe today? What can we learn about our world via Shakespeare's plays? How can his work help us understand and overcome today's crises? Such questions were directly reflected in the seminars offered by the partner institutions thanks to their academic staff's expertise as early modern scholars. The content of the seminars revolved around issues that included the importance of early modern literature and theatre for remembering and imagining European past and future, early modern literature and theatre in relation to European memories of crises, the role of dramatic crisis in early modern theatre and the representation of past and present political, social and ethnic clashes, the intercultural and transcultural nature of dramatic and literary sources and translation or production practices, to mention just a few. This section offers a summary of the project's seminar offer and an outline of the lectures, panels, conferences and other activities of the Intensive Programmes.

The pillars of the teaching-research programme each year were the seminars led by the scholars from the partner universities, accompanied by other academic and non-academic activities. Students had a range of topics and approaches to choose from, their choice having been restricted only by the rule that they were not allowed to select the seminar led by teachers from their own universities. Seminars were in some cases co-taught by colleagues from different institutions to highlight the value of transnational cooperation and exchange of good practices, both on the level of scholarship and on the level of teaching. Thus the students, who in this programme were expected to be ready for and encouraged to develop skills of collaborative work in international groups, were given an example of effective intercultural collaboration. In the course of the three years of the project's duration, most of the seminars were repeated, but some were modified or replaced by new ones. The following short outline will give a picture of the teaching programme's diversity.

The seminar "Crisis of Representation – Representations of Crises. Questioning Authorities on the Early Modern Stage," taught by Andreas Mahler from Freie Universität Berlin and Martin Procházka from Univerzita Karlova in Prague, addressed four history plays by Shakespeare, *Richard II*, *Henry IV* 1 and 2, and *Richard III*, with regard both to their depiction of a crisis of authority and to the crisis of representation in early modern England. *Richard II* was also read in the seminar by another teacher from Prague, Mirka Horova, who in her seminar "Play, Crisis and the State: Shakespeare's 'Gentler Gamesters' and Iser's Play Theory" approached the play in terms of Wolfgang Iser's concept of literary play to explore the possibilities of understanding politics and history and to discuss the findings against the current crisis of "post-truth" politics. History plays were also referred to in the seminar "Crown and Crisis in Shakespeare's England and Contemporary Europe" by Clara Calvo from Universidad de Murcia. The participants looked at how Shakespeare staged and interpreted the series of English medieval crises of political sovereignty in his two tetralogies and were invited to work on the links between these plays and some of their modern adaptations. A selection of early modern and postmodern plays were compared in the seminar "Laboratories of Identity: Early Modern and Postmodern Dramas and Theatricality as Experiments in an Age of Epistemological Crisis," offered by Attila Kiss from Szegedi Tudományegyetem, which focused on signs of the epistemological crisis in the representational techniques of these texts.

Nathalie Vienne-Guerrin from Université Paul-Valéry Montpellier 3 and Lieke Stelling from Universiteit Utrecht taught the seminar entitled "Crises in *The Merchant Of Venice* and *Othello*," which analysed the way crisis was represented in these two plays with special reference to the issue of religious conversion and the verbal aspects of expressing crisis. Marta Gibińska from the Jagiellonian University focused on the same plays in her seminar "Facing the Other: the Crisis of Acceptance and Understanding" which analysed the problem of the crisis in interpersonal relations based on racial differences. The plays were studied to diagnose various aspects of the crisis at encountering the other and to answer questions like how to stage the plays to enhance our recognition of the crisis of our time, and how to initiate possible processes leading to eradicating enmity and prejudice. The issue of otherness was undertaken also in the seminar "Intermedial Crisis: Visual Culture and Early Modern Representations – or, Gazing and/as Otherness in Shakespeare" taught by Rui Carvalho Homem from Universidade do Porto and Clara Calvo from Murcia. Their students discussed the close relation between the experience of seeing and the perception of otherness as represented in a selection of early modern texts and their stage and screen productions.

The seminar "[Un]Sustainable Human Social Institutions in Early-Modern Literary Utopias" by Paola Spinozzi from Università di Ferrara focused on Thomas More's *Libellus vere aureus*, Tommaso Campanella's *La Città del Sole* and Francis Bacon's *New Atlantis* as works that shaped early modern thought in Europe and introduced philosophical and political concepts that had invited constant reconfigurations throughout the centuries. "Food and the Human Experience in the Early Modern and the 20th-21st-Centuries Utopian Literature and Imagination" was the seminar by Fátima Vieira from Universidade do Porto. It offered insight into food as a political issue and into the human experience of food by bridging utopian strategies for solving food crises over the past five hundred years with projects that are undertaken nowadays. "Shakespeare's *The Tempest* and Bacon's *New Atlantis*: a Collaborative Reflection on 'Responsible Science,'" by the same scholar, started from the concept of "responsible research and innovation" as one of the European Commission's priorities for the Horizon 2020 programme to propose a discussion on the interplay between politics and science in the two works mentioned in the seminar's title.

"Negotiating the Rhetoric of Blame: The Debate about Women in the English Renaissance" by Larisa Kocic-Zámbó from Szeged paid particular attention to the mechanics of epideictic rhetoric, especially of claims blaming and scapegoating women for crises of mankind and/or nationhood, and its negotiations by female authors. This seminar was an introduction to the work of Shakespeare's "literary sisters" between 1500 and 1700, while "Lucrece, Katherina and the Violence of Postfeminism" by Juan Francisco Cerdá from Murcia took contemporary debates on feminism as the starting point for the discussion of *The Taming of the Shrew* and "The Rape of Lucrece," their afterlives and their current significations as a renewed interest in feminism and gender violence had (re)emerged to be a central concern for the third wave of feminism of the twenty-first century.

Other scholars from Berlin and Utrecht, Sabine Schülting, Paul M. Franssen and David Pascoe collaborated on teaching the seminar called "Representing Social Crises, Past and Present." It focused on the representation of economic crises, and their entanglement with social, religious, racial and communal conflicts in *The Merchant of Venice*, *Coriolanus* and Christopher Marlowe's *The Jew of Malta* in order to explore how these early modern texts can be made meaningful for contemporary debates about economy, racial and religious differences, and civic unrest. Contemporary debt crisis was at the centre of the seminar taught by another scholar from Porto, Miguel Ramalhete Gomes, "Rethinking Debt and Exodus through Early Modern and Late Modern Responses." It offered a parallel discussion of concepts of usury and debt in early modern and late modern contexts and encouraged the participants to consider the recent upsurge of critical responses to the contemporary debt crisis in order to use them as theoretical and experiential tools with which to approach the early modern experience of indebtedness and its economic theories, especially as they are reflected in Shakespeare's plays.

"Exploring Censorship and Freedom of Expression through Shakespeare" by Jean-Christophe Mayer from Montpellier offered the opportunity to learn about a series of early censors of Shakespeare's texts and encouraged students to explore the workings of censorship, whether managed by the state, institutions, communities, or individuals themselves. The seminar hoped to demonstrate that what Shakespeare's censored and maimed texts tell us may inform our modern notions of artistic and political freedom of expression. A direct link between past and present was also established by Rui Carvalho Homem from Porto, the leader of the "Mobility, Fear and Laughter in Early Modern Drama" seminar, who proposed a discussion of mobile selves, especially those situated on the periphery of social inclusion (or beyond its range), as represented in early modern drama with a view to developing a historicized understanding of the challenges posed today by human mobility under current global circumstances. Bridges between the past and today were equally clear in the seminar "'With such large discourse.' Language as Negotiation and Representation of Identity in Early Modern and Postmodern Crises" by Richard Chapman from Ferrara who explored with his students how language was used to represent the self and interact with others, influencing and expressing ideas of difference and perceptions of roles that often remain implicit. They used tools deriving from discourse analysis, pragmatics and sociolinguistics to make explicit comparisons between early modern and postmodern modes of discourse.

"European Shakespearean Festivals as Alternative Answers to Contemporary Crises" was the seminar co-taught by Florence March from Montpellier and Agnes Matuska from Szeged which offered an analysis of the Elizabethan understandings of the *theatrum mundi* and discussed the diverse interpretations about the way onstage and offstage reality intermingle and the audience is involved in the public event of a play – both in the early modern context and in contemporary adaptations of Elizabethan drama.

Lastly, the author of this article led the seminar entitled "The Crisis of Death. Perspectives on Death and Dying in Shakespeare's Time and Today" which will be presented in more detail in the following section. Detailed descriptions of all the seminars, together with teaching materials, readings and bibliographies can be found at http://www.new-faces-erasmus-plus.fr/?q=content/seminars-summaries.

The project's Intensive Programmes included also lectures, panels and poster sessions, starting with the Szeged round tables that consisted of panels on theatre and crisis, socio-political crisis, crisis and otherness, and Shakespeare and crisis. The topics discussed ranged from various definitions of crisis, the importance of utopianism and the role of theatre in the face of crisis, to the specificity of Shakespeare's plays that lend themselves to appropriations which make them relevant in relation to current-day issues.

During the IP in Montpellier a one day international conference was organised, under the title "What can Shakespeare do for us? / What can we do with Shakespeare? New Faces in interaction." To broaden the scope of the project, popularise its ideas, and disseminate its results, this event gathered a number of scholars from universities other than the partners of the consortium, including the University of Kent and New Hampshire University (USA). Panel discussions related to topics like performing Shakespeare in refugee camps, Shakespeare read in captivity, Shakespeare for teachers and secondary-school students, Shakespeare and intercultural communication, as well as Shakespeare in politics and diplomacy. A parallel conference, "Shakespeare's World and Present Challenges," was held during the project's last IP in Porto, when the scholars involved discussed Shakespeare and the origins of European culture wars, Shakespeare and populism, "The Rape of Lucrece" in the age of #MeToo, issues of integration and the early modern crises of conversion, and Shakespeare on women's education. All these academic events gathered a wide audience of scholars and students who were actively participating in question sessions and discussions.

International Brainstorm or How Did We Work in Seminar Groups?

This section presents, using as an example "The Crisis of Death" seminar, some methods and procedures that were employed during the NEW FACES seminar sessions.

While in early modern Europe the commonness of death and dying was experienced on daily basis, it is often claimed that nowadays, with the unprecedented development of medicine and technology, mortality has become one of the modern taboos. Public executions, admonitory displays of dead bodies or mass graves of plague victims seem to be as remote from us as *ars moriendi* and ritualization of dying. The fact is that with terrorism, dangerous climate changes, unprecedented acts of violence disseminated via modern media, and the global spread of deadly viruses we are nowadays confronted with the omnipresence of death more acutely than we would like to admit. Therefore, the participants of the seminar "Perspectives on Death and Dying in Shakespeare's Time and Today" were encouraged to explore death both as a critical situation experienced universally and as one of the faces of today's crisis. On the basis of selected background and source readings they first examined individual and communal aspects of death in early modern culture and compared them with the approaches to death prevalent in our own times. Then, they analysed chosen plays by Shakespeare to establish how death and dying was depicted in them. The ultimate task was to scrutinise the ways in which this depiction is treated in Shakespearean productions for stage and screen in order to observe how Shakespeare is used in today's cultural discourse on mortality.

The reading list included, among others, selected passages from Philippe Ariès's *The Hour of Our Death* (1980), James Calderwood's *Shakespeare and the Denial of Death* (1987), Michael Neill's *Issues of Death: Mortality and Identity* (1997), and a collection of essays edited by Mia Korpiola and Anu Lahtinen *Cultures of Death and Dying in Medieval and Early Modern Europe* (2015). These readings, to be done in the months preceding the Intensive Programmes, were to introduce the students into the most important aspects of death and dying in early modern times and into the presentation of death and death-related topics in the literature of the period. At his stage of pre-IP preparations, each seminar participant was to formulate two to four research questions related to the assigned readings and to share them with the rest of the group so that everyone could prepare for the discussion during the Intensive Programme meeting. According to the objectives of the project, the idea from the very start was to prepare ground for establishing links between past and present which usually were, in part at least, suggested already at the level of formulating the questions, as can be seen in the following selection:

> What does it mean that death is a cultural phenomenon?
>
> How do people deal with the inevitability and the fear of death?
>
> How can death become culturally meaningful?
>
> How has public death (caused by natural disasters, terrorist attacks, refugee crisis) changed in the digital era? Are we more or less removed from death?
>
> How might our new mourning ceremonies for public death that appear on television shift our reading of death in the works of Shakespeare?
>
> What could "good death" be in today's culture if we are living in a death-denying society?

Is the medical technological progress the reason why people are unwilling to accept death?

Why and how does mourning change from one society to another, and from one period to another?

Are attitudes toward death directly correlated to the cause of death? What kind of responses do characters in Shakespeare's plays have to various kinds of death?

In what way do twenty-first-century Shakespeare adaptations fuse the early modern approach to death with the current one?

To what extent is nakedness linked with death and the annihilation of identity in Shakespeare's texts?

How does Shakespeare deal with brutality and "cruel death"?

What was the impact of the plague on people's perception of death? Why do some texts, when describing the mass of people who died from the plague, depict people as objects? Is it possible that although the plague intensified the fear of death, it also minimized the human aspect of mass death?

How did attitudes towards death progress from the tame death model to the invisible death model? How and why are the concepts of death and sexuality closely linked? How did the concept of privacy emerge in relation to death?

How did the Reformation and the concomitant fundamental religious and epistemological changes transform the perception of death and dying in the early modern epoch? How do these changes manifest themselves in Shakespeare's plays?

These and other questions were, during the seminar sessions, integrated with a discussion moderated by the seminar teacher. The discussion started from general issues connected with death as a cultural phenomenon, the warm-up task having been to consider if Gertrude's words to Hamlet, "Thou know'st 'tis common. All that lives must die, / Passing through nature to eternity" (1.2.72-73) testify to her understanding of death as a natural or as a cultural phenomenon. Then, the participants were encouraged to discuss the statement that for human beings (unlike for animals) death is not a natural experience, but "an idea that has to be constantly reimagined across cultures and through time" (Neill 1997, 2), and one that is culturally determined (Ariès 1981), and to think about possible implications of this fact for literature and theatre. As a mixture of "the spiritual highs and the corporeal lows, human beings seek to deny mortality by fashioning idealised images of themselves, while "the denial of death is a fundamental motive not merely of individuals but of their cultures as well" (Calderwood 1987, 4). Man as a self-conscious and symbolic animal, deprived of the "bestial oblivion" (*Hamlet*, 4.4.40) and capable of abstract thinking, does not need to survive death literally to overcome mortality (Calderwood 1987, 5). What strategies, then, do people employ to deal with the inevitability and the fear of death? As Calderwood (1987) puts it, the human need to deny death "is most apparent in myth and religion, and the fact that these are cultural institutions suggests that culture as a whole is in some degree a death-denying agency" (6). Perceived from this perspective, literature opens itself as the space where human death may become meaningful in that it becomes part of a story that is transmitted and remembered.

The second part of the discussion focused on death in times contemporary to Shakespeare. It started from a historical overview of the attitudes to death and dying from the mediaeval religiousness as a tool to tame death, so that an ordered and predictable framework lessened the fear of it and allowed to see it as a doorstep of eternity, to the late mediaeval obsession with death as a result of the plague, visible in the *danse macabre* paintings on which death was depicted as life's terminus, to the early modern crisis of death, characterised, on the one hand, by attempts to become indifferent to death as something natural and, on the other hand, by changes in death rituals that followed the Reformation, by problems with accommodating death within the humanistic worldview, and by the renewed fear of it as the only element that seemed to resist the boldness of progress (Calderwood 1987, 12; Neill 1997, 30). It then moved to discussing tragedy as the main tool of early modern reinvention of death. English Renaissance tragedy, "catered for a culture that was in the throes of a peculiar crisis in the accommodation of death – one that reflected the strain of adjusting the psychic economy of an increasingly individualistic society to the stubborn facts of mortality" (Neill 1997, 30). Tragedy was, then, the "essential secular instrument for confronting the agonising mystery of mortal ending" (Dobson and Wells 2001, 108), while the "psychological value of tragedy's displays of agony, despair and ferocious self-assertion [...] was that they provided audiences with a way of vicariously confronting the implications of their own mortality, by compelling them to rehearse and re-rehearse the encounter with death" (Neill 1997, 31).

Having established the above background, the seminar moved on to discuss various faces of death that Shakespeare and his contemporaries were confronted with. First, the plague. Feared so much not only as an uncontrollable and appalling incurable disease, but also because mass death would frequently mean abandonment of proper funeral practices and, by levelling identities and distinctions by burial in the common pits, threaten the hierarchy of social order. Second, public executions. While the plague had an indirect influence on theatre and on playwrights in that theatres would close at the times of bans of public gatherings, there was a direct link between theatre and public executions organized as admonitory spectacles. The very locations for public executions were organized as theatres of punishment, with the scaffold as a stage, viewers as audience and the procedure following a carefully prepared scenario. Public deaths of criminals or heretics and displays of their heads or quartered body parts were employed as demonstration of the power of the state and its legal system, as well as representation of the state's dominance over the individual's body. Third, anatomy theatres. Dissections of dead bodies amounted to elaborate shows, being carefully staged in well-organized purpose-built show-places as paid entertainment. Last, but not least, death in war and other bloody social conflicts, like religious wars was discussed, as well as short life expectancy, including infant death.

Another step in this phase of the seminar sessions was to study some of these aspects of death and dying as depicted in a selection of texts from the epoch. Two poems by Sir Walter Raleigh, "On the Life of Man" and "De Morte," were compared with regard to their employment of the *theatrum mundi* metaphor. Two short elegies by Ben Jonson, "On My First Son" and "On My First Daughter" were discussed with special attention focused on the difference in imagery and meaning of the poem mourning the death of a son with one mourning the death of a daughter, with reference to the then prevailing social norms concerning family life and gender roles. Michel Montaigne's *Essays* were consulted with a reading from chapter XIX of Book I, "That to Study Philosophy Is to Learn to Die" in an attempt to look for a philosophical consolation in the face of mortality. Selected passages were read from Thomas Dekker's realistic report of the plague in his famous 1603 pamphlet *The Wonderful Year*, as well as from John Donne's *Death's Duel*, together with his most famous poem about death, the "Death be not proud" sonnet. Shakespeare was represented by the unsettling images from *Romeo and Juliet* of the closeness of love and death that culminate in Juliet describing herself and being described as the bride of Death in 3.2., 4.5. and 5.3.

Other plays by Shakespeare were discussed as well, as during the months of pre-IP preparations students were asked to select episodes from a chosen play by Shakespeare in which death is foregrounded and prepare an interpretative reading of it to be shared in form of a mini-presentation during the seminar session. Presentation topics prepared by the participants included, among others: Monstrosity and death. Death of monstrous females (Lady Macbeth); Death in Shakespeare's history plays, especially *Richard II*; Death scenes from *Titus Andronicus* and *Richard III*; Ophelia and Portia – women killed by elements; Polonius and Tybalt – deaths as turning points in the plot; Lady Macbeth and Cleopatra – comparison of their suicidal deaths; The Princes in *Richard III* and Prince Arthur in *King John* – death and children; Death in *The Timon of Athens*; Macbeth's Witches and premonitions of death; "The Rape of Lucrece" and the death of shame; Mortality and death in *King Lear*; The gravediggers in *Hamlet* – death and laughter; Juliet, Desdemona and Hermione – death and sexuality; Shakespeare's on-stage and off-stage deaths.

Finally, the participants were also to prepare short reports on how today's theatre, film, visual arts or other forms of culture present death and dying in Shakespearean or Shakespeare-related productions and projects and what their popular and critical reception tells us about the use of Shakespeare in today's discourse on death. Students analysed, among others, Ralph Fiennes's *Coriolanus* (2011), Justin Kurzel's *Macbeth* (2015), Ian McKellen's *Macbeth* (1995), Verdi's *Macbeth* in the Prague National Theatre (2015), Thomas Ostermeier's *Hamlet* in Berlin (2008), RSC's *Anthony and Cleopatra* (2017), RSC's *Julius Caesar* (2017), Richard Eyre's *King Lear* (2018), *Macbeth* at Teatro Nacional de São João (2018), the Hungarian version of the French musical *Roméo et Juliette: de la Haine à l'Amour* (2001), Jonathan Levine's zombie version of *Romeo and Juliet*, *Warm Bodies* (2013), Akira Kurosawa's *Throne of Blood* (1957), Jo Nesbø's thriller *Macbeth* (2018), death and suicide in *Hamlet* compared to David Foster Wallace's *Infinite Jest* (1996), representations of Ophelia's death in the famous paintings (e.g. by John Everett Millais, Paul Albert Steck) and their influence on stage adaptations.

At each phase of the Intensive Programme's seminar sessions students were encouraged to establish bridges between past and present. Are we so much different? Can the commonness of early modern death be really contrasted with death's alleged invisibility nowadays? The following aspects would repeatedly emerge in our discussions: causes of today's apocalyptic fears, global spread of diseases as a result of easy travel, destruction of the planet due to climate changes, dangers linked to modern war technology and developments in medical sciences, ageing of societies and prolonged dying in institutions, and the global media's role in publicising death and violence. The seminar allowed the students to acquire knowledge about the attitudes to death and dying in early modern culture, especially about the treatment of this topic in early modern literary texts. They also learned about how Shakespearean depiction of death and dying was interpreted nowadays on stage and screen in various places in Europe which enhanced their knowledge about how today's political and social crises are reflected in and commented on via theatre and film. They had an opportunity to develop their critical skills while commenting on the reception of Shakespeare's plays, mainly in stage and film adaptations of the last twenty years, and presenting creative interpretations of Shakespearean productions with reference to a range of today's crises.

Conclusions

By focusing on the topic of crisis and the ways crises were and can be confronted and managed in Europe from the early modern period to our time, NEW FACES promoted empowerment, participation and active citizenship of young people. It invited a community of scholars to work on a topic that is relevant to current European life with the purpose of providing a better understanding of the crises of the past in order to face and solve the crises of the present and future more efficiently. Gathering scholars and students from nine European countries, all working on crises in Shakespeare's world in relation to present challenges, not only improved the quality and relevance of higher education but also offered students the opportunity to work with other European students and thus to develop their intercultural competences and prepare them for future transnational work towards securing a better future. The NEW FACES Strategic Partnership's main aims were achieved by applying modern technologies in learning and teaching. The teaching was project-oriented and thus encouraged students to cultivate initiative, dialogue and responsible leadership and to share with others their original ways of thinking and working. The meetings and workshops with associate partners provided non-formal training and contributed to gaining and developing other than academic competences by the students.

The impact of the project on its participants, partner institutions, associate partners and other target groups is long lasting. Among the students of the Jagiellonian University the project has raised awareness of the possibility to discuss the current European crises through the lens of historico-literary and theatre studies. Thanks to the pre-IP preparations period, students became better aware of the intellectual potential of the interdisciplinary perspective, as well as of the pragmatic potential of the transnational approach. They developed critical thinking, writing skills, media literacy and skills in digital humanities. During the Intensive Programmes students had a chance to develop their intercultural understanding, skills in collaborative work, abilities to carry out projects, and to enhance their linguistic competences in a multilingual context. The meeting with the associate partner motivated the students to think about practical problems connected with the current refugee crisis. The Intensive Programmes encouraged them to consider the most acute European problems from the perspective of the history of culture, while the requirements for their seminar presentations and essays helped them to construct bridges between past and present in order to equip them with a repertoire of tools that will be helpful in solving the problems of the future.

References

Ariès, P. 1981. *The Hour of Our Death*. Translated by H. Weaver. New York: Random House.

Calderwood, J.L. 1987. *Shakespeare and the Denial of Death*. Amherst: University of Massachusetts Press.

Dobson, M., and S. Wells (eds.). 2001. *The Oxford Companion to Shakespeare*. Oxford: Oxford University Press.

Neill, M. 1997. *Issues of Death. Mortality and Identity in English Renaissance Tragedy*. Oxford: Clarendon Press.

NEW FACES, http://www.new-faces-erasmusplus.fr/.

Shakespeare, W. 1997. *Hamlet*. Edited by P. Edwards. Cambridge: Cambridge University Press.

Strategic Partnerships, https://ec.europa.eu/programmes/erasmus-plus/opportunities/strategic-partnerships-field-education-training-and-youth_en.

Index

Editor
Rafał Pawluk

Proofreading
Katarzyna Jagieła

Typesetting
Hanna Wiechecka

Jagiellonian University Press
Editorial Offices: Michałowskiego 9/2, 31-126 Kraków
Phone: +48 12 663 23 80, Fax: +48 12 663 23 83

GPSR Authorized Representative: Easy Access System Europe, Mustamäe tee 50, 10621 Tallinn, Estonia, gpsr.requests@easproject.com

www.ingramcontent.com/pod-product-compliance
Lightning Source LLC
Chambersburg PA
CBHW060834120626
46548CB00001B/2

* 9 7 8 8 3 2 3 3 5 0 0 1 9 *